BRITAIN'S BEST SMALL HILLS

A GUIDE TO WILD WALKS • SHORT ADVENTURES SCRAMBLES • GREAT VIEWS • WILD CAMPING & MORE

PHOEBE SMITH

Bradt

AUTHOR

Phoebe Smith knows good hills. For over ten years she's been exploring Britain extensively and has written about them in a range of magazines and newspapers in the UK, USA, Canada and Australia as well as being the author of eight books – all on the British wilderness and the joys of camping, including Bradt's *Wilderness Weekends: Wild Adventures in Britain's Rugged Corners* and *Extreme Sleeps: Adventures of a Wild Camper*. In addition to writing Phoebe has frequently appeared on radio and TV talking about wild camping, travel and women in the outdoors. She is an award-winning editor, motivational speaker, filmmaker and presenter. In 2015 and 2016, she was shortlisted for the National Adventure Awards in the Inspiring Others category. In 2016 and 2017, she was named an Ordnance Survey #GetOutside Champion for her work encouraging everyone to have adventures in the UK. Follow her adventures on www.phoebe-smith.com.

ACKNOWLEDGEMENTS

Thanks to my dad, Brian Smith, for taking me on a walk up Bryn Euryn when I was six. Neither of us knew it at the time, but it's the reason this book exists at all. Massive appreciation to Neil S Price for helping me get some of the wonderful photos in this guide despite the bad weather, and to all the other photographers who helped with images when my hard drive died! Huge gratitude also to the entire team at Bradt for asking me to write another book championing the British outdoors – special shout-outs to Rachel for signing me up, Anna for putting up with my blatant disregard for deadlines, Pepi for the great job on design, James Lowen for editing me with such finesse, empathy and patience, and Adrian for continuing to believe in my work. Honourable mention to my friend and mentor MC, without whom this book would have been written much faster…

FOREWORD

By Ed Byrne

It's rare for a person to feel that a book has been written just for them. There's good reason for this. Aiming a book at a potential readership of one person is a bad move professionally and tends not to be considered commercially viable by most publishers. However, this book has come along at just the right time in my life as to feel specifically designed for me alone.

Since I started getting into hillwalking back in the early noughties, I decided I wanted to do the biggest ones the UK had to offer and became an avid Munro-bagger (challenging myself to summit all 282 Scottish peaks over 3,000ft so compiled in a list in 1891 by Sir Hugh Munro). I've been well served in this endeavour by a wide range of guidebooks and resources – Munro-bagging has, after all, been a well-known sub-genre of mountaineering since long before I was born. If you want the tallest, the most extreme, the gnarliest, there's a plethora of publications catering to your needs. Since becoming a dad, however, it's become much harder to fit enormous mountains into my life. I just don't have as much room for them as I used to. That's where Phoebe's latest book comes in.

Britain's Best Small Hills is an excellent catalogue of those bite-sized peaks that are not just easily reached, but often easily overlooked by adventure seekers. This book shows you that you don't need to spend all day hauling yourself to the top of an Alpine giant in order to enjoy the sense of achievement and adventure that hillwalking offers. A peak is a peak, no matter how high, and communing with nature isn't something that happens exclusively at altitudes over 3,000ft.

What makes this book perfect for me is that it offers a list of peaks that I can take my kids up. A hillwalking starter kit, if you will. I've already dragged the boys up a few of the hills contained herein and can't wait to introduce them to the rest. I foresee evenings spent with the three of us leafing through these pages, planning our next excursion.

So I thank Phoebe for writing this book just for me, and I hope one day my kids will thank her, too.

Ed Byrne

– Comedian, Munro-bagger and newly converted small hills lover

CONTENTS

INTRODUCTION

PART 1: ENGLAND

↑ Small and sweet – the tasty summit of 596m Sugar Loaf, Monmouthshire. (Leighton Collins/D)

PART 2: WALES

Checking out the epic views from the 405m Helm Crag in Cumbria. (Neil S Price) ↑

PART 3: SCOTLAND

↑ Far from the driving crowd... enjoying Snowdonia views from the minuscule Bryn Euryn. (Neil S Price)

INTRODUCTION

Everyone should love mountains as much as me. It's no secret that I adore high places. Few activities can beat the buzz of being the loftiest living thing for miles around. Investing physical effort in return for world-class views that only those who take the time to clamber up slopes can enjoy is something that I seek out in every bit of free time I get. But I'm going to let you into a secret that few know and many forget… some of the best views, greatest walks and most memorable adventures can be had on small hills. Really.

Many famous mountain walking lists out there are based on height: think of the 'National Three Peaks' (the highest mountains in England, Wales and Scotland), the 'Yorkshire Three Peaks' (the loftiest three in Yorkshire), the 'Welsh 3000s' (all 14 mountains in Wales over 3,000ft/914m) and the Munros (the 282 peaks in Scotland that are over 3,000ft/914m with a specified amount of prominence on all sides). This might make you doubt that smaller peaks can be any good.

But those who shun peaks based on their vital statistics are truly missing out. Small absolutely can be beautiful. For a start, summit views can be fantastic on shorter peaks. And there's a whole host of other reasons to check them out:

1. You can take as long as you want over small peaks. A quick fix after breakfast, something to do in your lunch hour or an opportunity for fresh air after work? No problem. Or you can take your time, making the walk last a whole day. Small hills are as quick or as slow as you want them to be.
2. Small hills usually enjoy better weather. Clouds (including those pesky ones bursting with rain) often linger around the highest thing around.
3. Practise on small hills will make taller ones easier. Walking up them helps keep you fit (a regular ascent of even a tiny hill will burn off the calories) but they're also great for honing skills such as map reading and navigation too.
4. Introduce a friend, partner or child to a small hill first and you will more likely get them interested in doing adventures with you rather than if you try a baptism of fire on a giant mountain.
5. Forget measurements: height really doesn't matter. What hillwalking is really about is getting outside and exploring some of the beautiful countryside that is (often) right on your doorstep.

Pick any one of the 60 small hills described here then follow the corresponding route in this book. Do so and I guarantee that you will be persuaded that size really doesn't matter when it comes to adventure. Walk this way…

Phoebe Smith, May 2017 www.phoebe-smith.com

SMALL HILLS: THE ESSENTIALS

The best thing about walking is that it's such a deliciously simple way to get active, requiring very little in the way of equipment. If the mood takes you, you can simply grab a jacket, pull on your boots, and get started. When walking in the hills, however (even little ones like those in this book), the weather can be more unpredictable. So it pays to give a little more thought to the gear you might want to take with you in order to make your experience all the more enjoyable. After all, you want to encourage your companions to come with you more than once so keeping them warm and dry makes sense. So while hiking up small hills certainly shouldn't mean investing in lots of expensive kit, here's the gear you should consider having packed and ready to go…

KIT TALK

RUCKSACKS

The key piece of kit needed for carrying your jacket, water bottle and camera. Rucksacks come in all different sizes, shapes and colours of the rainbow, each vying for your attention in the outdoor shops. It can be difficult to know what to look for, so here's a few tips on key features.

❶ **Wand pockets and compression straps** On the side of the rucksack look for at least one – if not two – large pouch-style pockets made out of fabric or mesh. (These are called 'wand pockets' as they were originally designed to enable explorers to carry wands – aka canes – for marking out routes on glaciers, including on the first Everest ascent.) Wand pockets are really useful for carrying a water bottle on the outside, avoiding you having to root around for it inside the bag. They are also good for carrying walking poles and a small tripod (key for photographers). Compression straps above the pockets not only help cinch the excess fabric of your bag when it's not full (making it more streamlined), but also help secure tripods and poles to the pack so that they don't wobble as you walk.

❷ **Back length and system** Some packs offer various back sizes, mainly small, medium and large. ('Back size' is measured as the length of your back from the bone that sticks out at the bottom of your neck – known as the seventh cervical vertebrae – to the top of your pelvis, known as your iliac crest.) Others have a 'one-size-fits-all' approach. Either way, try several packs on first to ensure you get one that sits well on you.

Most rucksacks have a ventilated-back system – either a sculpted mesh and foam panel or a metal or plastic curved structure that holds the pack away from your body to allow air to circulate. These are useful to stop you getting too

sweaty when walking uphill. But again 'try before you buy' to make sure it's comfortable on your back.

3 Shoulder straps and hip belts The shoulder straps balance the pack on your body (you actually carry most of the weight on your legs and hips). So look for padding that provides comfort and ensure the shoulder straps don't cut into your armpits as they could cause rubbing sores. The hip belt helps support and stabilise the load, so make sure it's comfortable when full and fits well without restricting your movement.

4 Lid Not all small packs will have a lid – some you just access via a zip. But it can be a handy extra as you can keep frequently used items in its pocket or place wet garments under the lid so that the everything else stays dry.

5 Size The perfect pack is one that holds all the belongings you need. For these walks anything between 15 and 25 litres should do the job nicely – though if you are opting for one of the suggestions in *Added adventure* then you will need to choose something larger (approximately 40 litres).

6 Pockets Depending on the design, daypacks can boast few or many. They are useful for organising your kit, but too many pockets can be a faff as you won't remember where you put everything! So decide what balance works best for you. Inside some may have a pouch at the back that is compatible with hydration bladders (an alternative to using a water bottle); even if you don't use one it can be a great place for storing a map or indeed this book!

7 Fit There is no such thing as a unisex pack – anything claimed as such is designed for a man. Women carry weight differently from men due to their muscle structure, taking more on the hip than the upper body. Depending on your shape this may not be an issue ('unisex' packs tend to have a hipbelt designed for narrower hips, and shoulder straps designed for broader shoulders). But women and men alike may find it worth trying on any available women-specific packs too.

DRYBAGS

There's a wonderful line in Bill Bryson's seminal Appalachian Trail book *A Walk in the Woods* where he goes into a gear shop to buy a rucksack and is horrified to learn that one that costs US$250 (£190) is not waterproof. But the reality is that very few backpacks are – just water resistant. So if you want to keep kit inside dry you need to invest in drybags (or use plastic bags – not as effective but certainly a cheap alternative). There are different sizes available. A large one is a good start as it will keep everything inside it dry, but you may want to opt for a pack of four varied sizes and colours which will help organise your kit so you can find things quicker, eg: blue for food, green for first-aid kit, orange for accessories etc.

FIRST-AID KIT

Even on a short walk, it's always worth carrying a small one with you. You can easily make your own consisting of plasters, blister plasters, a tick remover, insect repellent, suncream sachet, and antiseptic wipes.

ACCESSORIES AND EXTRAS

As British weather can be unpredictable it's worth carrying a warm hat (or a summer hat/cap in warm weather), gloves (if you feel the cold a good option is to have a thin warm pair of 'inners' – made of fleece – or fingerless ones which are good for photographers, plus an outer wind- and waterproof pair).

A small headtorch is recommended, just in case you get caught out – especially if you are walking in winter when it goes dark early – or in case you fancy doing a night hike. Remember to check the batteries before you head out.

↑ A sample small hills kit bag. (Phoebe Smith)

Consider taking walking poles. Though some people think they look a little lame (and for older walkers only), they can reduce by nearly one-third the pressure on your knees. Their use should allow you to walk more hills for longer and avoid problems later in life. On flat ground – if used correctly – they can also help you walk quicker. They are also handy in the unfortunate event that you take a fall. And they help exercise your upper body too – bonus!

A small pair of binoculars will help you spot wildlife if that interests you. Finally – don't forget your camera (or camera phone) to record your adventures!

If combining one of these hills with a wild camp, you will also need a tent or bivvy bag, plus sleeping bag, camping mat, stove, mug, spoon and – of course – extra food.

FOOD AND DRINK

Walking uphill means you will get hungry so make sure you take plenty of snacks to replenish energy levels. Dried fruit, nuts, chocolate and sweets are all useful. And remember to take a water bottle (or hydration bladder) and fill it before you start. You should take at least one to two litres with you.

CLOTHING

When walking it's best to wear layers that you can remove if you get hot (or to which you can add if cold). Start with a thin baselayer, which sits next to your skin, but avoid cotton as this will stay wet if you get sweaty. Instead go for synthetic fabric or merino wool, which wicks sweat away from your body and helps regulate your temperature.

Above this you need a warming mid-layer. Micro-fleece is best for this as it packs down small and is nice and cheap. But a jumper can do the job too.

Finally you'll need waterproofs for when the British rain kicks in. This means both jacket and trousers. Look for fabric that is waterproof and breathable too – such as Gore-Tex or eVent. There are lots of cheap versions available that will work to stop rain getting in, though can end up feeling a little damp. This is typically because they don't allow sweat and heat to get out as effectively, which – in our typically damp but humid conditions – causes condensation to build up.

FOOTWEAR

For some of these hills you will likely be fine in a pair of trainers or multi-activity shoes – it is a case of personal choice. But if you are carrying a heavier rucksack (perhaps because you are planning to wild camp) or if your ankles are not particularly strong, then walking boots or at least mid-height footwear (where the cuff comes up around your ankle) are recommended. For routes featuring a scramble or rocky section, boots would certainly offer more support.

NAVIGATION

Usually on smaller hills finding your way is a straightforward affair – with some tracks and paths being waymarked. However, it's always worth knowing some basic navigation skills just in case. Plus getting used to map-reading on pint-sized peaks like these can help you confidently progress to walking higher hills.

WHICH MAP?

The most commonly used mapping products are the excellent options from Ordnance Survey, which offer maps at both 1:25,000 and 1:50,000. The former shows the most detail so is recommended for these small hills.

GETTING ORIENTATED

A great way to help you begin to grasp navigation is learning how to make the map in your hand 'fit' the landscape that you see in front of you. This is called 'orientating the map'. Simply open the map and turn it so that it fits the direction you are facing: all the features you see should be in the line suggested by the map. This enables you to actually see what tightly knitted contours, say, look like on the ground, and how the streams and walls line up. Do this every time you stop to try and work out your location. The more you do it the easier it will become. Over time, this will make route planning back at home much easier. It's also a great way to help others feel involved in the walk.

PLANNING TIMINGS

A rough timing for each of these walks is given on the relevant page. This is worked out using Naismith's Rule which is that the average person walks 4km/hour on flat ground, but then adds an extra minute per 10m going uphill, then factors in extra time for camera stops and food breaks. This is not an exact science, but is a good way to guestimate how long you might take. Do bear in mind, though, that when first starting out you may cover distances slower than when your fitness and skill levels are higher. Walking in the snow and in the dark will also take longer.

GPS/RECOMMENDED APPS

Both GPS devices and smartphone apps are improving all the time as navigational aids. They can be a good way of checking progress and testing yourself when you've orientated your map. One recommended app is OS Maps. For a modest annual subscription, this offers mapping for the whole of Britain plus the ability to plot routes. However, do make sure you always have a back-up paper map and compass too, as paper will never run out of batteries! If using a phone, protect it from the rain with a weatherproof case.

SAFETY

Walking up any hill is a hugely rewarding experience and the chance of things going wrong are low. But do remember to dress appropriately, and don't be afraid to turn back if the weather turns, you feel underprepared or are not confident in you (or your group's) ability. 'Enjoy not endure' is what I always say – the hills, after all, will always be there for another day.

Note: The routes in this book do come with manageable risks and sometimes take place in remote locations. The author and publisher have done all they can to ensure the accuracy of route descriptions, but they cannot be held legally or financially responsible for any accident, injury, loss or inconvenience sustained as a result of the information or advice contained in this book. Any outdoor activity – whether walking, wild camping or backpacking – is always undertaken entirely at your own risk.

USING THIS GUIDE

In this guide you'll find my personal picks of 60 of the best small hills that mainland Britain (England, Wales, Scotland) has to offer – each one carefully selected to inspire you to get outside more. You'll find every one of them offers something special – from intriguing history, unique landscape or geological features, to epic views, the chance to spot wildlife, try scrambling, sleep out on a wild camp and more. My aim is to start you off with these so that you'll develop the courage and confidence to go and walk further peaks – whether big or small. For those already bitten by the hillwalking bug these peaks have been chosen to demonstrate that you can enjoy fantastic views from and hiking on some of Britain's more height-challenged summits. They also prove that small hills also offer some great spots for wild camping and provide a way to persuade your friends, children and loved ones that the British outdoors is a jaw-droppingly magnificent place in which to spend time.

For each hill, as well as step-by-step instructions for summit success, you'll also find suggestions for *Added adventure* and *For adrenaline lovers* which both up the thrilling ante – whether by identifying bivvy spots for sleeping out or proposing ways to challenge yourself.

You'll note that a lot of routes take you up to the summit in the most direct – if not always the most visually stimulating – way. This is done on purpose. As a hill guide, specifically to get as many people as possible into the outdoors, I wanted to make it easy and quick to reach the top – minimum effort for maximum payoff. However, there are also options to *Make it bigger* for those demanding

KEY TO SYMBOLS

↔ Total distance of walk
↗ Total ascent during walk
↕ Total height of hill
↻ Duration of walk (estimated)

a longer and more varied stroll. And there are recommendations for *Little adventurers* – nearby places/points of interest to fill one or even several days in the area. I've also included practicalities such as recommended campsites (for those who like a secure place to pitch up), nearby places to eat and pick up snacks and supplies (pre- and post-walk) and any available public transport. As a package, this aims to enable you to fit a walk up one of these worthy hills into your next weekend, holiday or lunchbreak.

ADDED ADVENTURE

Under this heading you'll find a way to make your visit to the particular small hill more exciting. This could be a night walk, a winter hike, or – more often than not – a wild camp spot/quirky place to sleep. I adore wild camping (often my main motivator for getting outside) and find that small hills offer some of the best spots to enjoy a night under the stars, so for those of you looking to sleep out, this is the section for you.

Bear in mind if you head out wild camping it's legal in Scotland (everywhere except for many of the loch shores around Loch Lomond and the Trossachs National Park sadly, following introduction of a new byelaw in March 2017) and on Dartmoor, but elsewhere in Britain you are technically supposed to ask the landowner's permission, though this is not always practical. Wherever you sleep out, *please* follow the wild camper's etiquette. Namely – arrive late, leave early; take out all rubbish with you; don't light a fire without permission;

↑ Wild camping is the ultimate way to add adventure – but do ensure campfires are allowed before you light one. (Phoebe Smith)

sleep well away from people's houses and tracks; bury your toilet waste and pack out all loo roll with you; be respectful at all times – and if asked to move on, do so.

If walking in winter, bear in mind that even on small hills it can be too snowy/icy to be safe – especially on rocky areas. You may need to use (and know how to do so properly) an ice axe and crampons. Don't be afraid to turn back if the skills needed to complete the walk are beyond your capabilities. Nightwalking is fun, but do be sure to take warm layers, extra food and a headtorch – and tell a responsible person where you are going and when you expect to be back, just in case.

FOR ADRENALINE LOVERS

There's always one member of a group who likes to take their adventures a little further towards the realms of the extreme. If this is you, then check out this section for recommendations of activities on the hill or nearby with added exhilaration; from skydiving to caving, fell running to mountain biking, there's plenty to up the thrill factor, even on small hills.

FOR LITTLE ADVENTURERS

If taking children with you, remember that the whole point is for them to have a good time so they want to come again. Don't force them up a hill and have them refuse ever to go out with you again! Here are some top tips in doing this effectively:

- Consider a treasure hunt – do the walk yourself before them and hide some sweets at various points that you then get them to locate on the map. That will spur them on to keep going, distract them from the effort of the climb, and even get them excited about map-reading.
- Try geocaching – basically a global treasure hunt. Seek out co-ordinates online then find hidden 'caches' and log them (geocaching.com). Some caches contain toys, others expect that you bring something to exchange. All in all, a great way to encourage kids to get outside and clamour to do more.
- Get them involved – show them this book and invite them to pick the hill they want to climb. Or let them hold the map on the walk, and allow them to bring their own rucksack (even if it only has a couple of items in it). The key is to make kids feel that this is their adventure, rather than that they are being dragged on yours.
- Make a wildlife ticklist – a list of five wild things to spot on the walk. From worms to ants, birds or molehills, such a goal will keep them going.
- Praise them – you want them to remember the walk for all the right reasons. So encourage them by celebrating when they make it to the summit. And if they don't make it, make them feel good for getting as far as they did. It's about getting out there, so remember to make it fun!

AND FOR THE UNWILLING...

We all have friends, family or other halves that aren't convinced the outdoors is for them. Hopefully these little peaks – which boast maximum rewards for minimum effort – will help.

It's worth using some of the same tips for kids – praising them, getting them involved, showing them wildlife or points of interest. But also:

- Take rewards. Surprising them with their favourite chocolate bar or sandwich. Or take them to an unexpected point of interest or time arrival for sunset. Anything to make sure they remember the highlights of the experience – and yearn for more.
- Give them your better kit. Though it's hard to surrender your favourite waterproof, chances are they have no specialist gear so if you want them to have a good time, give them the best you have so that they stay warm and dry along the way.
- Let them choose the hill. Rather than enforce your favourite, ask them what interest they have – wildlife, fort, view, or the promise of a good pub at the end – and let them decide. Or try showing them the promise of 'Added adventure' to excite their inner explorer.

PLAN YOUR OWN SMALL HILL WALK...

Once you've ticked off a few (or dare I say all) of the small hills in this book, chances are you'll be hungry for more. To plan your own foray into the hills I suggest you simply...

- Get a map of your local area and look for summits close to home, where the contour lines bunch up nicely. Keep an eye out for trig points – denoted on OS maps by a blue triangle with a dot in the middle. These can be a good way of pinning down a good view as the Ordnance Survey needed to pick visible spots from which to triangulate the land when making maps.
- Look for bridleways/footpaths that will lead you to the top. Then match this up to a car park for a start/finish point and get plotting your route. Access land – where walkers have the right to roam off-path – is indicated by a yellow shading on OS maps. Remember to look for other points of interest and cafés/tearooms/pubs to start, end or break up your walk.
- Get yourself outside! Then share the hill you've climbed with me (see *Feedback request*, opposite).

(Phoebe Smith) →

FEEDBACK REQUEST

Been inspired to climb one of Phoebe's Best Small Hills? Or want to recommend one that you feel should have been included? Or fancy sending an update about conditions on the route? You can send your feedback direct to Bradt; contact us on 01753 893444 or info@bradtguides.com. We will forward emails to Phoebe who may post updates on the Bradt website at bradtupdates.com/smallhills. Alternatively you can add a review of the book to bradtguides.com or Amazon.

Communicate your adventures on Twitter, Instagram, Facebook and YouTube using the hashtag #BestSmallHills and we'll share it for you.

Bradt Travel Guides
@BradtGuides & @PhoebeRSmith
@bradtguides & @PhoebeRSmith
bradtguides
YouTube www.youtube.com/user/extremesleeps

A WORD ABOUT HILL SELECTION

The 60 specific hills found in this book have been chosen for three reasons. The first is that they represent a good geographical spread around the UK – I hope that all of you will find one within a few hours' drive from your doorstep. The second is that they all offer a little added incentive to climb them – from hillforts, to wild-camp spots, fascinating history or legends, local wildlife – and all offer superlative vistas without excessive ascents. The final reason is that this is my list of personal favourites, which I truly wanted to share with you all.

But like all lists I know that I can't include everyone's personal preferences so my hope is that you use this guide as a jumping-off point to start finding your own hillocks and adding them to your bespoke list of Britain's Best Small Hills. Since telling people I've been writing this book I've noticed that every time I mention the title someone always immediately says: 'Oh! Have you included [Insert your local little hill here]?'. I find this wonderful. It seems we all have favourite little peaks near to us, so please do send me your recommendations – sharing good hills with each other is my ultimate goal. I am always excited to climb new peaks – no matter how tall they are...

Standing atop the 'Lion and the Lamb' on the Lakes' Helm Crag. (Michael Hilton/D)

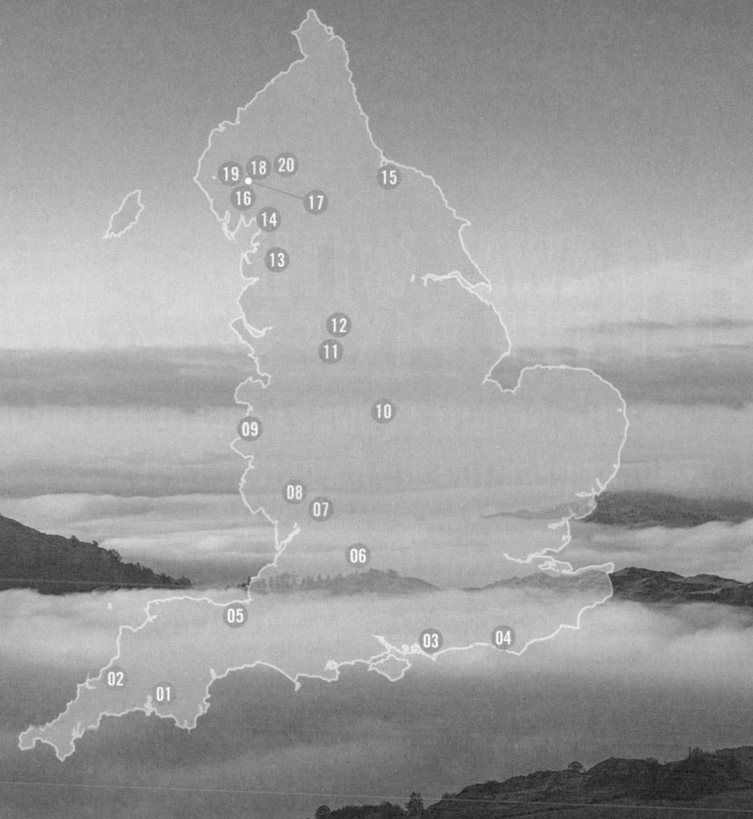

ENGLAND

01 AWAY WITH THE PIXIES

EXPLORE THE GRANITE CRUMBS BENEATH DARTMOOR'S LEGENDARY PEAK TO FIND A MAGICAL CAVE...

WHERE	Sheeps Tor, Devon
STATS	↔ 2km (1¼ miles) ↕ 360m ↗ 140m ↻ 1½ hours
START/FINISH	Sheepstor car park SX569689
TERRAIN	Grassy and rough paths through rocky ground
MAPS	OS Explorer (1:25,000) 20, 28; OS Landranger (1:50,000) 191

It's not often that a figment of local imagination makes it on to such an official document as an Ordnance Survey map. So take a look at Sheeps Tor on one of the OS Explorer 1:25,000 maps for this part of western Dartmoor and you'll notice something rather unusual. 'Piskies or Pixies House' is clearly marked south of the summit. Remarkably, this is not merely a nod to an oddly shaped rock, but an actual house (or, strictly speaking, cave). Venture down to that point from beneath the masses of granite shards that make up the summit, and you'll find a rectangular rock oddity that hides the house for the little piskies.The invisible creatures living inside the rocks at Sheeps Tor have featured in writing and tales since at least 1836. The 'cave' has – in reality – been formed by two slabs of granite that have fallen to create a narrow space about 1.8m (6ft) in length and 1.2m (4ft) wide. According to local legend, entering the cave requires you to make an offering to the homeowners. Failure to leave a gift (it used to be a pin or similar item, but now a biodegradable object is encouraged for the environment's sake!) is said to result in the pixies disturbing your sleep.

The dominating craggy granite tops will certainly be the thing that initially entices you to climb this Dartmoor peak. But it's the magical cave that is sure to entice you to explore further: just don't get carried away with the piskies...

↑ The clitter-strewn summit of Sheeps Tor hides a magical secret... (Craig Joiner Photography/A)

WALK THIS WAY

❶ From the car park in the forest east of Burrator Reservoir, turn left on to the minor road for 200m, then take the footpath on your left before Narrator Plantation, heading south. As you do, with trees on either side of you, keep a lookout for birds such as siskin, nuthatch and jay, plus the shy roe deer. Continue straight at the crossroads, to emerge from the woodland on to the lower fellside of Yellowmead Down. Here you can see the grass- and rock-coated hillside rising to Sheeps Tor summit. ❷ Skirt around the edge of the clitter-covered hill flanks bearing roughly southeast. Then, as the rocks start to relent, make a beeline for the summit, climbing steadily southwest. ❸ From the summit take the time to enjoy commanding views of the surrounding Dartmoor countryside – including the expansive Burrator Reservoir. Before you return (retracing your steps), consider indulging in a detour south to check out the Piskies House (see *Added adventure*).

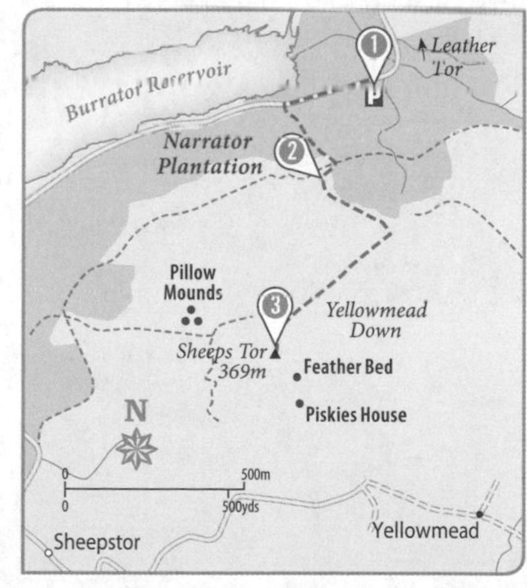

Gazing over to Burrator Reservoir from Sheeps Tor. (Neil Porter Photography)

ADDED ADVENTURE

Find the Sheeps Tor Piskies. From the summit, head to the southern slopes where – amongst the boulders and shards of granite – you can see the square formation of rocks that mark the entrance to Piskies House (around SX566681). It's a squeeze to get inside, but even today visitors leave offerings for the magic ones. The method is to go in on your stomach, backing inside. Only attempt it if you are not claustrophobic!

MAKE IT BIGGER

There's a wide choice of tors surrounding Sheeps Tor should you want to extend your walking, particularly, north of Burrator Reservoir. From the car park, head northwest to take in Sharpitor and, beyond that, Leeden Tor. Alternatively, cut north through the forest to reach Black Tor with its remains of multiple old settlements.

FOR LITTLE ADVENTURERS

Get your little ones to bring offerings for the Piskies to leave at the cave. I suggest a rock or flower so as not to litter the cave with non-biodegradables.

FOR CAMPERS

Sited on moorland owned by the Duchy of Cornwall, and with Dartmoor ponies roaming alongside cattle and sheep, Runnage Farm (runnagecampingbarns.co.uk; from £10pn) is the place for tent camping as well as offering camping barns and a granary bunkhouse.

FOR ADRENALINE LOVERS

If squeezing inside the cave is too easy, how about hauling yourself up and over granite rocks? Despite the lack of height (none exceeds 10m/33ft) there's an impressive 37 climbs to crack on this tiny tor's northern side – all at an acceptably low grade so good for beginner or intermediate crag rats. Recommended routes are Sheltered Crag and Mushroom Wall. For details see tinyurl.com/sheepstorclimbs.

FOR HUNGRY HIKERS

Pick up some cakes and savoury pasties (or indulge in breakfast or lunch) at Dartmoor Bakery in Yelverton (dartmoorbakery.co.uk). For poshed-up pub grub later try The Rock Inn (therockinnyelverton.pub). Yelverton also offers a Co-op for buying supplies.

OTHER PRACTICALITIES

The number 48 bus drops off near Burrator Dam, in the southwest corner of the reservoir, but only once daily so you wouldn't be able to get back the same day. Nearest toilets are in Yelverton.

02 PEAK WITH A PUN

HEAD FOR THE HIGHS OF BROWN WILLY, BODMIN MOOR'S PEAK WITH A BLUSH-INDUCING NAME

WHERE	Brown Willy, Cornwall
STATS	↔ 7km (4½ miles) ↕ 420m ↗ 192m ↻ 3½ hours
START/FINISH	Poldue Downs car park ⚲ SX137819
TERRAIN	Rough and often boggy ground on open moorland
MAPS	OS Explorer (1:25,000) 109; OS Landranger (1:50,000) 200

There's something very special about Brown Willy – and not just the name – though perhaps we should deal with this first. Yes, it regularly makes the list of the most curiously named places in Britain, and yes, it can be used in many a pun. The name, however, actually derives from one of two local Cornish names: Bronn Wennili (meaning 'hill of swallows') or *Bronn Ughella* ('highest hill' – it's the highest on Bodmin Moor and Cornwall as a whole). Honestly, though, where's the fun in that? In 2012, the idea was mooted to revert to a Cornish moniker but locals protested, inducing (pun-filled) newspaper headlines such as 'Hands off our Brown Willy'.

Names aside, despite its diminutive size this county top has plenty going for it. A monument near the start of the walk recounts the ghost story of Charlotte Dymond – a local 18-year-old murdered here in 1844 whose spirit is said to still wander Bodmin. There are Bronze Age settlements (hut circles, field systems and enclosures) including Fearnacre – one of the biggest in Cornwall. Pagans worshipped Roughtor Holy Well – on the northwest side of the fell of the same name – as a portal to another world. Then there's the summit of Brown Willy itself which, every 23 November, becomes a mecca for followers of the Aetherius Society, a UFO-based religion, who believe that the sun charges the peak with 'holy energy' on this date.

Then throw in a bit of wildlife to further enhance this raw, burnished green wilderness – from three types of deer (fallow, red and roe) to birds such as curlew, wheatear and stonechat. Finally, there are wonderfully shaped tors, carved by the elements over millennia, that adorn its summit and make this county top the ideal locality for a perfectly placed wild camp… More than a few reasons, then, why Brown Willy is one special, though small, peak – but then, size isn't everything… (sorry, I couldn't resist).

WALK THIS WAY

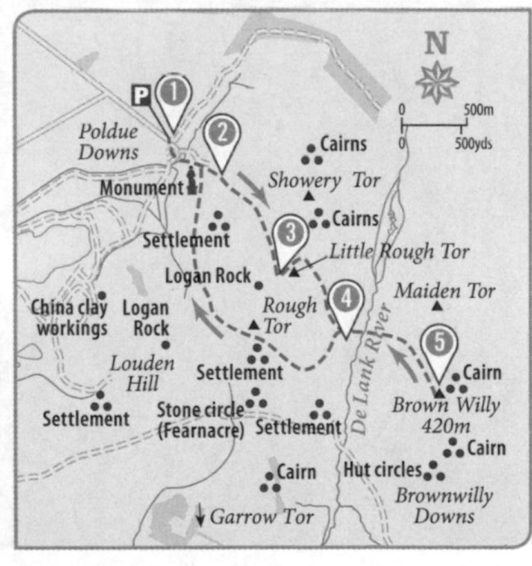

❶ From the car park at Poldue go through the gate and cross the bridge and follow the track southeast until it peters out after around 300m. ❷ Continue straight on, aiming for the space between the two rocky tors on the horizon in front of you (⚲ SX146808). Look out for reeds that surround the spring on Rough Tor and continue on to the rocky summit (400m) where Neolithic stone walls link the rocks together. This was the

← The wild expanse of Bodmin Moor, with Brown Willy looming in the background. (Helen Hotson/S)

site of a medieval chapel. 3 Here you can enjoy views north over to the Cornish coastline and, if the mood takes you, scramble around on the wind-scoured tors. Keep an eye out for wheatears flashing their white tails as they bounce from rock to rock; perhaps appropriately for today's walk, their name derives from 'white arse'. When you're done, bear northeast aiming for the col between here and Showery Tor, keeping to the rocky outcrop to your right. Descend to that tor (385m) then head southeast to the De Lank River, crossing the bridge. 4 There's a path here to follow southeast all the way to the summit of Brown Willy (420m). 5 From this summit, look west to see the china clay workings 1km beyond Rough Tor. Admire the landscape you've just traversed, which is smattered with evidence of prehistoric settlements, stone circles and cairns. To head back return to, and cross, the bridge. This time – rather than ascending Rough Tor – bear round the tor's southern edge then skirt the western slopes to gain more views over to the stone circle known as Fearnacre. Finally, walk north to rejoin the path back to your start.

↑ Watch the ground around the moor – it can become waterlogged. (Paul Nash/S)

ADDED ADVENTURE

With so much obvious history of our ancestors living out on Bodmin Moor, it would be rude not to take the tent and head out for a night on the moorland. Brown Willy itself makes a good spot given its proximity to a stream and a collection of tors beside which to hunker down and shelter from the wind. Alternatively you could try Maiden Tor, 1km (½ mile) north. At either site, the lack of light pollution should mean great stargazing.

MAKE IT BIGGER

Bodmin Moor was made for walking, but do be sure you are a confident navigator as the mist can come down suddenly – making finding your way confusing, even on smaller hills. Opt to check out nearby Garrow Tor and the intriguingly named King Arthur's Hall (2km and 3km to the southwest, respectively) before swinging back round to the north to pick up the bridleway that cuts past old settlements and stone circles at Highertown.

FOR LITTLE ADVENTURERS

Make this the place where you take the little ones on their first wild camp. Be sure to take plenty of layers so they don't get cold, along with any favourite toys so they have some home comforts. Then enjoy games such as shadow puppets on the tent walls and stargazing from the porch.

FOR CAMPERS

Cherry Cottage Campsite (🖱 cherrycottagecamping.co.uk; from £11pn) is a sheltered, family-run site with views of Bodmin Moor.

FOR ADRENALINE LOVERS

Every year, usually on New Year's Day, there's an annual fell run that takes place on Brown Willy, setting off from the Jamaica Inn (immortalised in Daphne du Maurier's novel of the same name, published in 1936). Take part in the real thing or simply grab your trail shoes and get jogging on this route.

FOR HUNGRY HIKERS

You can't beat a good bag of fish and chips – so why not try the award-winning Peckish (🖱 peckishfishandchips.co.uk) in Camelford, 4km (2½ miles) northwest. Here you'll also find pubs, restaurants and a Chinese take-away. There's a Londis shop for supplies.

OTHER PRACTICALITIES

There are no local buses to the start of the walk; the nearest place served is Camelford. There are no public toilets either, so try Camelford or Launceston before you start.

Roe are just one of three types of deer which call Bodmin Moor home. (Isselee/D) ↑

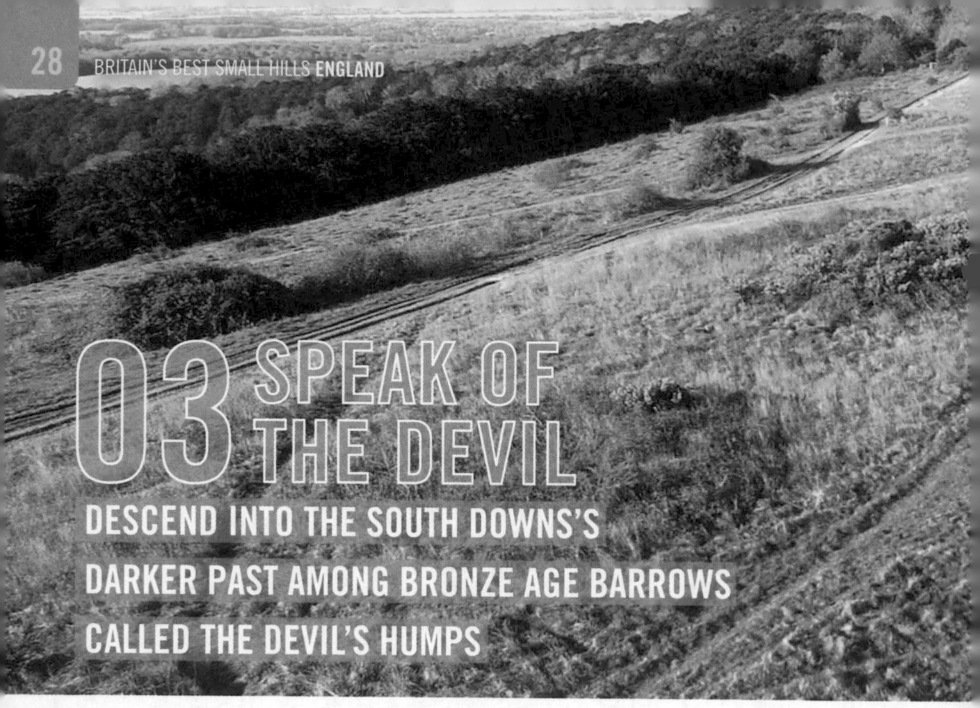

03 SPEAK OF THE DEVIL

DESCEND INTO THE SOUTH DOWNS'S DARKER PAST AMONG BRONZE AGE BARROWS CALLED THE DEVIL'S HUMPS

WHERE	Bow Hill, West Sussex
STATS	↔ 5.5km (3½ miles) ↕ 206m ↗ 159m ↻ 2–3 hours
START/FINISH	Kingley Vale Nature Reserve car park SU825087
TERRAIN	Clear track to start, then well-trodden trails on chalk hillside (can be extremely slippery when wet)
MAPS	OS Explorer (1:25,000) 8; OS Landranger (1:50,000) 197

Many people write off southeast England in terms of hillwalking – diminishing the area to simply London and Brighton, with no real outdoors adventures to be had – but they're very wrong. The chalk hills of the South Downs National Park of Hampshire and Sussex offer a whole bunch of great mini-peaks to check out – and sleep atop. Bow Hill is just one of these, albeit a very special one.

Bow Hill peeks up above the nature reserve at Kingley Vale, which is home to some of Britain's oldest yew trees – some 2,000 years young. Many yews were felled in the 14th century to make longbows, particularly after the government introduced a 'yew tax' of four bows for every cask of wine imported. This natural heritage imparts a distinctly ancient feel to Bow Hill, making visitors appreciate that they are somewhere worth cherishing.

And there is more than woodland coating the slopes of the down to conjure up Bow Hill's spellbinding atmosphere. On the summit itself are four Bronze Age barrows, which purportedly house the remains of Viking leaders that were vanquished by Chichester locals, with the intriguing names of Devil's Humps or King's Graves. Lore tells that the lesser Viking invaders who died on the slopes where the yews stand haunt the forest at night, when the trees themselves wander about. There's only one way to bear witness to the magic yourself – take a hammock and watch for spectres amidst the groves as night falls.

↑ The trail-covered Devil's Humps on Bow Hill. (Kevin Merrey)

WALK THIS WAY

❶ At the northern end of the car park, weave through the kissing gate to pick up the footpath that will lead you to Kingley Vale Nature Reserve. ❷ At the junction of paths there's a gate straight ahead. Go through it and into the forest. Here there's an interpretation hut with ample information panels on the area including details about the various archaeological discoveries here – Goosehill Camp (Iron Age settlement), the Bronze Age barrows of the Devil's Humps, prehistoric flint mines, old earthworks and the remains of a Roman temple – as well as insights into the wildlife you might see. Genned up, continue on the footpath until you emerge into a clearing, the slopes of Bow Hill rising in front of you. ❸ Here bear right, keeping the clearing to your left. If you are visiting in June or July, look for the stunning bee orchid flowering a few inches above the ground. In July, chalkhill blue butterflies flit across the chalk slopes alighting on wild thyme.

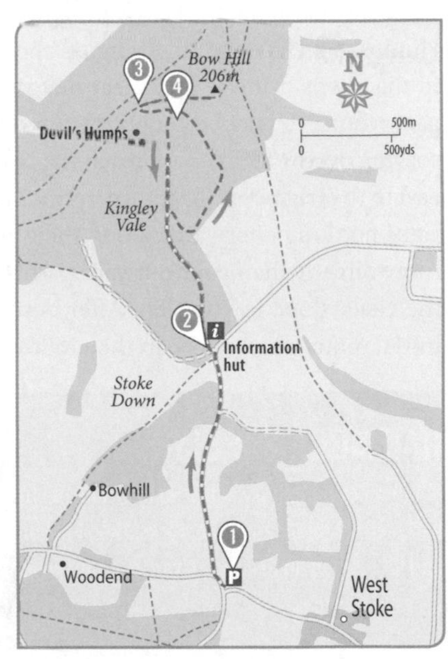

Then head uphill (northeast) towards a gap in the woodland that forms an archway of tree branches. Enter it to become engulfed by myriad trees: yew, oak, ash, holly and hawthorn. Pause to listen for the laughing call of a green woodpecker or the nervous tread of a roe deer. Continue uphill (take care after rain when the chalk-and-mud path can be very slippery) and you'll eventually emerge from the woodland on to more open downland. ❹ Turn left on to the path and follow it as coppices of trees flank both your sides. Go through a gate and continue along the grassy path up and out on to the tumuli cluster of Devil's Humps. ❺ Have fun lingering on these little lumps, watching the lights flicker in the towns below – on a clear day you can even see the Isle of Wight. As you gaze, your eye may be caught by a red kite tacking past or a common buzzard soaring overhead. Then, to reach the true summit, take the path bearing roughly east to the trig point. To return, retrace your steps through the gate but then turn right not long afterwards along the obvious track that heads downhill (south) more directly than your outward path. Look again for orchids and butterflies on the chalk slope to your left. After descending the slopes, the path rejoins your initial route, which you can then follow back to your start.

HAMMOCK SAFETY

If hammock camping, you'll need to ensure the tree is strong enough: check for signs of rot – crumbling bark, lighter colour, multiple cracks. Then hold on to the trunk around which you'll lash your hammock and lift yourself up to ensure it can take your weight without bending or snapping. Once you're satisfied, it's time to pitch.

↑ Kingley Vale is home to the oldest yew trees in Britain. (Sophie Lake/Footprint Ecology)

ADDED ADVENTURE

Take a hammock; as long as you're careful, the trees around this fell offer excellent scope for swaying yourself to sleep. This means you're in prime position to watch the sunset, then the lights of Chichester and the Isle of Wight begin to twinkle in the dusk... and then to see the perfect sunrise in the morning.

MAKE IT BIGGER

Kingley Vale Nature Reserve is a place to linger. Take your time exploring the various pathways and bridleways that vein the ground, check out the other Bronze Age spoils (such as flint mines) and remains of the Roman settlement, or root around the downland for beautiful orchids. Then strike out into the groves themselves, ignoring the constraints of paths, to gain the unbeatable feeling of being lost in Britain's ancient trees that are among some of the oldest living things in the country.

FOR LITTLE ADVENTURERS

The interpretation hut is a good place to linger with little 'uns. As well as the information panels, there's a chalkboard where people share their animal sightings. You could convert what's been seen into your own wildlife ticklist for kids to check off as you explore, or why not make a lean-to den in the trees – as others have done before you.

FOR CAMPERS

The nearest available camping is at the Camping and Caravanning Club's site, 8.3km (5 miles) away at Southbourne, west of Chichester (campingandcaravanningclub.co.uk/chichester; from £8.80pppn). Otherwise try Wicks Farm Holiday Park (wicksfarm.co.uk; from £18.50pn), 15.6km (9¾ miles) away, which also offers camping pods to rent.

FOR ADRENALINE LOVERS

Want to see the South Downs from a different perspective? The local gliding club offers two-seater trial flights or lessons where you'll cruise over these chalky mounds (southdowngliding.co.uk).

FOR HUNGRY HIKERS

There's nothing in the immediate area, but nearby villages offer a number of hostelries worth checking out. Try the Hare & Hounds in Stoughton (hareandhoundspub.co.uk), which serves local ciders, ales and good portions of stodgy post-walk (or post-hammock) grub. For a lighter bite head to Wellies Café (welliescafe.co.uk), a converted barn on the road from West Stoke to Chichester, which offers locally sourced breakfast, lunch or afternoon tea.

OTHER PRACTICALITIES

Although there is no public transport to Kingley Vale, you can take Bus 54 from Chichester to East Ashling (daily except Sunday and bank holidays), from where it is a 1km walk to West Stoke car park. If you drive, don't leave anything on display as signs warn of opportunistic thieves in the area (that said, the author has never had any issues even on overnight stays). There are no public toilets in the area.

04 AVALANCHE HILL

WITH NEGLIGIBLE EFFORT, SCALE THE SITE OF ONE OF BRITAIN'S WORST AVALANCHE DISASTERS

WHERE	Cliffe Hill, East Sussex
STATS	↔ 3km (1¾ miles) ↕ 164m ↗ 114m ↻ 1 hour
START/FINISH	Glyndebourne car park ⚲ TQ451107
TERRAIN	Grassy field paths; watch out for flying golf balls
MAPS	OS Explorer (1:25,000) 122; OS Landranger (1:50,000) 198

With a golf course sprawling over most of the summit (making walking here more akin to an unsolicited game of dodgeball than a pleasant country ramble), and vast quarries gouged out of the peak's northernmost flanks (scarring the would-be grassy slopes), you'd be forgiven for giving Cliffe Hill something of a wide berth. But allow me to try to persuade you otherwise.

For this minuscule bump hides something of a dark (indeed, tragic) past that is quite unexpected. Despite its limited stature – just 164m – Cliffe Hill lays claim to being the site of one of the worst avalanches in UK history.

↑ The unassuming Cliffe Hill – hard to believe that snow has formed cornices on its edges several times. (Ken Taylor/D)

It started on Boxing Day 1836. A huge accumulation of snow that had built up on the hill's sheer edge, reportedly 20ft (6.1m) deep, broke off. This destroyed a timber yard, sweeping it into the nearby River Ouse. But worse was still to come. Residents of adjacent cottages refused to move and, the following morning, a second avalanche struck. It tore up the seven houses below, coating them in a heap of white powder. Records are sketchy but it's said that only seven of the 15 people estimated to be inside were dug out alive. One was a young girl called Fanny Boakes and the dress she was wearing at the time of her rescue is still on display in the Anne of Cleves House in Lewes. In South Malling parish church is a grave of those who perished and on Boulder Row where the houses once stood is now a pub called the Snowdrop Inn, so named in recognition of the fateful December morning.

If that wasn't enough, Cliffe Hill's history goes back even further and is arguably even darker. It is also home to a Bronze Age barrow – found to be holding remains of cremations during a dig in the 1930s – though this was sadly quarried away. However, the eagle-eyed may spot a suspicious-looking lump on the golfing fairway – used as a hazard – which is actually the remains of a long barrow. Finally, you'll note the obelisk on the hill's westernmost reaches just before the town of Cliffe. This marks the site of a former monastery that was one of many destroyed by Henry VIII during the religious Reformation of the 16th century. Somewhat macabrely 17 Protestant martyrs were burned alive here; they are now memorialised at the annual Lewes Bonfire Night.

Golf course notwithstanding, with so much history and views out to the coast to boot, this is one hill that's certainly not below par…

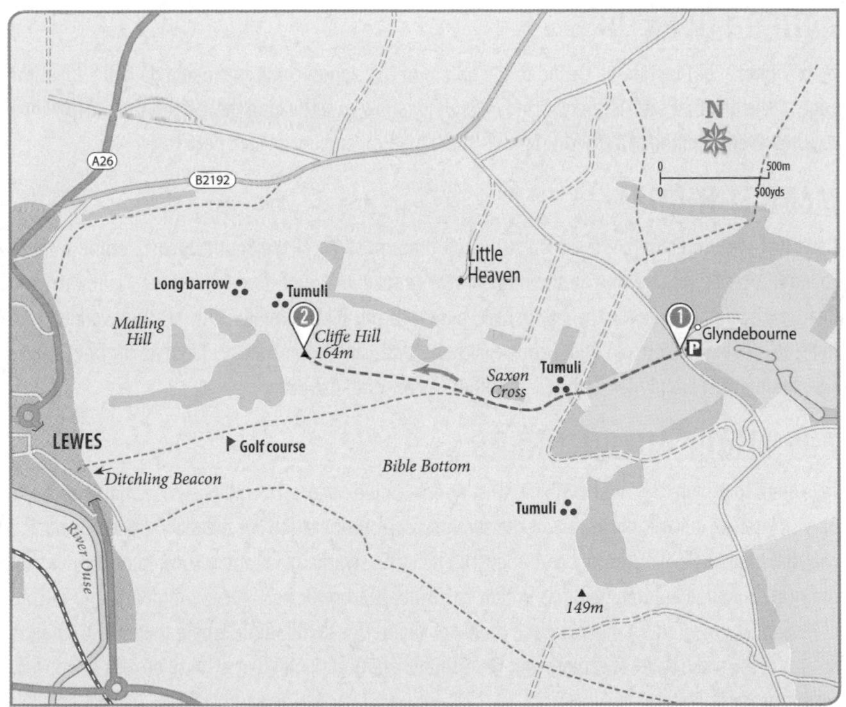

WALK THIS WAY

❶ From the car park at Glyndebourne, cross the main road to pick up the footpath heading west. As you steadily climb the grass-covered chalk downland you'll start to spy tumuli – raised earthworks – to your left. One even rises to 135m: its own mini-hillock. Though you won't see anything on the ground, the map gives a nod to this down's religious significance, with names such as Saxon Cross, Bible Bottom and Little Heaven lending an ecclesiastical nod to proceedings, even amidst the golf flags flapping in the breeze. ❷ At the summit, denoted by a trig pillar, you can gaze northwest along the rest of the ridge, out to the grassy fields and down to the quarry. Take note of the River Ouse to the west, into which the avalanche swept away the houses all those years ago. You'll also be able to spy the Snowdrop Inn (thesnowdropinn.pub) – the name of which is a nod to this infamous event. Further afield, enjoy panoramic views of the Sussex Weald and coastline and spot the impressive fort remains at Mount Caburn. Or look up and cloudwatch: how many different types of cloud can you spot (checking cloudappreciationsociety.org might help you differentiate them). When you're done, if you're not tempted to *Make it bigger*, simply retrace your steps back to the start.

ADDED ADVENTURE

Go in winter – but be careful. Owing to the nature of the slopes, cornices can and do build up on the edge of the hill. That said, it rarely is cold enough for snow to settle long these days! On a crisp winter day, however, a coating of fresh frost renders this a magical and uncrowded peak to explore.

MAKE IT BIGGER

Don't just stick to Cliffe Hill: head west to stroll through some of the South Downs's prime walking country. After Lewes you'll be on the ridge proper to take in Mount Harry, Plumpton Plain, Ditchling Beacon (the highest point in the Downs) and pass Jack and Jill Windmills (19th-century working corn mills; jillwindmill.org.uk) and a couple of pubs, and can end in spectacular style on Devil's Dyke (nationaltrust.org.uk/devils-dyke) – another worthy pint-size peak.

FOR LITTLE ADVENTURERS

Take them to explore the Sussex Wildlife Trust reserve called Malling Down (sussexwildlifetrust.org.uk/visit/malling-down), northwest of the summit. Go 'mini-beasting' for meadow grasshoppers and chalkhill blue butterflies (in July and August), enjoy the swathe of common spotted orchids or spot the richly coloured autumn gentians in that particular season. Or head for the ramparts and ditches of Mount Caburn's Iron Age hillfort just a couple of kilometres to the south, where there's also a nature reserve of the same name to explore that hosts Britain's largest population of burnt orchids (tinyurl.com/mt-caburn-reserve).

FOR CAMPERS

Blackberry Wood Campsite (blackberrywood.com; from £10pppn) is about 9.5km (6 miles) away, but located at the foot of the South Downs it's a wonderful place to stay with each pitch set in private glades. There are also two tree houses, plus a gypsy caravan, converted helicopter and curved wooden cabin.

FOR ADRENALINE LOVERS

Take your bike and, after hitting the summit, hit the road west up to Ditchling Beacon, which has roughly the same gradient as Mont Ventoux – the hardest of all the Tour de France climbs – but is about 14 times shorter. Do it 14 times for a real sense of achievement… and enjoy every swoop back down.

FOR HUNGRY HIKERS

The Lewes Arms (lewesarms.co.uk) has hearty, homemade pub grub from produce that, wherever possible, is locally sourced. For snacks your best options are in Lewes itself where there are loads of options. Try the Flint Owl Bakery (flintowlbakery.com) for handcrafted, organic and preservative-free bread, sandwiches and snacks.

OTHER PRACTICALITIES

Lewes train station connects with London Victoria, Eastbourne, Brighton and Gatwick Airport. If needs be, you can approach the walk from the west, straight from town, picking up the footpath that goes over Cuilfail Tunnel and ascends the west side of Cliffe Hill. The nearest toilets are in Lewes train station.

The 19th-century Jack and Jill windmills are famous landmarks on the Downs. (Philip Bird LRPS CPAGB/S) ↑

05 HEAD FOR THE NECK

SET YOUR COURSE FOR SOMERSET'S QUANTOCKS TOP, TO SPY RED DEER ROAMING WILD

WHERE	Wills Neck, Somerset
STATS	↔ 3km (2 miles) ↕ 386m ↗ 61m ↻ 1½ hours
START/FINISH	Triscombe Stone car park ST164359
TERRAIN	Well-defined bridleway all the way to the summit
MAPS	OS Explorer (1:25,000) 140; OS Landranger (1:50,000) 181

Although Wills Neck is rumoured to be a battleground between the Romans and local Weales (an Anglo-Saxon word for 'foreigner' and the origin of today's name) around 55BC, it is now a place of pure peace. Its rump-like slopes rise steadily to become the highest point in Somerset's rolling Quantock Hills. In summer Wills Neck glows almost purple from the heather that coats its flanks, which, come autumn, darken to form a thick russet blanket.

From the summit of Wills Neck you can see a sprawling panorama of other lumps and bumps around the countryside – from Dartmoor to Exmoor, the Mendips to the Brecon Beacons. The trail is even mountain-bike friendly and you'll often see lycra-clad two-wheelers bounding over the ridgeline. It also follows part of a walk known as the Macmillan Way, which links Boston in Lincolnshire to Abbotsbury in Dorset to raise money for the cancer-relief charity of the same name.

As you skirt the southwest corner of Great Wood, keep a lookout for roe deer slinking between the trees or a sparrowhawk soaring overhead before plummeting to cause chaos among a flock of small birds. Buoyed by this blend of landscape, vistas, exertion and nature, embrace being a foreigner to this high land and indulge in a wild adventure – in every sense of the word.

WALK THIS WAY

❶ There are numerous paths from the car park – make sure you take the one immediately uphill bearing south, steering a course between Great Wood to your left and the (concealed) Triscombe Quarry to your right. After a few hundred metres on open hillside, you will pass a cairn – a good way to confirm you are on the right track. ❷ At the summit drink in the expansive views. To the west is Exmoor, south the nearby Blackdown Hills, with the high plateau of Dartmoor beyond, to the north the Bristol Channel with the Brecon Beacons behind and, to the east, the equally tempting Mendips. Once your thirst has been quenched, consider whether or not you want to continue. If so, check out the tumuli to the southeast and perhaps journey to more of the Quantock Hills beyond. If not, simply retrace your steps.

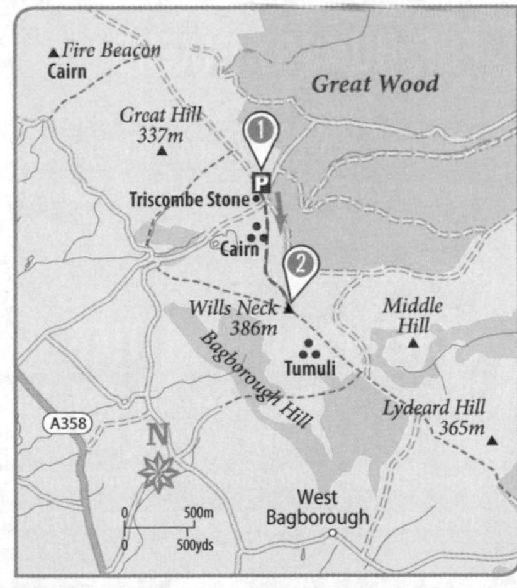

← A heathery haze at Wills Neck. (Derek Stone/A)

ADDED ADVENTURE

Bring your bivvy to claim a wild camp spot at the very top of the Quantocks, from where you can watch the lights from Taunton start to twinkle at dusk and perhaps feel smug at your escape from urbanity. For those who want a slightly more active night, you could try a summer walk listening for and potentially seeing nightjars, a fabled nightbird informally known as 'goatsucker', which occur in the Great Wood, just northeast of this walk.

MAKE IT BIGGER

The Quantocks Ridge stretches northwest and southeast from the summit so choose your direction and get hiking. Hit the former and you'll end at Somerset's wonderful coast. Choose the latter, and you'll finish on Colthelstone Hill where you'll likely find a herd of Exmoor ponies.

FOR LITTLE ADVENTURERS

Within a short drive (27km/17 miles away, in Minehead) is the West Somerset Steam Railway (west-somerset-railway.co.uk) – a rewarding post-walk treat for short and long legs alike.

FOR CAMPERS

Fourteen kilometres (9 miles) away, Moorhouse Campsite (moorhousecampsite.co.uk; from £13pn) is well located and dog-friendly. As well as space for tents, it offers two camping pods, small animals for kids to pet, and a wooden climbing area. You can even buy fresh eggs and home-brewed cider from the farm.

FOR ADRENALINE LOVERS

Take your mountain bike, as the Quantocks are a great place to explore on two wheels as a bridleway runs the length of the summits. Pack a bivvy or tent too and you can really make a day (and night) of it.

FOR HUNGRY HIKERS

In Nether Stowey (12km/7½ miles away), Quantock Tea Room (quantocktearoom.co.uk) offers sandwiches, cakes and drinks. For a pub meal try the Carew Arms (thecarewarms.co.uk) in Crowcombe, 7km (4½ miles) away along the road to Minehead. Be sure to try the Wills Neck golden ale – named after the hill you've just climbed. Supplies can be picked up in the supermarkets in Taunton.

OTHER PRACTICALITIES

There are some sporadic local buses (including the 23, operated by Hatch Green Coaches, which runs daily on weekdays; tinyurl.com/willsneckbus) from Taunton to West Bagborough, the nearest village, but otherwise you need to drive to the start of this walk. There are no public toilets on the walk, the nearest being in Taunton.

Exmoor ponies can be spotted near this pint-size peak. (Mike Charles/S)

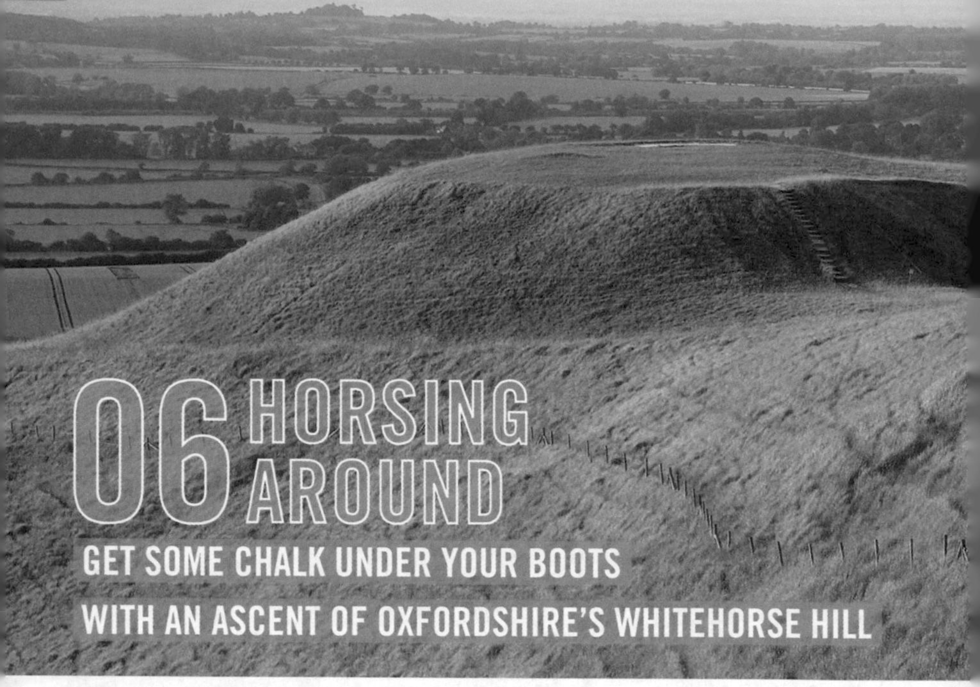

06 HORSING AROUND

GET SOME CHALK UNDER YOUR BOOTS WITH AN ASCENT OF OXFORDSHIRE'S WHITEHORSE HILL

WHERE	Whitehorse Hill, Oxfordshire
STATS	↔ 1km (¾ mile) ↕ 261m ↗ 50m ↻ 1 hour
START/FINISH	National Trust car park ⚲ SU293866
TERRAIN	Steep up and downhill on grassy tracks, small section on minor road
MAPS	OS Explorer (1:25,000) 170; OS Landranger (1:50,000) 163

Little hills usually need to have something going for them to make them worthy of a climb, but Whitehorse Hill (sometimes called White Horse Hill; nationaltrust.org.uk/white-horse-hill) has two worthy interest points. The first is that, despite its diminutive size, the hill is the highest point in Oxfordshire, giving you a 'county top' for your effort (as well as offering views over six counties). Even more distinctive is that, as the name suggests, it's also the site of a giant white horse carved into the underlying chalk.

Initially thought to have been made in the Iron Age (between 800BC and AD100), carbon dating has shown that the carving dates from the Bronze Age (probably 1200–800BC). Whitehorse Hill is often touted as one of the finest (and best-preserved) examples of this form of chalk art. And the best news? You can get an intimate view over this giant equine for the bare minimum of walking – no trotting needed.

WALK THIS WAY

1 From the car park head south on the minor road. Ignore the first turning but at the crossroads bear left (east), bidding farewell to the Lambourn Valley Way as it bears off to the right. **2** Continue on, heading uphill along what is

↑ The flat-topped Dragon Hill sits alongside Oxfordshire's Whitehorse Hill. (Whiskybottle/D)

now the Ridgeway National Trail. Skylarks may provide acoustic accompaniment to your walk: see if you can spot one singing high in the sky. **3** Look for the gate at the top of the hill and head north through it to access the remains of Uffington 'Castle' hillfort and obtain views of the White Horse itself from the 261m summit. If you walk in summer, admire three types of orchid (common spotted, chalk fragrant and pyramidal), other plants such as various birdsfoot trefoils and knapweeds, plus butterflies including Adonis blue and marbled white. **4** From the summit take in the views of the feature called The Manger and even as far as the Cotswold Hills. Skywatch for birds of prey such as red kite and common buzzard, or perhaps a kestrel hovering in the breeze. Then either cut down the north side of the hill to join Dragonhill Road and turn left to go back to your start, or retrace your steps from the summit going back the way you came. Dragon Hill is worth a minor detour *en route*; this flat-topped little chalk hillock is said to be one of many places in the UK where St George slayed his dragon (they point to the path where no grass grows as being the place where blood spilled).

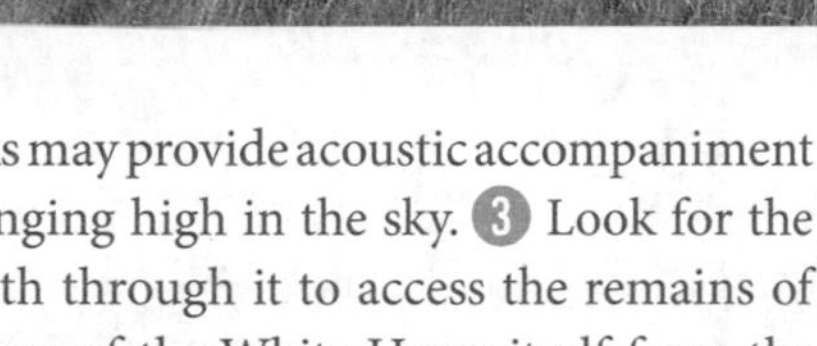

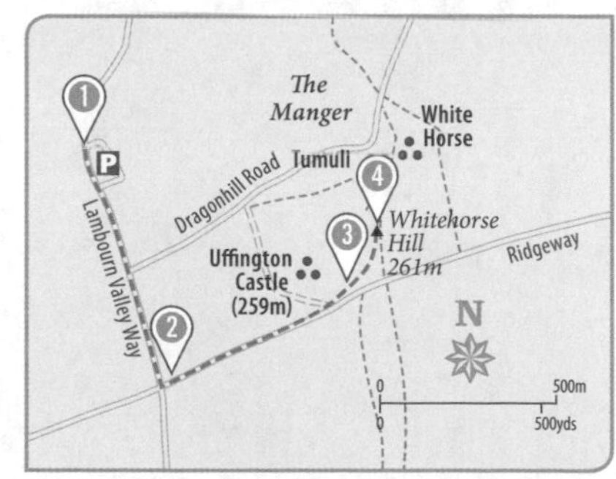

ADDED ADVENTURE

As if you needed reason to linger after dark but... one legend has it that once a year the chalk horse comes to life and leaves the hillside to go and feed on the slope below (known as The Manger) – but is always back in position by first light. So take your warm clothes, camping mat and sit out to watch this equine giant when night falls.

MAKE IT BIGGER

The chalk horse lies alongside a much longer route, the Ridgeway National Trail (nationaltrail.co.uk/ridgeway). Believed to have served as a road for over 5,000 years this is the oldest still-used path in Britain. The total distance is 139km (87 miles), running from Avebury (Wiltshire) to Ivinghoe Beacon (Buckinghamshire). You could trek this part of that route or follow the waymarked 'Ridgeway Circular Route' for a shorter (7km; 4¼ mile) loop around the nearby countryside.

FOR LITTLE ADVENTURERS

The White Horse adjoins Uffington 'Castle'. Although all that's left of this Iron Age fort is essentially a single ditch and rampart, it nevertheless gives your little ones something to explore.

FOR CAMPERS

Britchcombe Farm (britchcombefarm.co.uk; from £8pppn) offers camping seasonally and is neatly located for this hill and walking trails in surrounding Oxfordshire.

The best view of a white horse is often from above. (John Henshall/A)

FOR ADRENALINE LOVERS

What better way to experience the landscapes surrounding the chalk horse than on a real horse? Local outfit Asti Equestrian (asti-equestrian.co.uk) offers lessons and hacking in the area.

FOR HUNGRY HIKERS

Just over 1km from the car park (walking – carefully – north along the minor road) is Woolstone, where you'll find an oak-beamed, thatched-roof pub called the White Horse Inn (whitehorsewoolstone.co.uk; booking advised), which serves lunch and evening meals featuring fresh Cornish fish. Britchcombe Farm (see opposite) offers cream teas and snacks on weekend afternoons. For supplies Ashbury's Village Shop (ashburyshop.co.uk), 5km (3 miles) southwest, has some basics. For more choice Swindon, 19km (12 miles) away, is your best bet.

OTHER PRACTICALITIES

There are no toilets on this route; the nearest ones are in the pub at Woolstone (customers only). Public transport is limited to Saturdays, when Bus X47 calls in three times between Swindon and Ardington.

07 EDGE YOUR BETS

HEAD TO SHEER-SIDED CLEEVE HILL FOR THE CHANCE TO BE A ROCK STAR...

WHERE	Cleeve Hill, Gloucestershire
STATS	↔ 7km (4¼ miles) ↕ 330m ↗ 56m ↻ 3 hours
START/FINISH	Cleeve Common car park ⚲ SO989271
TERRAIN	Open hilltops, grassy paths
MAPS	OS Explorer (1:25,000) 179; OS Landranger (1:50,000) 150

When is the high point of a walk not actually a high point? Answer: when it's Cleeve Hill. The highest point is 330m and sits south of the ridge, with a crowd of three tall radio masts adorning its flanks – but the summit is not the reason you'd come (good thing too because believe it or not, there's actually a golf course at the top!). Here on the dramatic Cotswold Edge escarpment is a sprawling common of Jurassic limestone interspersed with rare orchids, making it a biologically and geologically rich Site of Special Scientific Interest (SSSI). The limestone edges are what appeal: protruding like yellowed teeth from a grassy green gumline, they add a shot of unexpected drama in the otherwise rolling Cotswold hillsides. Yet more interest is provided by old settlements in the form of an Iron Age hillfort, The Ring (a circular earthwork believed to have served as an enclosure for animals in the early centuries AD), and the Neolithic long barrow of Belas Knap. There's even a series of tricky but short climbs on Castle Rock that add further drama to a flattened summit that many overlook.

This walk across an SSSI is also brilliant for fauna and flora. The limestone grassland has never been fertilised, sprayed or ploughed, so contains a wondrously diverse range of wildflowers. Wander with your nose to the ground in summer and you should see birdsfoot trefoils, wild thyme, burnet-saxifrage, carline thistles and harebells. Look a bit closer to discern bee or pyramidal orchids. Walk with an expert and you may spot the rare musk orchid or purple milk-vetch.

↑ Looking out from Cleeve Common on Cleeve Hill. (Andrew Roland/S)

WALK THIS WAY

1 From the car park head southwest on the track to take you up on to Cleeve Hill (part of which is sadly a golf course!). It won't be long before you reach a trig point above The Ring. **2** The trig does not actually mark the highest point on Cleeve Hill, but it does offer the best views from the top. From here you can see Exmoor, peer down to Cheltenham and its racecourse, and look west to the River Severn and the Welsh hills beyond. When you're ready, continue along Cotswold Edge (often called Cleeve Cloud – and marked as such on the OS map) to walk above the impressive limestone escarpment. **3** You'll come to the mound of what was once an Iron Age hillfort. It is clear from the vista why this made a particularly good stonghold.

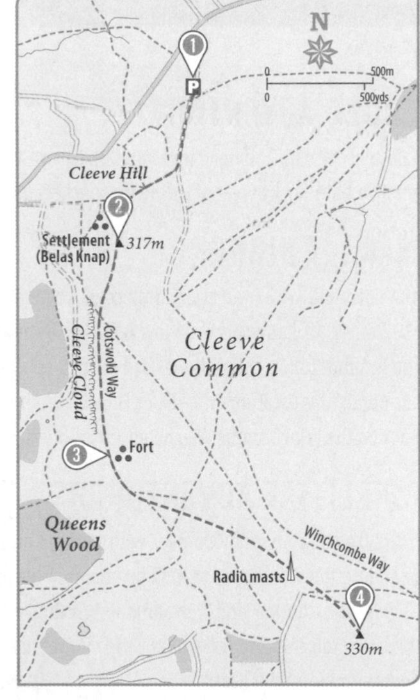

ADDED ADVENTURE

Take a bivvy bag, and head up after dark to find a perfect spot to spend the night – near the fort – or set up a hammock in one of the nearby pockets of woodland.

MAKE IT BIGGER

The Cotswold Way (nationaltrail.co.uk/cotswold-way) that runs across this summit offers 164km (102 miles) of pathways to follow between Bath and Chipping Campden. Rather than rushing up to the summit, follow this national trail southeast from the car park to take in some of the woodland that surrounds the escarpment – Elder Grove, Woodpeckers and Breakheart Plantation – before looping back on the Winchcombe Way heading northwest to claim the top.

FOR LITTLE ADVENTURERS

If they're not so easily won over with hillforts and summits, head into the woodlands to look for common butterflies such as peacock, comma and red admiral, which are abundant in this area. You can also (carefully) watch for reptiles – slow worms, adders and common lizards.

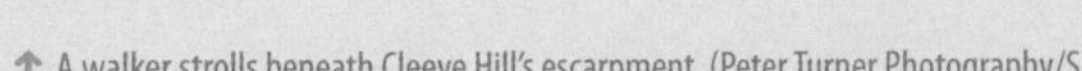

↑ A walker strolls beneath Cleeve Hill's escarpment. (Peter Turner Photography/S)

FIND A GOOD BIVVY SPOT

The perfect place to site your bivvy bag will be as flat as possible – check for lumps, bumps or uncomfortable rocks. If pitching on a slope make sure your head is elevated rather than your feet and consider taking tent pegs to anchor your bivvy. It's always nice to position yourself either west facing (for sunset) or east facing (for sunrise). Put your sleeping mat inside the bivvy for maximum comfort.

Continue on the path past two tall beech trees called 'The Twins', then cut southeast, heading towards the three radio towers. Continue past both masts and car park to reach the trig point, which marks Cleeve Common's highest spot, at 330m. ④ Unfortunately there is not much of a view from this rounded peak from where you can take the obligatory summit shot. However, excitement is not provided by a stationary trig point, but rather by things that move. In late winter and early spring, adders bask in secluded sunny spots. Burnet moths and dark green fritillaries visit purple flowers in summer. Skylarks serenade from upon high. Greater and lesser horseshoe bats inhabit some of the caves. There are four badger setts (stay after dusk for the chance to see them), while roe deer and muntjac browse the shrubbery. To return you can either retrace your steps or vary your route by picking up the Winchcombe Way heading northwest back towards The Ring and your start point.

FOR CAMPERS

Folly Farm Camping (cotswoldcamping.net; from £15pn) is a quiet family-run site just west of Bourton-on-the-Water, 17.7km (11 miles) away.

FOR ADRENALINE LOVERS

Castle Rock is the one face on this Cotswoldian hill that is ripe for climbing, so take your rope and harness and check ukclimbing.co.uk for routes.

FOR HUNGRY HIKERS

There is a bar at Cleeve Hill Golf Club (cleevehillgolfclub.co.uk/restaurant) that non-members may use. Otherwise try The Royal Oak (royal-oak-prestbury.co.uk), a 16th-century inn in Prestbury considered by *National Geographic* to number among England's top ten pubs, or The Apple Tree Inn in Woodmancote (tinyurl.com/appletreewood).

OTHER PRACTICALITIES

Nearest toilets are in the Golf Club. Bus 606 runs daily between Cheltenham and Winchcombe: ask for 'Golf Club junction'. For supplies, the nearest place is Cheltenham.

← Dark green fritillaries can be seen during the summer months. (Rudmer Zwerver/S)

08 MALVERN MAGIC

SUMMIT THE HIGHEST POINT IN WORCESTERSHIRE FOR A VIEW OVER 13 COUNTIES

WHERE	Worcestershire Beacon, Worcestershire
STATS	↔ 3km (1¾ miles) ↕ 425m ↗ 115m ↻ 1½ hours
START/FINISH	Upper Wyche car park SO768439
TERRAIN	Road to start then grassy paths to summit
MAPS	OS Explorer (1:25,000) 190; OS Landranger (1:50,000) 150

It might be tempting to think that the majority of the little peaks celebrated in this book have been used – at some time or another – as a warning beacon. And with a name like Worcestershire Beacon (or, for locals, simply 'The Beacon'), this one is no exception. However, this particular hill has served a great many other purposes too. During World War II air raids on Birmingham, it was a lookout for fire. In the late 2000s, the BBC parked its transmitter van here to cover the horse racing at Worcester. And in 1968–69, the hill itself was a location for another BBC programme, *Doctor Who*.

Nowadays The Beacon's main role is to provide some excellent walks and 360-degree views down to the surrounding towns and beyond. And it certainly delivers. On a clear day you can see over to the Shropshire and Cotswold Hills, the Bristol Channel and out to Birmingham too. Indeed, eagle eyes have apparently discerned parts of 13 counties from the top. Take note of the toposcope on the summit. It was designed by Malvern architect Troyte Griffith, who was friends with another local man – perhaps Britain's greatest composer – Edward Elgar. To gain inspiration for his compositions, Elgar would wander these hills for hours, listening to the sounds of the wind in the trees.

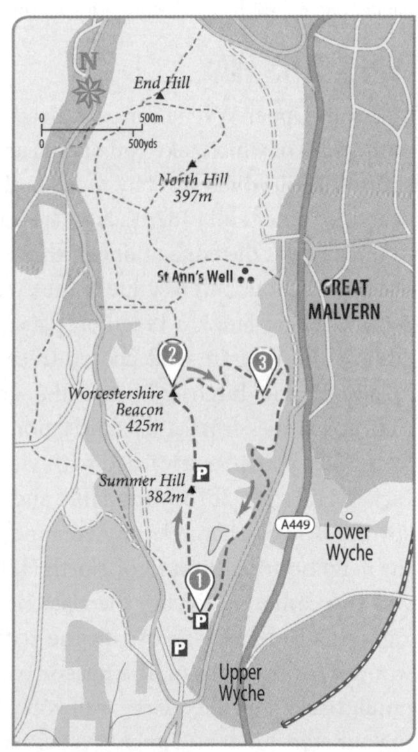

The hill is looked after by a local group called the Malvern Hills Trust (malvernhills.org.uk) formed in 1884 to protect the land. Old laws allow commoners to graze on the Malvern Hills, so you could be sharing summits and slopes with sheep or even Galloway cattle – the latter brought in to 'mow' the grass in a more natural haphazard fashion than the lawnmower-like technique of sheep.

There's decent wildlife to see too – whilst hazel dormice remain concealed, ravens (which are going from strength to strength), peregrines and common buzzards are all visible. Stonechats flit between the tops of bushes, clacking at your approach. In April, birdwatchers seek ring ouzels, a montane thrush that pauses here on its northwards migration. In high summer, grayling is a speciality: the Malvern Hills harbour an isolated population of this supremely camouflaged butterfly.

← Peering along the ridge of Worcestershire Beacon. (James Osmond/A)

When strolling on the summit, try to spy any indication that a café used to sit here – as it did until 1989, when destroyed by a fire. Perhaps thankfully, the owners were refused permission to rebuild it. Now you'll need to take your own cuppa to celebrate bagging this county top – or drink in the uninterrupted views that make this such a worthy walk.

WALK THIS WAY

❶ From Upper Wyche car park head north to be presented with several path options, all of which take you on and around Worcestershire Beacon. Follow the summit trail, which directly ascends the hill, crossing over a subsidiary bump called Summer Hill (382m). Note how the land drops away in dramatic fashion to the east. It's the edge of one of three disused quartzite quarries (now Sites of Special Scientific Interest due to the extensive amount of exposed meta-igneous rocks). If you fancy a breather, pause on the west slope of Summer Hill to admire the veteran wild cherry trees, which interpolate the more common sycamore and birch. ❷ From the grassy, round, bald summit (the name Malvern comes from a bastardisation of the Celtic term *moel-bryn*, meaning 'bare hill') you'll be rewarded with views of nearby hillocks such as Redditch's Lickey Hills, the Shropshire Hills and the Cotswolds. You may also be able to spy the Bristol Channel, the Avon and Severn Valley, Worcester Cathedral and the neighbouring summit of North Hill. You could return straight to the car the way you came, but to vary the vista, head downhill instead, bearing east on the zigzag path. ❸ Cut across on the path now heading south, which skirts the wooded lower flanks of The Beacon, ventures close to the road, passes the little pond (backed by the quarry wall you passed above on your ascent) and returns to your start point at Upper Wyche.

↑ The summit makes a great spot to grab a cuppa. (Pippa Sanderson/S)

ADDED ADVENTURE

Take your bivvy and bed down for the night on this county top: you'll have to go late and stay away from the track. There's a series of springs and water sources on the Malverns – traditionally used by locals – so sourcing water here should not be an issue. The nearest is St Ann's Well (which is marked on the OS map).

MAKE IT BIGGER

Why stop at just one Malvern when you can have two? North Hill offers a natural extension: from Worcestershire Beacon simply follow the col north. But why limit yourself to two? Check off End Hill, northwest of North Hill, and you'll have completed a triple billing of northern Malverns. Still want to walk more? Head south from Upper Wyche, across the B4232, to tackle the rest of the ridge of peaks.

FOR LITTLE ADVENTURERS

Southwest of Malvern Wells, check out the nearby Iron Age hillfort earthworks of British Camp (SO760400), and explore the ramparts of a Norman castle, which has shaped the hill itself.

FOR CAMPERS

Out to Grass is not the closest campsite but provides a good base (outtograss.com; from £9pn). It is self-catering but on Friday nights there's a communal campfire that serves homemade stew, toasted marshmallows and hot chocolate. Tasty.

FOR ADRENALINE LOVERS

Sign up for the annual race on this little peak (worcester-ac.co.uk) or just go with your fell shoes and get jogging for a surprisingly tiring workout – especially if you team this beacon with some of the additional fells.

FOR HUNGRY HIKERS

St Ann's Well Café (stannswell.co.uk) is an elegant hillside offering that's good for vegetarian and vegan snacks, cakes and fairtrade coffee. To get supplies pre-walk there are several supermarkets in Malvern.

OTHER PRACTICALITIES

There's a train station in Great Malvern from where you can walk or take the 44 bus to start the walk from the east side of the hill (at the information centre SO774460). Nearest toilets are in the British Camp car park, 3.5km (2¼ miles) away.

Keep your eyes peeled for common buzzard. (James Lowen) ↑

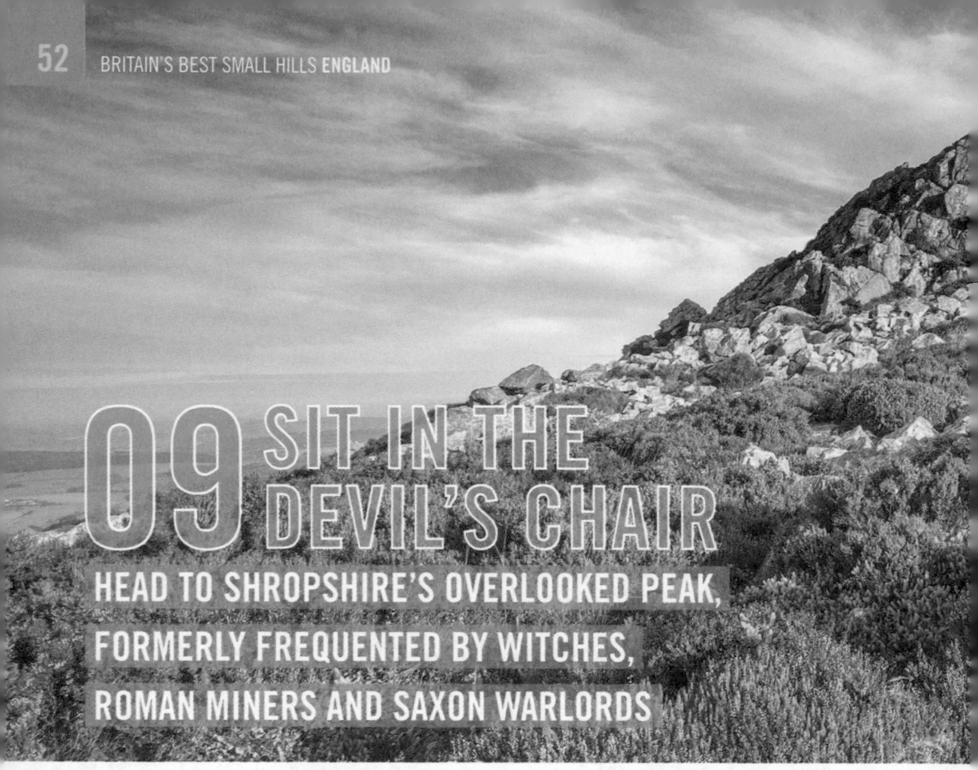

09 SIT IN THE DEVIL'S CHAIR

HEAD TO SHROPSHIRE'S OVERLOOKED PEAK, FORMERLY FREQUENTED BY WITCHES, ROMAN MINERS AND SAXON WARLORDS

WHERE	The Stiperstones, Shropshire
STATS	↔ 3.5km (2 miles) ↕ 536m ↗ 144m ↻ 1½ hours
START/FINISH	Bog Centre car park ⚲ SO358977
TERRAIN	A climb on grassy paths to the ridge, then undulating along the tops
MAPS	OS Explorer (1:25,000) 217; OS Landranger (1:50,000) 126

With your first glimpse of Shropshire's often-overlooked Stiperstones you know you've arrived somewhere very special. For amidst the rolling hills and tree-covered slopes, protruding above this particular ridge is a knot of jagged quartzite rocky tors, clad with a fuzzy blanket of heather that flushes purple in late summer. It's no wonder then that such an otherworldly, out-of-the-way spot, would be the catalyst for many a local legend. Take the Devil's Chair, said to be the spot where Beelzebub himself would appear and where local witches would gather in anticipation of his coming. Then there are the Roman lead miners who toiled away on these slopes; many believe their souls linger here. Factor in a smattering of burial cairns from the Bronze Age plus a proliferation of red grouse uttering their haunting 'go-back' call and you can't help but feel that someone (or something!) is out on this hillside with you. All the more reason to go, I say: well, that and the chance to scramble on some of these tors. Oh and the views. And I haven't even mentioned the lack of crowds…

WALK THIS WAY

❶ From the car park take the footpath southeast (the opposite direction to the visitor centre), climbing gradually. ❷ When you reach a junction, take the

↑ Heather carpets the bewitching Stiperstones in summer. (EddieCloud/S)

path to your left, cross the road and ascend steadily along the Shropshire Way. Along the route look out for ample wildlife. As well as red grouse, birds such as stonechat and meadow pipit frequent the heather, while curlew and lapwing may call evocatively from neighbouring fields. Common lizards sunbathe on bare ground, scuttling away if you tread too heavily. Green hairstreak butterflies sit tight on gorse bushes in spring, when a flaming-orange male emperor moth may tear past, hell-bent on finding a female. You'll pass a cairn, then hit your first rocky cluster at Cranberry Rock, followed by the summit at 536m. Look around you at the shattered shards of white quartzite, caused by the continuous cycle of freeze/thaw that occurred during the last ice age. **3** From here you can, of course, retrace your steps straight back to the car park. But I recommend continuing for another couple of hundred metres to check out the fabled Devil's Chair where the only proper thing do is take a seat on top of it. Then simply turn around and return back the way you came or pick up another path (eg: one heading west then another south) to loop back to your car.

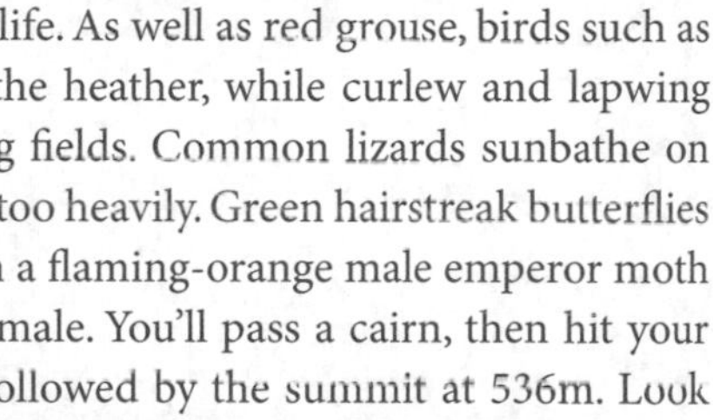

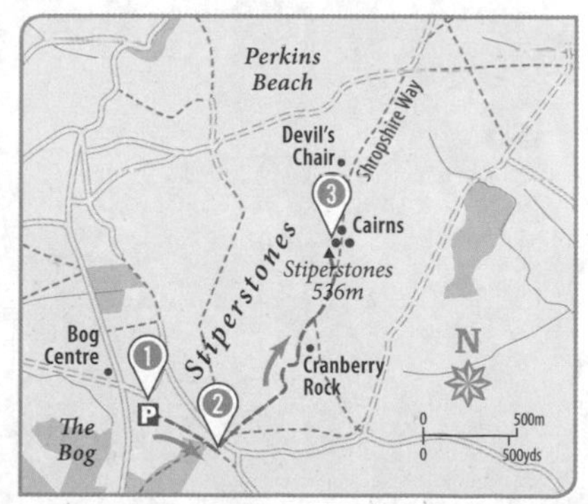

Listen for the call of red grouse as you ascend this little peak. (Andy Butler)

ADDED ADVENTURE

Be sure to head down into The Hollies (SO379991), where wizened holly trees – three or four centuries old and interspersed with rowans – stand ghost-like in the fields. Linger here into the evening, and maybe longer.

MAKE IT BIGGER

The route up into the Stiperstones partly follows the Shropshire Way (tinyurl.com/shropshireway) – a network of 224km (139 miles) of intersecting paths that easily divide into 27 linear sections and ten circular walks. Integrate one of them – or several – into your walk.

FOR LITTLE ADVENTURERS

Inspire young minds by taking them to the Stiperstones in time for dusk. Legend has it that a Saxon noble (and warlord) known as 'Wild Eric' once owned this land, but when defeated by William the Conqueror he was imprisoned by witches in the lead mines – which is where he remains even today. As the sun goes down he is said to ride the hills in a green cloak and feather cap.

FOR CAMPERS

Brow Farm Campsite (browfarmcampsite.co.uk; from £6pppn) in Ratlinghope, 5km (3.1 miles) east, offers pitches and pods spread across two tranquil hectares, with a pub (The Bridges) within walking distance.

FOR ADRENALINE LOVERS

Head over to Snailbeach Mine (01952 405105; daily, with visitor centre Jun–Oct 11.00–16.00 Sun & bank holidays). Here you can explore the old lead-mine buildings and, when tours are available, venture underground.

FOR HUNGRY HIKERS

The Bog Centre (bogcentre.co.uk) is a visitor centre with a café serving drinks and cakes, the latter including Bog Bake – a cake as famous as Wild Eric. For something more substantial check out The Stiperstones Inn (stiperstonesinn.co.uk), a 19th-century pub, for full pub fare and afternoon tea as well as morning coffee and real ales. Pick up supplies in Church Stretton, 14km (8½ miles) east.

OTHER PRACTICALITIES

From Church Stretton (where there is a train station), the Shropshire Hills Shuttle Bus 780 (tinyurl.com/shuttlestiperstone) runs on weekends and bank holidays from Easter to September (but not, oddly, in June). The nearest public toilets are inside The Bog Centre.

10 MINI-MOUNTAIN

TACKLE LEICESTERSHIRE'S SURPRISINGLY CRAGGY BEACON HILL, A VOLCANIC LEGACY AMIDST ENGLAND'S NATIONAL FOREST

WHERE	Beacon Hill, Leicestershire
STATS	↔ 1km (¾ mile) ↕ 248m ↗ 28m ↻ ½ hour
START/FINISH	Beacon Hill car park ⚲ SK509146
TERRAIN	Grassy paths and woodland tracks
MAPS	OS Explorer (1:25,000) 245; OS Landranger (1:50,000) 129

Given its seemingly small size, this minuscule mountain is unexpectedly, impressively and excitingly craggy. Formed by a volcano that exploded 6km (4 miles) northwest, its grassy rampart-like edges make way for clusters of jagged igneous rock that recall a giant serpent trying to break through the ground beneath your feet. In 2005, Beacon Hill was even voted one of the 'seven wonders of the Midlands' for its distinctive shape (although I honestly couldn't tell you what the other six were – though a quick Google search may inform those dying to know!).

Just as excitingly, there is more to Beacon Hill than its peak. It is the site of a Bronze Age hillfort and, from the top, a toposcope draws the eye towards landmarks such as Lincoln Cathedral and the Peak District. This new 128-hectare country park – part of the National Forest (tinyurl.com/beaconhillcp) – also boasts a network of trails for walking, cycling and horseriding, that links its range of landscapes (forest, heath, grassland, wetland and more) with nearby woodlands and farmland. All in all, Beacon Hill is definitively a place that demands lingering long after you've checked off the summit.

WALK THIS WAY

❶ Starting at the main (western) car park, accessed from Beacon Road, simply follow the path heading north towards the summit. You'll pass through

↑ A Highland cow belies the small stature of Leicestershire's Beacon Hill. (Graham Oliver/A)

woodland that includes 8,000 trees from 28 native British species, planted in 1996. ❷ Soon another path merges from the right. Continue straight on and, in less than 0.5km, you will reach the craggy summit. ❸ From the top you can get some great views over to the Peak District to the north and Lincoln Cathedral to the northeast – and you should even be able to spot steam trains coming and going along the Great Central Railway To go back to the start simply retrace your steps, or embrace the possibilities offered by the network of footpaths and make the summit merely the start of exploring the wider area.

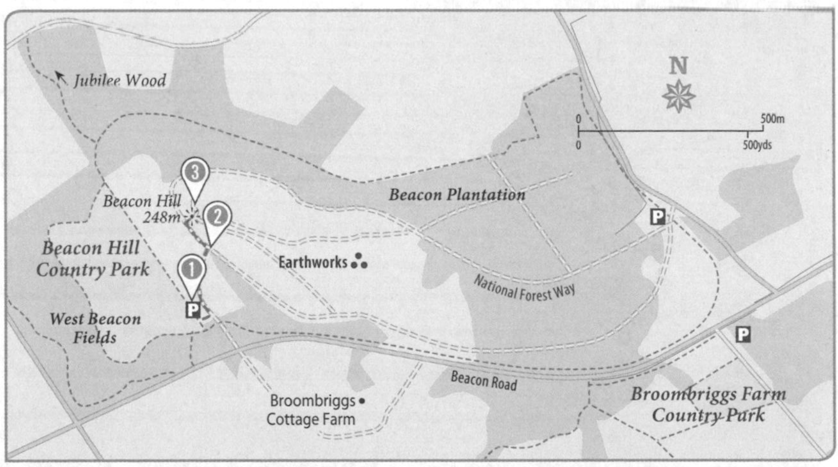

A rhododendron labyrinth at Beacon Hill. (Vicky Norton)

ADDED ADVENTURE

Test your scrambling. Small though Beacon Hill may be, the rocky outcrops that adorn its summit are an excellent training ground for testier hands-on action. Rather than simply walk up to the summit, why not have a go making your way across the rocks.

MAKE IT BIGGER

The summit sits in the midst of Beacon Hill Country Park, which offers a trail-veined network of woodland paths. From the Broombriggs Farm Trail to Jubilee Wood beyond the confines of the park (2km to the north; tinyurl.com/jubileewoodbeacon), there are many ways to extend your walking.

FOR LITTLE ADVENTURERS

There's a children's play area in the Country Park complete with a hazel maze, a rhododendron labyrinth and unique wooden sculptures – perfect to occupy little ones (just don't lose them!). Alternatively, you could peer carefully into the field ponds for newts, frogs and diving beetles, or try to creep up on ever-alert dragonflies that perch along the watery fringes. Also check out the West Beacon Fields area a few minutes' walk southwest of the car park and visitor centre. This area was included in the park in 2000 to re-establish an old hedgeline used as an important corridor by native wildlife. A great place to sit and try and spot some 'locals'.

FOR CAMPERS

Proctors Park in the Soar Valley (proctorspark.com), 7.9km (5 miles) east, offers riverside pitches from just £13pn.

FOR ADRENALINE LOVERS

Enjoy the feeling of getting bark under your fingers. Pick a (well-established) tree from the many that form Beacon Hill's sprawling canopy and get climbing. Just be sure not to ascend what you can't descend and consider taking a bouldering crash mat and a friend to help 'spot' you.

FOR HUNGRY HIKERS

There's nothing in the immediate area but nearby Leicester and Loughborough offer many options both to grab a pub meal and pick up supplies in one of the many supermarkets.

OTHER PRACTICALITIES

Some buses – Centrebus 154 and Kinchbus 123 – run close to the park. Toilets can be found in the car park at the start.

11 ACCESSIBLE REEF

CELEBRATE COUNTRYSIDE RIGHTS OF WAY ACT FREEDOMS BY WALKING ON A 300-MILLION-YEAR-OLD CORAL REEF

WHERE	Chrome Hill, Derbyshire
STATS	↔ 7.2km (4½ miles) ↕ 425m ↗ 285m ↻ 3 hours
START/FINISH	Hollinsclough layby SK065664
TERRAIN	Mainly clear paths up and on the ridges of two hills, with some steep sections with big drops either side
MAPS	OS Explorer (1:25,000) 24; OS Landranger (1:50,000) 119

Being a limestone protrusion, Chrome Hill was once under the sea. But, unlike many others, this Peak District summit still looks like it could be lifted up and placed back there without marine creatures thinking it odd. With sheer drop-offs plus nooks and crannies in seemingly every rock face, it's not hard to imagine a wealth of saltwater life lurking inside the crags. During the Carboniferous era (a massive 340 million years ago), this coral reef once edged a shallow lagoon. Nowadays this hulking wedge of rock bursts through the grass like a rocky sea serpent.

Impressively ancient though it may be, this is not the only incredible piece of history that this summit claims. By walking to Chrome Hill's summit along with the equally striking Parkhouse Hill – its former undersea mate – you're committing an act that would have been illegal as recently as 1999. Last Millennium, both hills were private land – with access prohibited to hikers. However, when the Countryside Rights of Way Act (CRoWA) came into force in 2000, the duo were designated as 'access land', meaning that walkers were entitled to freely explore them.

↑ Looking over to the former coral reef of Chrome Hill from Parkhouse's summit. (Phoebe Smith)

One remaining (and quite fitting) quirk, however, is that Chrome Hill is still something of an island. It cannot be reached by any current right of way and access to it is still via private land. But given that so many people used to trespass to reach it, the Peak District National Park admirably negotiated an access arrangement with landowners. A concessionary path now takes you to the start of the ridge. So celebrate your freedom to walk on this rocky reef – without even making a splash…

WALK THIS WAY

1 From the layby on New Road follow the road north and approximately 200m after the road that turns right/east (into the village) you'll see a small gate on your right, marked with a bridleway post. Go through it. You'll get your first glimpse of Chrome Hill here. You'll be on Staffordshire gritstone at first. Following the track as it cuts across the slope below Hollinsclough Rake, past a Moorside Farm outbuilding, and veering northeast to cross the River Dove, you'll transition seamlessly into limestone country. Continue straight, climbing the steep slope up to a farm track at Fough.

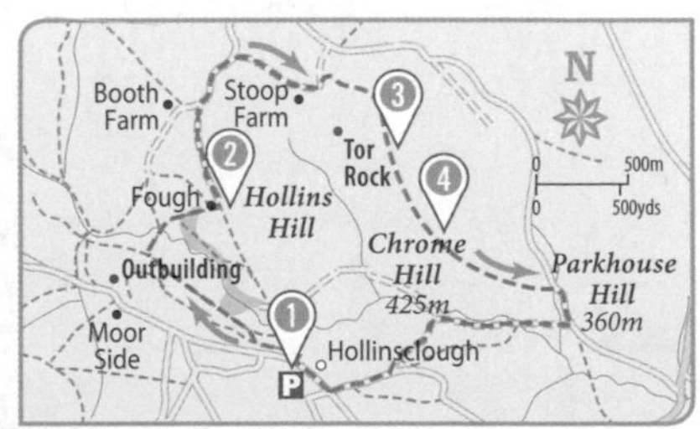

2 Turn left on to a track that bends round Booth Farm, heading to Stoop Farm. Note the white limestone rock beginning to protrude from the grass either side – a hint of what's to come. The footpath leaves the road to your right then briefly joins a farm track. Leave the track to continue on a faint path above Stoop Farm; this path is not marked on the OS map but is signposted on the ground. Continue to the north of Tor Rock then descend into the next field, and along the bottom of the following one. A concessionary path then takes you to the start of Chrome Hill's ridge. 3 The ground gets steeper as you ascend the obviously well-used path. Take time to embrace the power of CRoW and find your own route up. Get to grips – literally – with some of the rocky outcrops: use your hands to gain height, peer into the myriad nooks and crannies, and teeter as close to the edge as you dare. At Chrome Hill's highest point, celebrate by taking in the phenomenal views of neighbouring Parkhouse Hill to the southeast. 4 Descend southeast to Dowel Dale Road. Follow it south then head west along the farm track. This crosses the River Dove then branches left at a signpost. Follow this track to Hollinsclough and, at the top of the village, turn right to get back to the start.

CROWA LAND – KNOW YOUR RIGHTS

The Countryside Rights of Way Act (2000) designated swathes of Britain as 'Access Land' meaning walkers had the right to hike wherever they liked within it – be it on or off designated paths. Access Land should be signposted as such on the ground, but you can also find it easily by looking on an OS Explorer map (1:25,000) for yellow colouring: these patches show the boundaries. Note that in some areas access can be restricted for conservation purposes.

↑ Taking in the views from the former coral reef of Chrome Hill. (Phoebe Smith)

ADDED ADVENTURE

Combine neighbouring Parkhouse Hill which offers an even greater sense of exposure. Once you reach Dowel Dale Road, cross it heading southeast to stand at the nose of Parkhouse. By far the easiest way to ascend the hill is to veer to the left around the rock face then curve right to reach the ridge. There's a faint path; for the best views stick to the edge. From the summit, you'll get the classic shot of Chrome Hill. Linger here enjoying this perfect view of your entire walk, then retrace your steps to where you joined the ridge but this time veer left on a well-trodden (but steep) path to rejoin the road.

MAKE IT BIGGER

You can do the route in reverse, but after summiting Chrome Hill, continue west, piecing together the many footpaths and bridleways to reach the little-visited areas of Axes Edge Moor and Cheeks Hill, sandwiched between the A537 and A54. For something even longer, an ascent of Shining Tor – the highest peak in Cheshire (and a much-loved bivvy spot) – is certainly possible.

FOR LITTLE ADVENTURERS

Head here in the late afternoon in summer to watch the sun set on Chrome Hill. For it's at the pairing of these two peaks that writer Jeff Kent witnessed a 'double sunset': from the southern flank of Parkhouse Hill, the sun can be seen to set twice in the same place (this is due to the rotation of the earth, so as the sun sets the planet continues rotating, allowing the sun to become briefly visible again). It's said that on Chrome it sets to the southwest of the summit before re-emerging on the northeastern slope – only to reset again at the foot of the hill.

FOR CAMPERS

Longnor Wood (www.longnorwood.co.uk; from £18pn) is nearest (5km/3 miles from the start) and has good tent pitches away from the caravans, although it is for adults only. If you have little ones try the very family-friendly Knotlow Farm (knotlowfarm.co.uk; from £10ppn) 11km (7 miles) east.

FOR ADRENALINE LOVERS

Climb it. Take your rope, harness and helmet and head for the southwest ridge where a couple of limestone slabs offer a tricky and entertaining way to reach the top. There's also a challenging pinnacle on Parkhouse.

FOR HUNGRY HIKERS

The Pack Horse Inn (www.thepack-horseinn.co.uk) just outside nearby Longnor offers good pub grub and locally brewed ales. There is a good chippy in town too. For supplies there's a small shop in Longnor; for supermarkets and camping gear, the nearest town is Buxton to the north or Leek to the south.

OTHER PRACTICALITIES

There are no toilets in Hollinsclough; the nearest are in Longnor. Buses go from Buxton to Earl Sterndale, then take a Moorland Connect bus to Hollinsclough (www.travelinemidlands.co.uk; Mon–Fri).

12 A VISIT TO MOTHER

BE WOWED BY LANDSLIPS AND CAVES ON THE PEAK DISTRICT'S FAMOUS SHIVERING MOUNTAIN

WHERE	Mam Tor, Derbyshire
STATS	↔ 4.5km (2¾ miles) ↕ 517m ↗ 97m ↻ 3 hours
START/FINISH	Mam Tor car park ⚲ SK123832
TERRAIN	Stone steps to start, flagstones along ridge and well-marked paths
MAPS	OS Explorer (1:25,000) 1; OS Landranger (1:50,000) 110

Sandwiched between the Eden Valley to the north and Hope Valley to the south stands the little hill of Mam Tor. Made up of fragile shale and corrosive sandstone it has been the site of a series of dramatic landslips over the years that have created smaller hillocks around it. Hence its name, which means 'Mother Hill' – one that has given birth to several others.

Mam Tor's fragile nature has also resulted in another moniker, Shivering Mountain. To understand why, visit the hill's southern slopes from the village of Castleton below. Here you'll see evidence of the old Mam Tor Road, which was constructed in the 1800s and rebuilt many, many times following regular landslides, before being closed for good in 1979. Even four decades later, beneath Mam Tor's ever-crumbling flanks, you can still see the painted tarmac and cat's eyes along this road to nowhere. The slopes are still moving today at an estimated rate of around quarter of a metre every year. So don't put off a visit to mother any longer; climb Mam Tor soon, before it disappears entirely.

WALK THIS WAY

❶ Climb the steps at the top end of the car park (which is a good place for flocks of brambling, a pretty finch, in winter), following the footpath next to the road until you come to a gate. ❷ Go through the gate and ascend the steps on the rounded and open hillside. You'll notice the National Trust (the landowner) has chiselled pictures into some of the flagstones as a nod towards the Iron Age people who constructed the fort whose remains you are now scrambling over. Be sure to stick to the path all the way to the summit as the cliffs to the south (your right) are very unstable. Keep an eye on the skies for raven and peregrine, while, in summer, birds at ground level may include meadow pipit, wheatear and whinchat. ❸ Once you've reached the summit and trig point you will be rewarded with some stunning views across to Edale and Kinder Scout to the north, along the ridge to Hollins Cross and Lose Hill (see *Make it bigger*) to the northeast and down into Castleton and the Hope Valley to the south. Enjoy the views then simply retrace your steps to the car park.

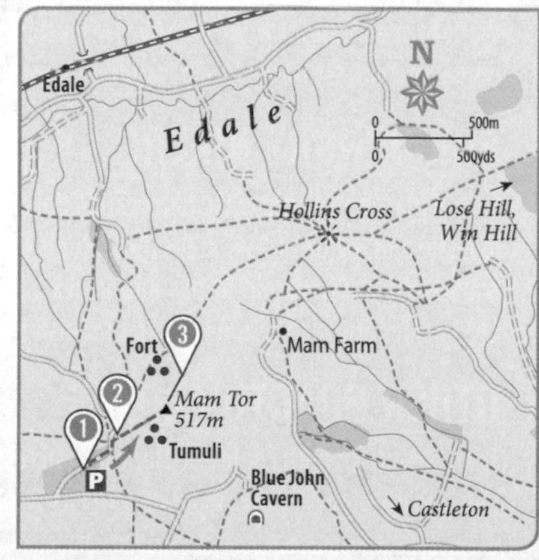

← Looking out across The Great Ridge and Mam Tor from Lose Hill. (Ed Rhodes/A)

ADDED ADVENTURE

Go underground: Castleton is home to a number of caves worth exploring. Take a boat trip 450m below the ground at Speedwell or gawp at Peak Cavern (both speedwellcavern.co.uk), which boasts the UK's largest cave entrance. Be sure to check out the old Mam Tor Road between Mam Farm and Blue John Cavern (marked as a public access route – green dots on the OS Explorer) to truly appreciate the destructive heritage of Mam Tor.

MAKE IT BIGGER

So many options. For a little bigger, don't stop at Mam Tor. Continue northeast to Hollins Cross then along the ridge to Lose Hill – from where you can gaze over (or, should you want to make it a really big walk) to its rival, Win Hill, north of the railway line. Want more still? Head downhill, northwest into Edale. Here you can pick up the Pennine Way from where you can summit the sprawling Kinder Plateau to the northwest – the place were protesters trespassed *en masse* in 1932, a direct action that marked the start of the right-to-roam movement in England and Wales.

FOR LITTLE ADVENTURERS

A visit to Blue John Cavern (bluejohn-cavern.co.uk) is a great option to explore the limestone and mineral formations. For fresher air, head to Peveril Castle (tinyurl.com/eh-peveril) and let the nippers burn off energy running around the imposing castle remains.

FOR CAMPERS

Waterside Farm Campsite (01433 670215) offers a basic option with flat ground and free showers, all in the shadow of Mam Tor (Easter–Sep; £5pppn).

FOR ADRENALINE LOVERS

Want to see Mam Tor from the sky? Derbyshire Flying Centre (d-f-c.co.uk) offers taster days where you can try hang- and paragliding around this distinctive summit.

FOR HUNGRY HIKERS

Lots of places available in Castleton and Edale. Both the cosy Penny Pot Café (01433 670293) in Edale and the award-winning Three Roofs Café in Castleton (threeroofscafe.com) are great choices for hot and cold drinks and snacks. For an evening meal head to Ye Olde Nags Head (yeoldenagshead.co.uk) for classic British pub grub and real ales.

OTHER PRACTICALITIES

Train stations in both Edale and Hope give access to Mam Tor. The nearest public toilets are in the pay-and-display car parks in Edale and Castleton.

The sun sets over mini, but marvellous Mam Tor. (Daniel_Kay/S)

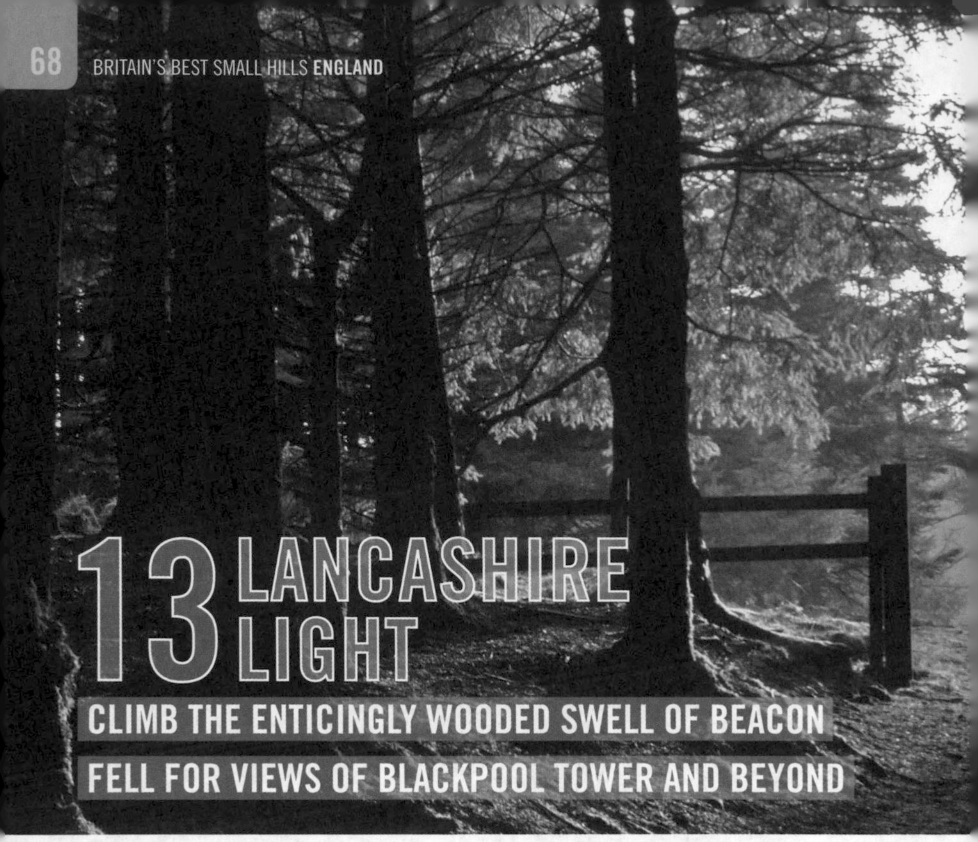

13 LANCASHIRE LIGHT

CLIMB THE ENTICINGLY WOODED SWELL OF BEACON FELL FOR VIEWS OF BLACKPOOL TOWER AND BEYOND

WHERE	Beacon Fell, Lancashire
STATS	↔ 2km (1¼ miles) ↕ 266m ↗ 48m ↻ 1 hour
START/FINISH	Beacon Fell car park ⚲ SD565426
TERRAIN	A mix of clear trails and grassy paths
MAPS	OS Explorer (1:25,000) 41; OS Landranger (1:50,000) 103

With views supposedly reaching as far as Snowdonia and the Isle of Man, it's not surprising that this unassuming Lancastrian hill was chosen, as early as 1002, to sport a literal beacon that would form part of a warning system across Britain. Reportedly, the site even played a role in alerting residents to the invading Spanish Armada in the late 16th century.

Since then Beacon Fell, an isolated hill on the edge of the Forest of Bowland, has been handed from one owner to another until, in 1970, Lancashire Country Council opened it as one of the UK's first country parks. Today the site boasts 75 hectares of moorland and coniferous forest, readily explored via a network of trails sprawling out from six car parks. A good variety of mammals reside here – from roe deer to badger and weasel – but seeing them may be easiest around dusk. The tarn holds an abundance of dragonflies, while the pond outside the visitor centre is occupied by frogs and newts in spring.

Beacon Fell is also home to a series of sculptures by local artist Thompson Dagnall. Most have a wildlife theme, but one – *Orme Sight* – is a human head with an open eye through which you are said to see the Great Orme (page 178). (In reality it's not *that* good a viewpoint.) Other landmarks to spot

↑ The woodland-rich Beacon Fell makes for excellent hiking. (Donna Clifford/S)

from the top are Blackpool Tower, the Forest of Bowland, Pendle Hill and the Lake District. In short, a great and supremely easy fell to claim in a leisurely morning stroll.

WALK THIS WAY

1 From the car park by the visitor centre (where you'll spot Dagnall's *Orme Sight* sculpture) you can take a number of paths, all of which are themed (sculpture, woodland, fellside etc). The quickest route to the summit is to take the Sculpture Trail path heading southeast. 2 After a couple of hundred metres, at the junction of tracks, turn left to head uphill. Ignore any other turnings, keeping straight to reach the summit. 3 From the top enjoy the views – which sadly nowadays don't include those as far reaching as Snowdonia or the Great Orme in Llandudno, but do offer panoramic vistas over the rounded bumps of the Bowland fells and Parlick Fell opposite. When you've had your fill, simply retrace your steps or pick up one of the other paths to lead you back to the start.

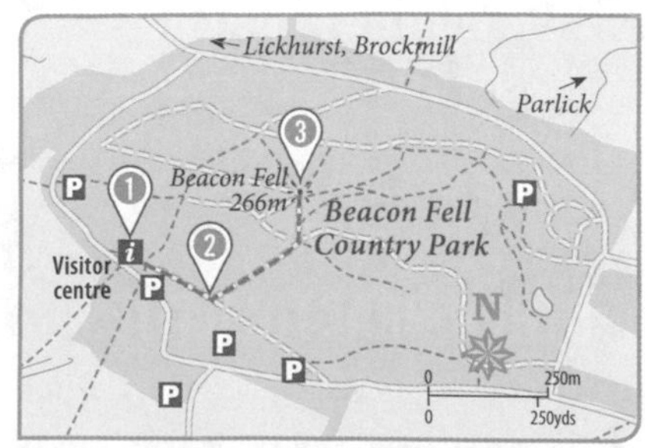

ADDED ADVENTURE

The nearby hill of Parlick, 4km (2½ miles) northeast, and its rolling ridgeline of Fair Snape Fell and Holme Moss Fell, offer possibilities for a discreet wild camp. There's a crumbling shelter on top of the former that can act as a handy windbreak. You may also want to try a night walk at Beacon Fell, the perfect time to try to spot the mammals that call the woodland home.

MAKE IT BIGGER

Take the public footpath out of the country park to undertake a round of the villages and woodlands in the area. From the visitor centre head north then west towards Lower Lickhurst and Brockmill (the site of an old cotton mill, and, even earlier, a paper mill). Follow the River Brock south before cutting back east over Lower Trotter Hill. Pass the (currently closed) Cross Keys Inn at Whitechapel and head via Crombleholme Fold back to the car park.

FOR LITTLE ADVENTURERS

Head to the visitor centre first where free family-friendly events – such as bushcraft, bat walks and scarecrow making – take place on various weekends and public holidays throughout the year. Otherwise discovering the wooden sculptures along the trail helps divert small minds from the uphill climb and gives them something to hunt for. Look for wildlife at the waterbodies: spot amphibians in the pond by the visitor centre or gawp at speedy dragonflies at the tarn. If you're after some Roman remains then head to Ribchester 16km (10 miles) away. This is one of Lancashire's most important such sites and is home to a museum and various excavations.

FOR CAMPERS

One option is Beacon Fell View Holiday Park (☎ 01772 783233; from £23pppn, 11.7km (7¼ miles) away, but it's a bit too 'holiday park'. For something classier – if there's a group of you, say – consider Bark and Brook (🖱 barkandbrook.co.uk), 10.6km (6½ miles) distant, which offers exclusive hire of their woodland and shower/toilet facilities from £150.

FOR ADRENALINE LOVERS

For something really extreme you could parachute over the hills. Black Knight Parachute Centre (🖱 bkpc.co.uk) offers the highest skydive in the UK from 15,000ft (approximately 4,570m), from £150.

FOR HUNGRY HIKERS

The visitor centre café serves hot and cold drinks as well as ice cream. For something more substantial check out the award-winning Ye Horn's Inn (🖱 hornsinn.co.uk) in Goosnargh for food and drink from their micro-brewery; it even has a store for bikes. For pre-trip supplies Preston is your best bet.

OTHER PRACTICALITIES

Public toilets are at the visitor centre. There is no public transport available to access this hill.

Looking over to Parlick from the top of Beacon Fell. (Lancashire Images/A)

14 PIT-STOP PEAK

NUDGING THE M6, FARLETON OFFERS A FAST-LANE FELL *EN ROUTE* TO THE LAKES

WHERE	Farleton Fell, Cumbria
STATS	↔ 4km (2½ miles) ↕ 265m ↗ 83m ↻ 2 hours
START/FINISH	Park before top of hill (SD552787) on road outside Clawthorpe
TERRAIN	A mix of paths – some clearer than others, plus limestone pavements
MAPS	OS Explorer (1:25,000) 7; OS Landranger (1:50,000) 97

There are not many hills you'd lavish with praise due to their proximity to a motorway – but Farleton Fell is one. Sat right above the M6, you're likely to have seen this little bump many times, but never paid it any heed. A shame indeed, because this Cumbrian hill offers a chance for fresh air for those travelling north or south.

It's not merely ease of access that makes this hilltop a winner. Climb it and you'll not only garner great views of the Lakes, Morecambe Bay, the Howgills and Forest of Bowland, but, as a bonus, you'll also find a sprawling limestone pavement – one of Britain's best-preserved examples of this geological feature, with its clints and grikes.

You'll see footpaths marked on the map – but don't be fooled into thinking this a routine stroll. To reach the top of this expressway summit requires following your nose, picking one of a number of hidden passageways and possibilities among the limestone rocks. Keep a lookout for the foliage too. Depending on when you visit, you might come across unusual plants such as fly orchid, lily-of-the-valley, rigid buckler-fern or dark red helleborine. Miles better than a stop at any service station!

WALK THIS WAY

❶ Start at the small layby (with space for several cars) on the road between Newbiggin and Clawthorpe. (If the layby is full, an alternative parking option is at Plain Quarry, 2.5km south at SD552763, from where you'd have to cut through Hutton Roof Crags – see *Make it bigger*.) Cross the road to pick up the track heading roughly north. Ignore the footpath that cuts east–west and continue towards Newbiggin Crags.

❷ Follow the track around, up and between the bare, grey slabs of limestone pavement until it peters out. ❸ Thread your own way through and over the limestone, bearing northwest until you reach the edge and the summit of this fell.

❹ Enjoy the views in all directions – including that of the M6 where all the cars are rattling past, unaware of your joy of climbing this tiny top. Then simply pick your way back over the limestone to return.

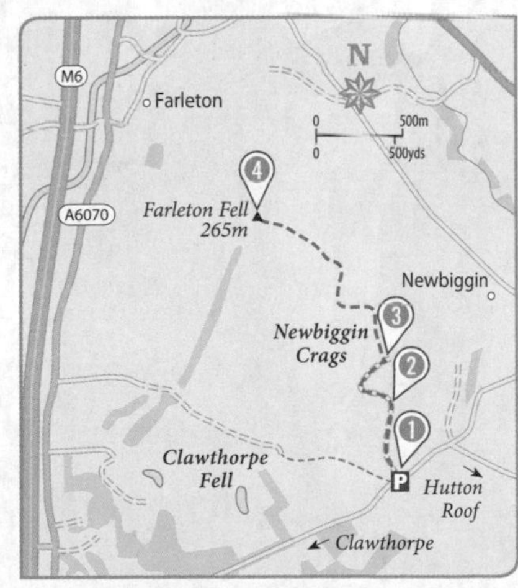

← Standing on the clints and grikes of Farelton Fell, looking east. (BRIAN ORMEROD PHOTOGRAPHER/A)

Approaching the limestone shards on Farleton Fell's slopes. (Andrew Graham)

ADDED ADVENTURE

Try bouldering – climbing rocks that usually don't require ropes. The whole area is littered with limestone geology perfect for cutting your teeth at the sport. You will need a crash mat, some chalk and a friend who can 'spot' you (position themselves behind you to catch, deflect or slow your fall should you need it). Bouldering is a great way to improve your scrambling and climbing techniques, enabling you to practise holds and moves in relative safety.

MAKE IT BIGGER

Rather than finishing at the car, continue across the road and on to Hutton Roof, the adjacent cluster of tightly knit limestone pavement. Except for a footpath below its northern edge, this area is also devoid of paths, so ascending Hutton Roof is a proper make-your-own-adventure exploration.

FOR LITTLE ADVENTURERS

Head to the woodland on Uberash Plain (found by heading southwest on the path just up the road from the layby), where, in the right season, you can feast on wild raspberries and blackberries. The nearby Lancaster Canal is also a great place for a stroll, watching the narrowboats saunter by.

FOR CAMPERS

The nearest campsite is Waters Edge Caravan Park at Crooklands (watersedgecaravanpark.co.uk; from £10pppn). Although a bit caravan-heavy, it has ample on-site facilities including pool room, bar and TV lounge.

FOR ADRENALINE LOVERS

As well as bouldering there are a number of climbing routes on Farleton Crags; for detailed routes and levels see ukclimbing.com.

FOR HUNGRY HIKERS

For a coffee and light bites head to the Hideaway Coffee House – family-run with beautiful views – on the A65 near junction 36 of the M6 (hideawaycoffeehouse.co.uk). For more options and to pick up supplies head to Kirkby Lonsdale where there is a supermarket and several pubs.

OTHER PRACTICALITIES

There is no public transport to the starting point; the best is Stagecoach Bus 555 (Lancaster–Kendal) which calls at Burton-in-Kendal, approximately 4km away. There are no public toilets nearby; it is best to use M6 services.

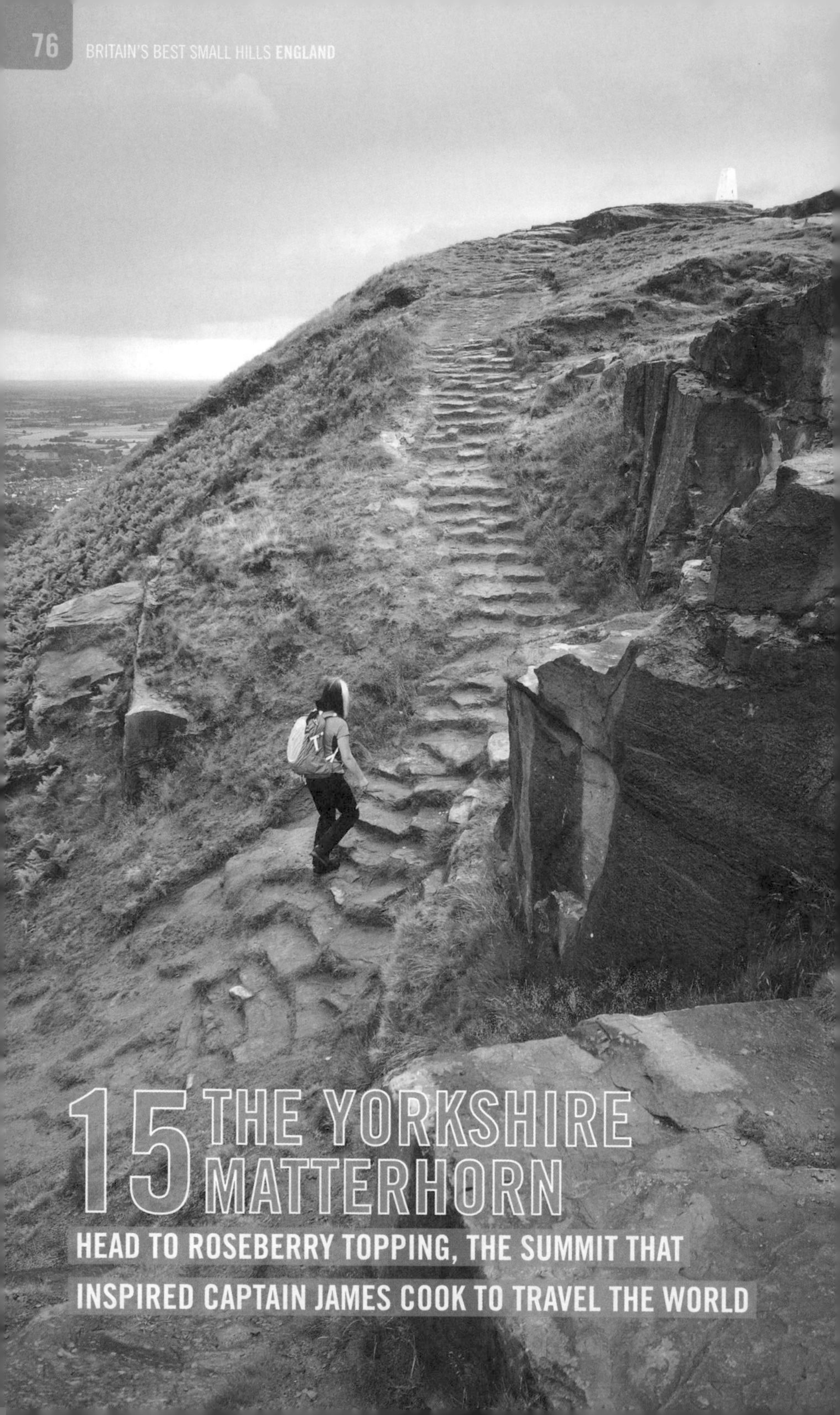

15 THE YORKSHIRE MATTERHORN

HEAD TO ROSEBERRY TOPPING, THE SUMMIT THAT INSPIRED CAPTAIN JAMES COOK TO TRAVEL THE WORLD

WHERE	Roseberry Topping, North Yorkshire
STATS	↔ 2km (1¼ miles) ↕ 320m ↗ 220m ↻ 1 hour
START/FINISH	Newton under Roseberry car park NZ570128
TERRAIN	Short but steep climb to the summit. Path clear but can be slippery.
MAPS	OS Explorer (1:25,000) 26; OS Landranger (1:50,000) 93

Evidence that the British have a tongue-in-cheek sense of humour includes the sheer proliferation of so-called 'Matterhorns' that seem to exist on our shores. From Wales to Scotland (via many places in between) several are locally (and sometimes more widely) known as 'The Welsh Matterhorn' or other similarly grand moniker – no matter that ascending them demands none of the months of training, risk-taking and experience involved in conquering their Alpine namesake, which is among Europe's loftiest peaks. But perhaps the British summit most deserving of the title is Roseberry Topping, 'the Yorkshire Matterhorn'. It is meritorious not because of its height, but because of the sense of adventure, exploration and discovery it inspired within a young tyke called James Cook.

To many the name will be familiar. The boy went on to become Captain Cook, the famed navigator who negotiated no end of unchartered waters and discovered new territories – and who even has the Cook Islands in the South Pacific named after him. The seed from which Cook's travels grew was planted on this summit scarred by an ironstone mine. In 1736, when Cook was eight, his family moved to Aireyholme Farm in the town of Great Ayton below the flanks of Roseberry Topping. One evening, Cook decided he would climb the hill – something he did regularly thereafter – where, it is said, he first

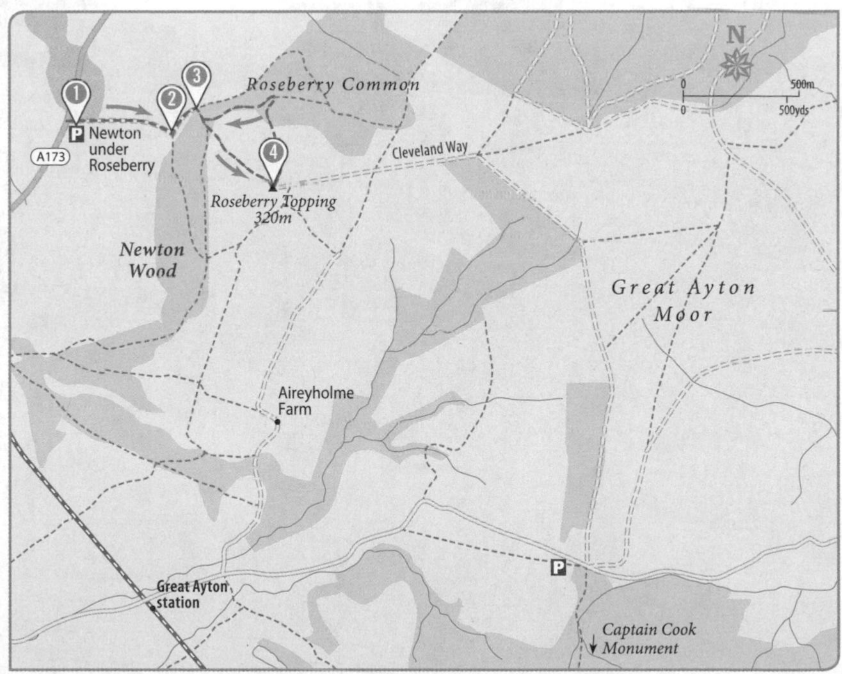

← Climb Roseberry Topping for travel inspiration. (Neil S Price)

If you really squint and look at Roseberry Topping, it could pass for the Matterhorn (sort of). (Colin Carter/NYMNPA)

discovered the rewards of a challenge, a realisation that set him on a course to become a great explorer. Such history is impressive, but the profile of Roseberry Topping (a name derived from a Viking word for the Norse god Odin plus the Yorkshire dialectical version of the Old English topp) is just as striking. Comprising shale and clay, and protected under a sandstone helmet, Roseberry is distinctly conical. The Topping's rugged appeal is enhanced by its sharp nose – the result of a geological fault and the collapse of a nearby ironstone mine in the early 1900s – and a series of rough pittings and scars.

'The Yorkshire Matterhorn' inspired a young James Cook to explore the world. Just think what epiphany might greet you on the summit...

WALK THIS WAY

❶ From the car park turn right on to Roseberry Lane and follow it east towards the hill. ❷ At the end of the lane, you'll come to a set of steps. Climb them and cross the gate into Newton Wood. Turn left at the top and follow the path through the oak trees, keeping an eye out for roe deer, woodpeckers and, in spring, bluebells. ❸ Turn right to follow the path along the woodland edge, then follow the stone path that turns left through a gate on to Roseberry Common. Take the track – a series of steep slopes and stone steps – all the way to the summit. The climb to the top is sudden and sharp, but finishes just as soon as you start getting a sweat on. ❹ At the top, grant yourself time to sit for a while to see whether inspiration or a thirst for exploration finds you, as it did James Cook. When it has (and if it hasn't what better excuse could you have for climbing Roseberry again?) then choose from any number of the paths back down. You could sweep to the southeast, the east, northeast or opt to walk further to see the monument dedicated to Cook (see *Make it bigger*). The quickest route, however, is to take the path northwest down to the wood then retrace your steps to the start.

↑ Claiming the stony top of Roseberry Topping. (Neil S Price)

ADDED ADVENTURE

Run it: the tracks around the hillside make this the perfect training hill for any would-be fell runners. Start with Roseberry Topping, doing hill reps, or – if you're feeling ambitious – check out the Roseberry Romp, an 8km (5 mile) running trail (see nationaltrust.org.uk/roseberry-topping).

MAKE IT BIGGER

Think like James Cook and let the exploration continue by following the path east from the summit heading then curving round to bear south on the Cleveland Way headed for Cockshaw Hill (NZ591109). Cross the minor road (that leads back west into Great Ayton) to follow the path up to Captain Cook's monument on Easby Moor (NZ590100). From there head northwest on the path to take you back into Great Ayton, from where you can pick up the footpath that fittingly cuts alongside Cook's Aireyholme Farm then traverses west through Newton Wood and back to your start point at Newton under Roseberry.

FOR LITTLE ADVENTURERS

On the hill get them to keep an eye out for fossils that are often found in the rocky shards. Elsewhere, nearby Dalby Forest (forestry.gov.uk/dalbyforest) is traffic-free and perfect for a family bike ride. Dalby Bike Barn (dalbybikebarn.co.uk) rents bicycles so there's no problem if you didn't bring your own. Prices from £10 for under 15s.

FOR CAMPERS

A number of nearby options include Kildale Camping Barn, Byre and Campsite (at Park Farm; kildalebarn.co.uk; from £6pppn) within viewing distance of the Captain Cook monument.

FOR ADRENALINE LOVERS

At least once a month in the summer, Pinpoint Adventure (pinpointadventure.com) offers abseiling down the sandstone face of Roseberry Topping – all 12 knee-trembling metres. No experience needed.

FOR HUNGRY HIKERS

The Kings Head Inn (kingsheadinn.co.uk) is at the foot of the peak in Great Ayton and offers great-value grub post-walk (though you might need to climb Roseberry Topping several times to work off an enormous roast dinner). Food supplies can also be picked up in the village.

OTHER PRACTICALITIES

There's a train station in Great Ayton (on the line connecting Middlesbrough and Whitby) from where you can walk approximately 3km northeast, via Aireyholme Farm, to Roseberry Topping. Bus 81 also connects Great Ayton with Middlesbrough. Toilets in Newton under Roseberry car park are open by day.

The great-spotted woodpecker can be heard among the branches of Newton Wood. (Monica Viora/S) →

16 A WALK WITH A RING TO IT

GET YOUR HANDS ON SOME REAL ROCK BY SCRAMBLING UP THIS CONISTON SUMMIT

WHERE	The Bell, Cumbria
STATS	↔ 2.5km (1½ miles) ↕ 335m ↗ 85m ↻ 1 hour
START/FINISH	Walna Scar car park (SD289970), Coniston
TERRAIN	Well-defined track to start, then pathless grass and a pick-your-own scramble to the top
MAPS	OS Explorer (1:25,000) 6; OS Landranger (1:50,000) 90, 98

It's not often that a small fell can delight in a hands-on ascent, but The Bell is no ordinary summit. Almost pimple-like in form, this peak sits aside a well-trampled track – along which many a hiker will have strode *en route* to the larger Coniston fells in this well-visited chunk of the Lake District – yet few ever bother to climb it due to its minuscule size.

That is a mistake. The rocky nose of The Bell hides considerable excitement in the form of a Grade 1 scramble. 'Scrambling' covers the middle ground between walking and climbing. Simply put, a Grade 1 scramble is like an easy climb without ropes, a sort of step up from simply hillwalking but not as tricky as a climb. You will need to use your hands as well as feet for at least some of the moves. In sum, a Grade 1 scramble will thrill but not terrify.

'Scrambling' can certainly be an exciting way to add some adventure to walking up little mounds – and you never know, you might discover that you have quite the taste for it, which could mark the start of a whole new hobby. At just 30 minutes to climb it via the scramble this is the perfect introduction to this grey area between walking and climbing and a handy skill to have.

WALK THIS WAY

❶ From the car parking area at Walna Scar take the former quarry road to your right and follow it as it heads north. The Bell will be in front of you. ❷ You'll soon notice a wide grassy track leading off to your right. Follow this past a ruined homestead, walking along the stone wall until you come to a bracken-coated and fairly boggy clearing just below the base of the hill. ❸ The fun begins here. There really isn't a set path to the top so you will need to pick your own way, making it as hands-on as you wish. A good route can be gained by starting slightly left of the rocky ridge then scrambling up for a few metres beside a couple of juniper bushes before reaching a flattened, grass-covered section. Go straight up to another terrace then bear to the right to take on the ridge proper where you can scramble up for a few more metres. You'll reach a flattened section with an obvious tree. Keep this to your right to climb up again until you reach some rocks with well-positioned

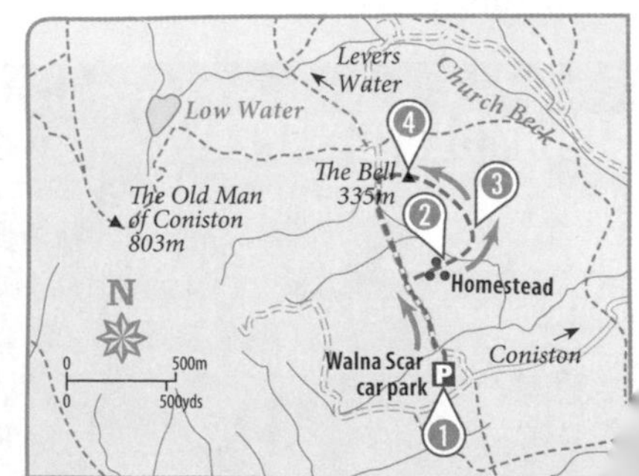

← Hands may be required on the rocky ridge of The Bell. (Neil S Price)

hand- and footholds. Soon you'll emerge on to some stone slabs where the scramble ends; from here, it's a walk to The Bell's unmarked summit. ❹ Enjoy the views and adrenaline rush from a job well done, before continuing northwest off the back of The Bell. From here, it's an easy walk down to rejoin the old quarry road you followed at the start. Turn left on to this and continue south to the starting point.

SCRAMBLING SAFELY

When using your hands on rock for the first time remember the golden rule: don't attempt to climb up what you can't climb down – it's always easier to ascend than descend so don't get caught out. Look for natural hand- and foot-holds, but don't commit without checking it's strong enough first. If there's more than one of you, send the weakest up first so you can spot them, pointing out places to put their feet as they go.

...ll but perfectly formed (and often ignored) – Coniston's The Bell. (Tranquilian Photography)

ADDED ADVENTURE

There is so much scope to vary the route that you can make it as adventurous as you like. If you are after a wild night out then Levers Water, less than 2km northwest, can make the perfect sleeping spot.

MAKE IT BIGGER

Being in Coniston means you're surrounded by a host of excellent hillwalking opportunities. If The Bell has whetted your appetite for more height, head northwest on the path up to Levers Water and then take the path that leads west up to the col at Levers Hawse. From there follow the ridgeline south to tick off the muscular Old Man of Coniston, an 803m giant that offers supreme views down to Coniston Water as well as over the route you'll have just ascended, and even down to The Bell you scrambled on. On the way down, the slopes are littered with spoils from its mining past – including buildings, shafts and tools – explore them with care.

FOR LITTLE ADVENTURERS

The Bell will prove quite a mission thanks to its scrambly summit. Ensure that you don't climb up what you can't climb down and, just in case, always position yourself behind children to catch them if they fall. It's always worth pointing out the route, though often children are more confident than grown-ups. The more cautious may prefer to approach via the west face, where a grassier slope requires walking rather than scrambling. For more tips on safe scrambling, see opposite.

FOR CAMPERS

The National Trust's nearby Hoathwaite Campsite (🖰 tinyurl.com/hoathwaite-campsite; ⏲ Easter–Sep; from £7pppn) offers back-to-basics camping or – at the other extreme – glamping in a Basecamp Tipi, both in stunnning locations.

FOR ADRENALINE LOVERS

Want to try your hand at gorge walking? Church Beck is a popular spot, but you will need a guide as access can be an issue otherwise. Local outfits River Deep Mountain High (🖰 riverdeepmountainhigh.co.uk) and Joint Adventures (🖰 jointadventures.co.uk) should be able to help.

FOR HUNGRY HIKERS

You can pick up food supplies at Coniston's Co-op (🖰 conistonCo-op.co.uk) or the Spar (in the petrol station). For a light snack/lunch head to the airy Bluebird Café in Coniston, which has lake views (🖰 thebluebirdcafe.co.uk). In the evening try Steam Bistro (🖰 steambistro.co.uk), which delights in serving local produce and where you can bring your own tipple. For a pint there's The Black Bull Inn or The Sun, both of which also serve food.

OTHER PRACTICALITIES

The Coniston Rambler (Bus 505, daily) connects Coniston with Hawkshead, Ambleside and Windermere. You'll find public toilets in Coniston village car park and at Coniston Boating Centre.

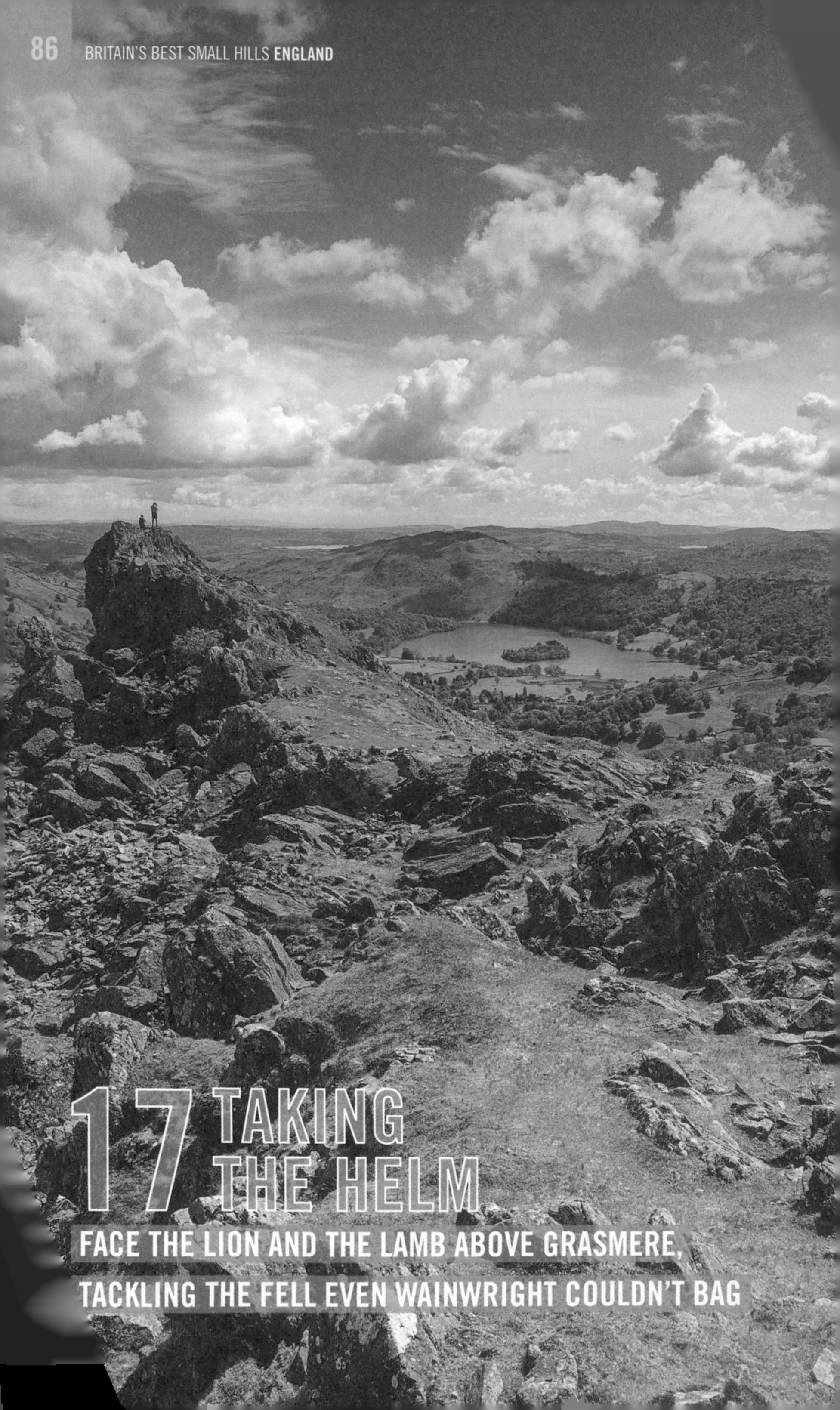

17 TAKING THE HELM

FACE THE LION AND THE LAMB ABOVE GRASMERE, TACKLING THE FELL EVEN WAINWRIGHT COULDN'T BAG

WHERE	Helm Crag, Cumbria
STATS	↔ 6km (3¾ miles) ↕ 405m ↗ 325m ↻ 2–2½ hours
START/FINISH	Broadgate car park NY338077
TERRAIN	Minor roads to start, then rough and rocky fell paths, culminating – if you dare – in a tricky scramble to the summit proper
MAPS	OS Explorer (1:25,000) 7; OS Landranger (1:50,000) 90

Rather than rush to the top of the Lakeland fell of Helm Crag, it pays to take a few moments to gaze up at it from beneath. For it's from the outskirts of the village of Grasmere that you can fully appreciate some of the nicknames given to the rock formations above. The first is 'The Lion and the Lamb' at the Crag's southern end. Viewed from the A591, in particular, the moniker is apposite, with one huge rock resembling the maned head of a majestic lion, in the front 'paws' of which sits a smaller rock recalling a woolly lamb. Reaching this pair of rocks is the first goal and – provided you use your hands – this landmark is a fairly easy one to stand atop.

The second target, however… well that one takes a little more guts, skill and determination. Depending who you ask it may be called 'The Old Lady Playing the Organ' (presumably on account of the rocky pipes that stick out from its squareish organ-shaped base) – or 'The Howitzer' (after the military firearm). There are even some who mistakenly refer to it as 'The Lion and the Lamb'. Regardless of the appellation, this rock formation marks the true 405m summit of Helm Crag and makes for a tricky ascent. Often you'll see people carrying rope to do it. Whether you work up the courage to try won't matter because even if you chicken out, as many people do, you'll be in good company: the Lakeland legend himself – guidebook writer Alfred Wainwright – was unable to climb it too. In any case, watching others try is way more fun anyway.

WALK THIS WAY

1 Starting from Broadgate car park in Grasmere turn left on to the B5287 and follow it to the crossroads. Here turn right on to Easedale Road; follow this for 1.5km (1 mile) out of the village towards Easedale. Following signs for Easedale Tarn and the YHA, pass through a small cluster of houses and farms. Ignore turnings to Easedale Tarn; where the road curves right you'll spy fingerposts to Helm Crag Path. Follow these through a gate then along a road that climbs to the right alongside further houses. **2** You'll come to another gate that leads on to a rocky bridleway. Follow this as it climbs uphill to an old quarry where a sign for Helm Crag will direct you to the right.

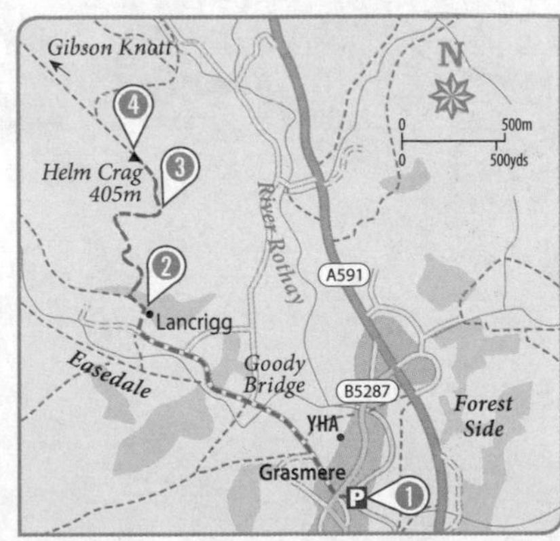

← Taking in the view towards Grasmere from the summit ridge of Helm Crag. (Richard Bowden/S)

Preparing to tackle the dreaded 'Howitzer', Helm Crag – the only summit Wainwright couldn't reach. (Neil S Price)

This zigzags up the fellside and – eventually – emerges on to an almost flat grassy shoulder. Make time to leave the path here to head southeast to a small depression (see *Added adventure*) for some of the best views of Grasmere you can get (more breathtaking than from the true summit). ③ Once you've had your fill of superlative-inducing landscape, turn your back on it and pick up the path in front of you, which now works its way up through the rocky outcrops. You'll pass The Lion and the Lamb first, which, of the two major rock formations, arguably offers the better views out to Grasmere and the surrounding Helvellyn fells. Then continue towards the summit where The Howitzer – due to its sheer size and scale – cannot be missed. ④ If it's wet or icy you're best leaving the rocky summit for another day, but if you are feeling adventurous then summon up your inner lion and give it a go (see *For adrenaline lovers*). Once you've finished – successfully or otherwise – simply retrace your steps to the start.

↑ Helm Crag from Grasmere. (Stewart Smith Photography/S)

ADDED ADVENTURE

Helm Crag is the perfect summit for sleeping out, with its far-reaching views of other fells and a beautiful depression halfway up it is an ideal place from which to admire the sunset. You will need to take your own water, however, as there are neither tarns nor streams along the route – and it's a fair old hike back down to the valley to get some.

MAKE IT BIGGER

Use Helm Crag as the first summit in a round of shapely crowns. Continue northwest to Gibson Knott and Calf Crag, before reaching Greenup Edge, then veer south to High Raise, before descending via Blea Rigg and Easedale Tarn along your return to Grasmere.

FOR LITTLE ADVENTURERS

There's a lot to keep little ones busy in Grasmere. Check out the famous Sarah Nelson's Grasmere Gingerbread shop, where the staff still dress in traditional period clothing. Visit Wordsworth's garden, which, fittingly, blooms yellow with daffodils in early spring, or his grave in St Oswald's Church. Or focus on water, by pottering along the pretty River Rothay or hiring a rowing boat at Faeryland (faeryland.co.uk).

FOR CAMPERS

The nearest campsite to Grasmere is at Rydal Hall (rydalhall.org; from £8pppn) just under 4.5km (3 miles) south. Bring your tent or hire a yurt, pod or shepherd hut.

FOR ADRENALINE LOVERS

Tackle the Howitzer: the two ways up are via the right edge (looking at it from the path) or, slightly more straightforward, up the central slab to the right of an obvious patch of moss. Both routes have serious consequences should you slip so only attempt the climb if you are confident and conditions are in your favour.

FOR HUNGRY HIKERS

Aside from the gingerbread – which cannot be recommended highly enough – Grasmere has plenty of cafés and pubs. To really treat yourself, head to the recently opened Forest Side (theforestside.com) across the A591 from the village. In this fairytale Gothic mansion, local chef Kevin Tickle has created a special forage-to-fork tasting menu, where you get to sample fell-found fare such as syrup made from birch-tree sap wild fungi, seafood from the Cumbrian coast and more. The menu changes seasonally; booking ahead is advised. For supplies there is a Co-op in the centre of Grasmere as well as numerous outlets selling take-away sandwiches.

OTHER PRACTICALITIES

Both the 555 bus from Lancaster and Kendal to Keswick and the 599 to Ambleside/Kendal call via Grasmere. The nearest public toilets are at Stock Lane car park in Grasmere.

18 BAREFOOT RAMBLINGS

TACKLE THE LAKELAND PEAK SO SMOOTH THAT FELLWALKER ALFRED WAINWRIGHT SUGGESTED ASCENDING IT SHOELESS...

WHERE	Hallin Fell, Cumbria
STATS	↔ 1.5km (1 mile) ↕ 388m ↗ 175m ↻ 1 hour
START/FINISH	Small car park on The Hause at Martindale ⚲ NY435191
TERRAIN	Steep push up grassy slopes
MAPS	OS Explorer (1:25,000) 5; OS Landranger (1:50,000) 90

Ullswater is one of the most popular spots in the Lake District, with many a hill-lover venturing to its shores to tick off the popular peak of Helvellyn from the knee-trembling ridges of Striding and Swirral Edge. But it doesn't have to be scary or even crowded if you know where to look...

Enter Hallin Fell. To a geologist it may simply be described as part of the ridge that runs down from Steel Knotts (435m), but to the more romantic among us – those who like to add a hearty dash of imagination to our landscapes – this portly peak stands proudly on its own, and is just begging to be climbed. This perspective derives from the depth of the col in which Martindale sits to the south and the cleft that the rivers of Rampsgill, Bannerdale and Boredale have gouged to the west – not to mention the expanse of Ullswater circumventing its remaining edges. From the summit, linger a while to watch the water and to see Ullswater's famous steamer boats gliding along its surface – an alternative way to start or finish this walk if you have the time (see *For little adventurers*). Better still, the location on the southern side of Ullswater means that this is one hill you can get virtually to yourself, as no road flanks the lake west of Martindale. Not a bad prospect for one of the busiest parts of the Lake District National Park.

↑ Hallin Fell seen from across Ullswater. (Harry Horton/A)

WALK THIS WAY

❶ From the car park opposite St Peter's Church, cross the road (ie: north) where you'll see a 'No cycling' signpost. ❷ From here you simply follow the broad grassy path that zigzags up to the summit of Hallin Fell, ignoring the turn off to the right (your return route), complete with its obelisk. The path passes through bracken with scattered rocks, whilst sheep graze over to one side, beyond a drystone wall. ❸ Resting against the Hallin Fell summit obelisk, take in the views of the fells that line the massive expanse of Ullswater, putting a name to each. Famed fellwalker Alfred Wainwright wrote of this cairn, which originally towered 4m high but is now barely half that, 'the man who built [it]... did more than indicate the highest point: he erected for himself a permanent memorial'. For the return, to vary your route take the path that first heads northeast but then cuts south downhill and back to your start point.

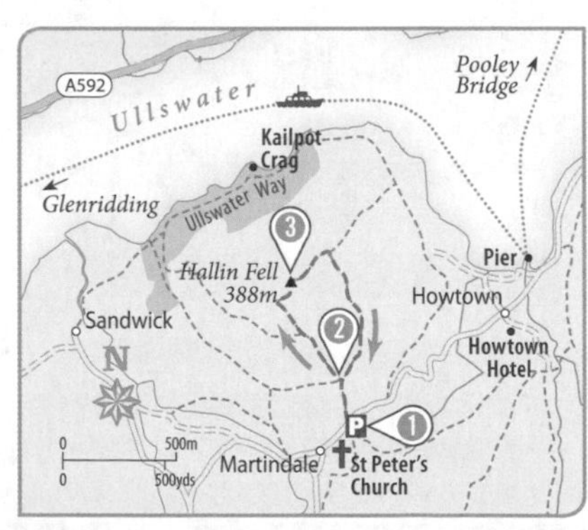

ADDED ADVENTURE

Leave the shoes in the car and heed famed fell-lover Alfred Wainwright's advice that Hallin Fell can be ascended 'comfortably in bare feet'. Literally feeling nature between your toes is said to help you connect with the landscape better – and certainly this hiker can attest to the keenest feeling with which you'll instantly detect every single stone, slightly sharp frond of bracken or bramble. For first-time barefoot bimblings it may be wise to carry your shoes in your backpack.

MAKE IT BIGGER

Officially opened in 2016, the Ullswater Way allows hikers to circumnavigate the entire body of water over a 32km (20 mile) route. There are options to add on even more adventure – this little hill for one, but also a trip to Aira Force waterfall north of the lake and to Gowbarrow Fell, (another lovely lump opposite Hallin Fell).

FOR LITTLE ADVENTURERS

A trip on an Ullswater 'Steamer' (starting in Glenridding; ullswatersteamers.co.uk) will be an added bonus. It is also a highly recommended way to start the walk from Glenridding (where you can leave your car) as it calls at Howtown pier, just east of Martindale. Alternatively, have a short walk along the northern shore of Ullswater at Gowbarrow Bay back towards Glenridding, with its copious pebble-strewn spits made for skimming.

FOR CAMPERS

Tucked away between the northern shore of Ullswater and Little Mell Fell, you'll find The Quiet Site (thequietsite.co.uk), an award-winning facility that offers tent camping as well as the opportunity to sleep in a heated camping pod.

FOR ADRENALINE LOVERS

Below Hallin Fell, Kailpot Crag is famous among intrepid wild-water fans for cliff jumping. There's even a little beach and woodland beside the Crag. If you're not 100% sure about jumping, go with a guide such as Swim the Lakes (swimthelakes.co.uk).

FOR HUNGRY HIKERS

The Howtown Hotel (howtown-hotel.co.uk) has a public tearoom that offers homemade cakes and light lunches (Mar–Nov). It lies in the nearby hamlet of Howtown and has been owned by the same family for more than a century. Alternatively, Patterdale Village Store and Post Office (patterdalevillagestore.co.uk), 6km southwest of Martindale, is one place to pick up supplies pre-walk if coming from the western or central Lakes, otherwise Penrith has a wider choice.

OTHER PRACTICALITIES

The 508 bus connects Pooley Bridge (the nearest village) to both Penrith train station and Windermere. However, reaching the start of the walk will mean a long walk (7km) or hitchhiking. The nearest public toilets are in Pooley Bridge, behind the information centre.

The views of Ullswater are greater than you'd think this small fell would deliver. (Acceleratorhams/D)

19 KING OF THE CASTLE

STROLL TO THE TOP OF LAKELAND'S ROCKY FORTRESS THEN DISCOVER THE CAVE HIDDEN BENEATH...

WHERE	Castle Crag, Cumbria
STATS	↔ 3.5km (2¼ miles) ↕ 290m ↗ 208m ↻ 2 hours
START/FINISH	Car park in Rosthwaite ⚲ NY257148
TERRAIN	Woodland paths, open fellside, rocky tracks (care needed when wet)
MAPS	OS Explorer (1:25,000) 4; OS Landranger (1:50,000) 90

It's impressive to think that in just 2 short hours of hiking you can gain the summit of the pleasing promontory of Castle Crag, which has two rather special claims to fame (one per hour, you might argue). The first is that it's the only Lakeland hill sitting under the 300m (1,000ft) threshold that makes it into author and illustrator Alfred Wainwright's *Pictorial Guides to the Lakeland Fells*. This immediately suggests that this is a summit well worth your attention. Known as a man of to-the-point phrasing, it was on this small hill that Wainwright seemed to let adjectives get the better of him, waxing lyrical about it being 'so magnificently independent, so ruggedly individual, so aggressively unashamed of its lack of inches'. And who could blame him? With a climb to the top featuring slate spoils seemingly arranged like an elaborate sculpture garden plus views from the top spanning the raw beauty of the exquisitely glacier-gouged, U-shaped Borrowdale Valley, you'll find yourself spouting summit superlatives with equal gusto.

But there's more to this hill than just a propensity to induce flowery phrases in even the most stoic of hikers. For those in the know (you imminently among them), Castle Crag's second unique selling point is perhaps even cooler. Underneath the summit, deep in the belly of this mini-mountain, hides a

↑ Looking up to the craggy Castle Crag (crows circling wouldn't look out of place). (Andrew Locking)

very spacious cave that served as the summer home for a man called Millican Dalton back in the 1930s. A self-styled and self-described 'Professor of Adventure', who always sported a wide-brimmed Tyrolean hat and smoked Woodbines (he was also a teetotal, vegetarian pacifist in case you were wondering), Dalton gave up a house and good job in London in 1904 to live an alternative lifestyle. From the place he reputedly dubbed 'The Cave Hotel', Dalton would take mixed groups of men and women out climbing, walking and camping – all at a time when doing so was particularly taboo.

Though Dalton died in 1947 his legend lives on. Indeed, Dalton commemorated his own residence of the cave by penning his own epitaph inside ('Don't waste words, jump to conclusions'). Look at the wall of the cave opposite and you'll also notice the letters AW carved into the rock – said to have been cleaved in by none other than guidebook writer Alfred Wainwright himself. He joked that it was a penthouse cave as it was split-level and had running water – which it does to this day – in the form of a continuous trickle that runs from top to bottom. Take advantage of your walk to climb down to the cave, enter and commune.

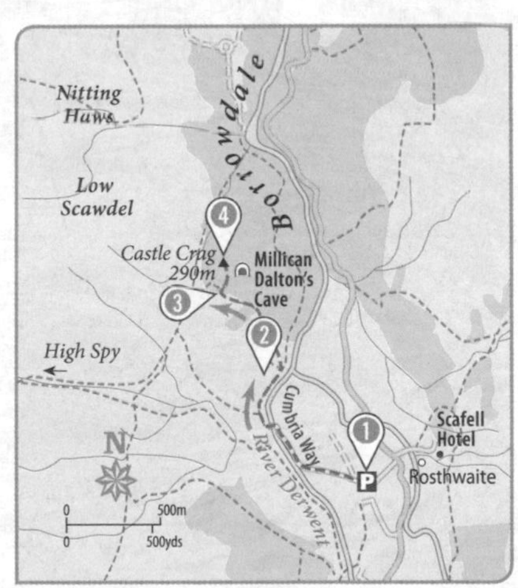

Ascending the slate paths – remains of its former quarry days – *en route* to Castle Crag summit. (Andrew Locking)

WALK THIS WAY

1 From the car park turn right to head up the narrow lane with the River Derwent to your left. Follow the babbling waterway as it winds alongside the green fields of the valley floor and you'll come to a stone bridge on your left. Cross it and follow the Cumbria Way (bridleway) along the west bank of the river. 2 After a couple of hundred metres, before you enter the woods, another track branches uphill to the northwest. Follow this as it steadily climbs, looking out for curly-horned Herdwick sheep, a breed unique to the Lake District, as you go. You'll pass through a gate, alongside a small stone shelter (to your left) and continue on the path as it zigzags uphill through a gap in the wall. 3 Turn right into the mature sessile-oak woodland and follow the well-marked path up to Castle Crag's summit, admiring the strange collection of manmade slatestone markers formed from the quarry spoils, presumably left by fellwalkers passing through on the way to the summit. Do note that the slate can be slippery in rain. 4 At the top is a memorial to the men from Borrowdale who died in World War I. The summit itself is said to have once formed part of a hillfort, although – due to quarrying – it is impossible to tell. What you will see for sure are far-reaching views down Borrowdale and over to the fells of Skiddaw at the opposite (northern) end of Derwent Water, and (to the south) Great Gable and the Scafells behind. If you don't wish to hunt for Millican's cave – see *Added adventure* – return to your car by simply retracing your steps.

↑ The entranceway to Millican Dalton's cave, hidden in the folds of Castle Crag's slopes. (Neil S Price)

ADDED ADVENTURE

For the ultimate it has to be spending the night in Millican Dalton's cave. You will need to arrive late and leave early, and ensure you take all rubbish out with you – even if it's not yours. Be discreet, do not go in a large group and make sure you take a bivvy with you as the cave is always damp and down-filled sleeping bags won't keep you warm if they get wet. To access it from the summit the easiest way is to retrace your steps back to the Cumbria Way. Turn left (north) on to this long-distance path and follow it until you see a faint path on your left (at around NY251159) that goes up to the cave.

MAKE IT BIGGER

For more height, head west from Castle Crag's summit, then south on the path that runs south–north until you reach Tongue Gill. Take the path on your right (west) heading uphill to Wilson's Bield then bear right (north) on to the tops of High Spy, Maiden Moor and Catbells. Then follow the ridge north, cutting down on the nose of Brandelhow to Derwent Water before taking the Cumbria Way south, along the lake, then by the river, back to your start point (passing Dalton's cave *en route*).

FOR LITTLE ADVENTURERS

The woodland beneath Castle Crag is perfect for spying roe deer, red squirrels and even foxes, making it ideal for a nature walk, particularly in high winds when the summit is best avoided. Race twigs down the river, meander alongside the stream and look for dens among the trees.

FOR CAMPERS

Chapel House Farm (chapelhousefarmcampsite.co.uk) is the perfect place to pitch for Castle Crag. Essentially just a field by the adjacent farm, it offers solitude, walks right from your tent door and a pub (Riverside Bar at the Scafell Hotel; see below) within a few minutes' stroll.

FOR ADRENALINE LOVERS

Think like Millican; the River Derwent is ripe for a water adventure. Grab yourself a packraft or inflatable canoe, find a safe entry (and exit) point and go with the flow

FOR HUNGRY HIKERS

The Scafell Hotel in Rosthwaite (scafell.co.uk) offers formal sit-down dinners for those who want them. More fresh-off-the-fells-friendly is the Riverside Bar next door, which will happily accommodate muddy boots. They do massive portions of hearty fare – and you can ask to carry out what you don't eat. Make sure you try the hot chocolate with a side of Grasmere gingerbread.

OTHER PRACTICALITIES

The nearest train station is in Penrith. Buses leave there for Keswick (Bus X5) from where you can get the Rosthwaite bus from outside Booths supermarket (handy for picking up supplies; booths.co.uk/store/keswick). There are no public toilets in Rosthwaite – the nearest are in Keswick, 10km (6 miles) away – though if eating in the bar or hotel you can use their facilities.

20 PENNINE PERFECTION

DETOUR OFF THE PENNINE WAY TO DUFTON PIKE FOR FAR-REACHING VIEWS OF THE EDEN VALLEY

WHERE	Dufton Pike, Cumbria
STATS	↔ 6.5km (4 miles) ↕ 481m ↗ 321m ↻ 2–3 hours
START/FINISH	Dufton village green car park NY689249
TERRAIN	Farmland (can be boggy), rough fell paths, section of Pennine Way
MAPS	OS Explorer (1:25,000) 19; OS Landranger (1:50,000) 91

You'd think that, being so close to both a car park and pub, this tiny top would be well climbed. But the Pennine Way long-distance footpath cleverly swerves people out of the way of this hill's summit – thereby streamlining walkers to its big attractions on either side. Sitting just a few kilometres to the east, 'England's Grand Canyon' (aka High Cup Nick) grabs most visitors, whilst to the west lies the triple crown of Pennine pinnacles – namely Little Dun Fell, Great Dun Fell and Cross Fell (the highest top in the range).

Contrastingly crowd-free, and boasting a distinctly shapely profile, Dufton Pike is an easy hill-climbing prospect offering a little-trodden grassy ascent with excellent views over the Eden Valley and beyond. It has another claim to fame, being made from some of the North Pennines' oldest rocks – dating from 420–480 million years ago. Indeed, when you look at these now, it's hard to believe that these were once merely volcanic ash and mud debris at the ocean edge. In short, it's the perfect place for a peaceful and reflective stroll.

WALK THIS WAY

❶ From the car park turn right on to the street. Follow the road as it bends left then follow the lane to the left of the village chapel, which is signposted for the Pennine Way to Garrigill and a public bridleway to High Scald Fell. ❷ Follow the country lane as it heads northeast, past Pusgill House, ascending steadily. ❸ Continue on to a kissing gate in the wall to your left where you'll be able to

↑ The far-reaching views of the Eden Valley can be taken in from shapely Dufton Pike. (Andrew Locking)

make out the faint grassy trail that takes you all the way to Dufton Pike's summit. **4** From this conical Pennine peak you'll be able to take in extensive views of the surrounding hillocks – such as Knock Pike – as well as more impressive mounds beyond. To the east is Great Rundale (once home to an active lead-mining industry and now covered in old workings), to the south the small town of Appleby-in-Westmorland can be glimpsed and, to the west, the beautiful rolling Eden Valley stretches out into the distance, from where the impressive Lakeland fells of the High Street range peek out. Once you've had your fill, locate a faded boot-beaten path heading northwest down the nose of the peak. Follow it downhill to the wall. **5** Continue on the signed route to the right to meet with the track running along Great Rundale Beck. Turn left on to it and follow it until it meets a wider vehicle track. At the junction of paths stay left to join the Pennine Way. Keep on the long-distance path until the main track swings to the right, at which point you continue straight on following the National Trail. Follow this past Coatsike Farm and all the way back into Dufton and your start point.

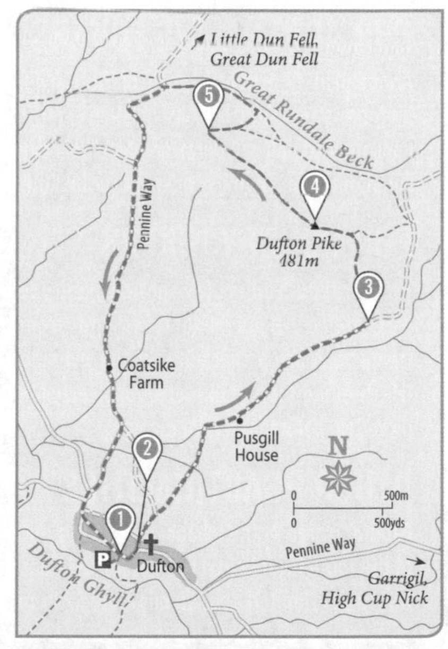

ADDED ADVENTURE

Nearby is a U-shaped valley or glacial trough that is often cited as England's own Grand Canyon. Take a stroll to see it from one of the many crumbling pinnacles and buttresses that line its rim then, for a real wild night, consider sleeping in a bivvy overnight (a safe distance from the edge, naturally) so you can watch its rocks change colour at sunrise.

MAKE IT BIGGER

Continue along the Pennine Way to pick off Little Dun Fell and Great Dun Fell before reaching the mighty Cross Fell (highest peak in the Pennines, at 893m). It's a long and committing walk with no real route-shortening escape routes, so plan ahead: either bring all your usual camping equipment, plus some fuel for a fire) or stay overnight in Greg's Hut bothy on Cross Fell's northern flanks. Then head back out on the lower Pennine Way the following morning.

FOR LITTLE ADVENTURERS

Check out Dufton Ghyll in the woods behind the car park (tinyurl.com/duftonghyll)– there's strolls to be had on the paths either side of the stream. Take a ticklist for little ones and look out for mature beech, oak, sycamore, sweet chestnut and elm trees plus the native red squirrel. In the stream you can spot fish and, in spring, the whole place is coated with bluebells.

FOR CAMPERS

Grandie Caravan Park (duftoncaravanpark.co.uk; camping from £7pppn) offers a truly sublime location at the foot of the Pennine fells, with this walk and others straight from your tent flap.

FOR ADRENALINE LOVERS

About 4km (2½ miles) north of Dufton Pike, accessed via the Pennine Way, is the fairly unimpressive Knock Fell. Its northern spur, however, hides an entranceway into Knock Fell Caverns, a complex network of 4.5km (2¾ miles) of passageways for the experienced caver only. For information, permits and maps contact the British Cave Research Association (bcra.org.uk).

FOR HUNGRY HIKERS

The Postbox Pantry (postboxpantry.co.uk daily except Thu) in Dufton serves teas, coffees, homemade cakes and scones as well as light lunch options. Traditional cream teas are a speciality. In the evening (and noon–14.00 Wed/Sat/Sun) The Stag Inn (thestagdufton.co.uk) serves up hearty fare and real ales. Booking advised. Supplies are best picked up beforehand in Appleby.

OTHER PRACTICALITIES

Parking is free in the village. If planning on walking to High Cup Nick bear in mind that part of the route is on land. Look out for red flags and heed advice on whether to continue. Public transport is limited, though bus route 573 runs from Appleby on Fridays only.

High Cup Gill flowing down from the head of High Cup Nick. (Clearview/A)

Assessing wild camp potential on 389m Yr Arddu. (Neil S Price)

WALES

21 JUST DESSERTS

DISCOVER THE TASTY-SOUNDING BLORENGE, A SWEET LITTLE OUTLIER OF THE BRECON BEACONS

WHERE	Blorenge, Monmouthshire
STATS	↔ 4km (2½ miles) ↕ 561m ↗ 51m ↻ 1 hour
START/FINISH	Cefn y Galchen car park ⚲ SO262107
TERRAIN	Grassy tracks
MAPS	OS Explorer (1:25,000) 13; OS Landranger (1:50,000) 161

Its name – Blorenge or The Blorenge – may sound distinctly dessert-like (I can't help but think blancmange) but the association with puddings doesn't end there. Look a little deeper at the geological make-up of this Brecon Beacons outlier and you'll discover that it is actually trifle-like below ground – with layers of mudstone, sandstone and limestone among its ingredients. Walking the easy few kilometres to the summit is equally as appetising, being a simple stroll over the steadily sloping grassy and bracken-coated ground, with a rough path cutting right through it for easy walking. You'll pass a little hut *en route* and maybe even some ponies that often graze here, before reaching the ancient stone cairn ring that sits atop the highest point.

From the summit you'll be able to see two of the other little hills in this guide – The Skirrid (page 112) and Sugar Loaf (page 116) – as well as the rest of the Black Mountains. Take some time to also peer down to the southeast of the summit where you can spy forest above a quirky feature known as The Punchbowl. During the last ice age, a glacier carved out this depression from an otherwise wedge-like hill. It is now a nature reserve maintained by the Woodland Trust (🖱 tinyurl.com/punchbowl-woodland) – well worth a wander. Inside you'll find a mix of beech, ash, downy birch and

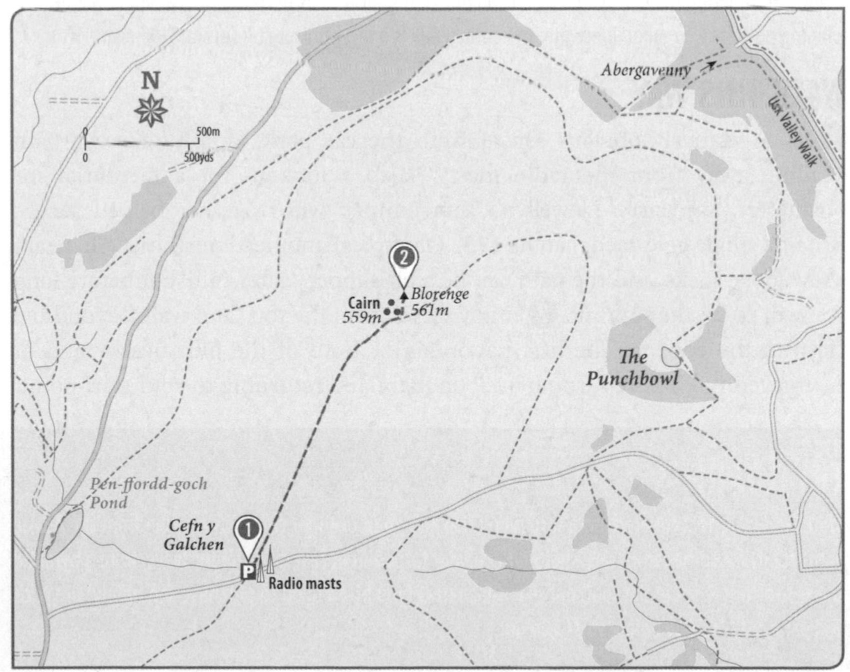

← Tasty views from Blorenge of the equally as sweet-sounding Sugar Loaf. (Jennifer Thompson/D)

occasional sessile oak, field maple and holly trees. Keep your binoculars handy for green woodpecker and, if visiting at dusk, pipistrelle bats too.

After completing the peak consider hitting one of the local pubs to track down a pint of the award-winning pale ale also called Blorenge. The entire walk is a tasty prospect from start to finish.

WALK THIS WAY

❶ It's a relatively obvious ascent from the car park. Simply take the path heading away from the radio masts (keep a lookout for a memorial for Foxhunter, Sir Harry Llewellyn's showjumper, who together helped secure Britain's single gold medal at the 1952 Olympics) and head northeast. There are a few loose rocks, and the path can be a bit slippery after rain, but before long you will reach the summit. ❷ Enjoy views from the top (and walk beyond the cairn to the edge for the best panorama) – both of the hills nearby and of Abergavenny – before turning back on them and returning to your start point.

TRY A TARP

Woodland is perfect for erecting a tarpaulin (also known in outdoor circles as a basha from the Aussie name for it) for some temporary shelter. Pitch your tarpaulin in several different ways, from a pyramid shape to a simple sheet flat roof, but essential extras (you often need to purchase separately) are pegs and paracord – so buy before you head out.

↑ The Woodland Trust's Punch Bowl is surrounded by an inviting fringe of trees. (Keith Huggett/WTML)

ADDED ADVENTURE

You'd have to be discreet of course – as with any wild camp – but it is possible to camp among the trees near The Punchbowl. Take a tarp and bivvy or a hammock for maximum options.

MAKE IT BIGGER

Beneath the slopes of The Blorenge runs the Usk Valley Walk, which runs 77km (58 miles) between Caerleon and Brecon. Slap this peak on to that (or part of that) longer trek and you're in for a winner.

FOR LITTLE ADVENTURERS

Head down from the summit as per the walk above, but rather than heading straight for your car, veer further west to Keepers Pond (⚲ SO254107; also marked on maps as Pen-ffordd-goch Pond), easily accessed from the same car park. Benches make it a great place for a picnic, and interpretation boards guide your walk. Eat your sandwiches and, in the summer, watch out for dragonflies such as common darter and birds such as meadow pipit.

FOR CAMPERS

Either of the sites recommended for The Skirrid (page 112) or Sugar Loaf (page 116) would be good. In case they are full or if you want somewhere nearer, in Llangattock try Park Farm (🖱 parkfarm-campsite.co.uk; from £7pn).

FOR ADRENALINE LOVERS

The Blorenge is a well-known spot for hang- and paragliding. Book at 🖱 tinyurl.com/powysparaglide (prices from £119 for a tandem flight).

FOR HUNGRY HIKERS

The Co-op in Blaenavon, 4km (2½ miles) southwest, is the place to get supplies before your walk. For a sit-down meal head to Butterflies (🖱 butterfliesblaenavon.co.uk), a great gastropub that also does a killer Sunday roast. You may also want to consider stocking up on snacks at Abergavenny Market (🖱 abergavennymarket.org.uk; Tue/Fri/Sat) to pick up a range of local cheeses and bread.

OTHER PRACTICALITIES

Public toilets are found in Blaenavon on Lion Street. Buses go from Abergavenny (where there is a train station) to Pontypool from where you can catch a connecting bus to Blaenavon. From here, walk to the starting point.

Wander down to Keepers Pond to spot birds such as the meadow pipit. (James Lowen) ↑

22 THE OUTLIER

TACKLE YSGYRYD FAWR, AN OBLONG HILL THAT REPUTEDLY CAME INTO BEING AS JESUS WAS CRUCIFIED

WHERE	Ysgyryd Fawr, Monmouthshire
STATS	↔ 4.5km (2¾ miles) ↕ 486m ↗ 293m ↻ 2 hours
START/FINISH	Car park beside the B4521 ♥ SO328164
TERRAIN	A steep climb on gravel and grassy paths; care needed in woodland (which can be slippery)
MAPS	OS Explorer (1:25,000) 13; OS Landranger (1:50,000) 161

Wedge-like hills are great, seeming to call out to us to be climbed, demanding that we feel their contours beneath our boots. Nowhere is this truer than Ysgyryd Fawr, an oblong hill often affectionately referred to as The Skirrid (tinyurl.com/skirrid). Isolated from the surrounding hills, it rises like a shark fin from the farmland – a sharp rocky mass coated with scree and woodland.

The hill's name has an intriguing (if geologically doubtful) origin. 'Ysgyryd' means something that has been shattered, divided or split. 'Fawr' means 'great', and – looking at the side profile of The Skirrid – it does look as if the little 364m nose has cracked off from the main oblong wedge. Local lore has it that this part of the hill's slopes split and fell off at the exact moment of the Crucifixion of Jesus. Geologists, however, would say that it is more down to the composition of the peak: a mix of sandstone on unstable mudstone.

The religious connotation doesn't end there. Most obvious are the remains of the 17th-century St Michaels Chapel, the Roman place of worship that graces the summit. Additionally there's a rock

↑ Ysgyryd Fawr aka The Skirrid, and its shapely summit. (Jeff Tucker/A)

formation known as the Devil's Chair, so-named after the Devil argued to a giant called Jack O'Kent that England's Malvern Hills were higher than the Sugar Loaf (page 116). When Jack was proved right the Devil scooped up some soil to drop on the Malverns to make them higher, but mistakenly dropped it on The Skirrid, thereby forming this little tump.

Given all this creative conjecture, it is unsurprising that some locals refer to this hill as the Holy Mount or Sacred Hill. One thing is for sure – while some of the steep ascents are a little devilish, the feeling you get from standing on this summit, with glorious views in every direction (Somerset's limestone Mendips to the south, Wales's Black Mountains to the west, the rest of the Black Mountains to the north and Forest of Dean over to the east) is much more heavenly.

WALK THIS WAY

1 Follow the gravel path northwest from the car park and cross the stile into Caer Wood. As you emerge from it the path splits, fittingly just under the cracked-off rock. Continue straight on the Beacons Way footpath (heading east and uphill; the other path is where you'll join this route on the way back). **2** Ignore other turn-offs and carry on, following the grass-covered ridge of Ysgyryd Fawr, across open hillside, up to the summit at 486m. **3** As well as views of the surrounding hills, this is where you'll find the remains of a church where persecuted Roman Catholics would hold their services during and after King Henry VIII's religious Reformation in the 16th century. There are also depressions marking an even-earlier Iron Age hillfort. After your exploration, take the steep path down from the summit, bearing northwest to join a grassy footpath. **4** Turn left on to this path, following it south into the woods as it contours around the eastern side of The Skirrid. After just under a couple of kilometres you'll reach the path that you left at the end of stage 1. Follow this back to your start.

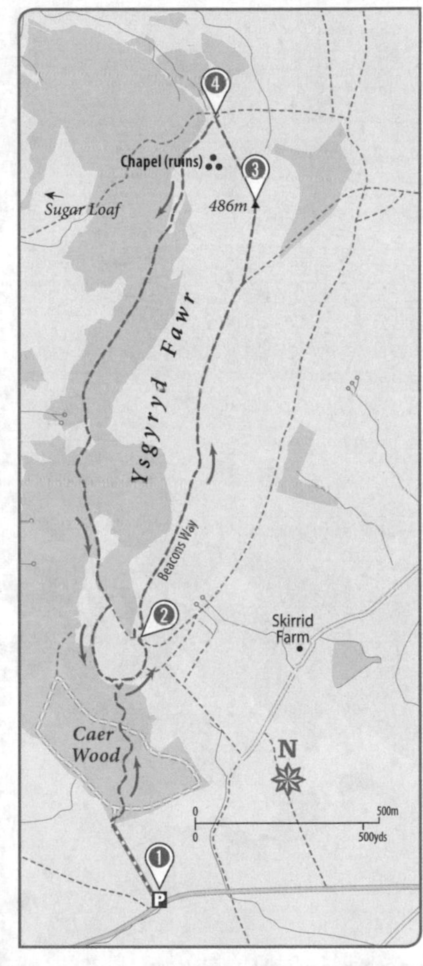

Ysgyryd Fawr as seen from Blorenge (combine the two for a perfect peak-bagging day). (Whiskybottle/D)

ADDED ADVENTURE

The woodland that blankets the western flanks of this mini-mountain can be a good spot for a hammock camp. Otherwise, take your bivvy and tuck yourself in near the remains of the chapel.

MAKE IT BIGGER

Similar to Sugar Loaf (see overleaf) you can combine this hill with any one of the other hills of Abergavenny – the nearest being Ysgyryd Fach (a couple of kilometres to the south) or Deri (4km to the west). Alternatively, you could add on a walk along the Beacons Way (breconbeacons.org/beacons-way) – a walking path that leads 152km (95 miles) from Abergavenny to Ashfield (near Llandeilo).

FOR LITTLE ADVENTURERS

Nearby Abergavenny Castle and Museum (abergavennymuseum.co.uk) offers the chance for kids to explore the ruins of a Norman castle and get creative in the small, child-focused museum where there's the opportunity to dress up in period clothing, and experience a World War II air-raid shelter.

FOR CAMPERS

You could try the campsite recommended for Sugar Loaf (see overleaf). Otherwise, The Rising Sun pub in Pandy (therisingsunpandy.com; end Feb–mid-Nov; from £8pn), 9.5km (6 miles) away offers award-winning B&B accommodation as well as a campsite, and serves hearty food.

FOR ADRENALINE LOVERS

Take on the Abergavenny fells on the back of a mighty steed (or a pony at least). Abergavenny-based Grange Trekking Centre (grangetrekking-wales.co.uk) offers guided pony-trekking for all levels and abilities over the Black Mountains and beyond. From £32.

FOR HUNGRY HIKERS

For breakfast or snacks try Crumbs Café (5 Market St, Abergavenny; 01873 854420) for their trademark 'Big Boys Breakfast'. For a heartier meal, it has to be the Skirrid Inn (skirridmountaininn.co.uk), which claims to be among the oldest pubs in Wales. Sharing its name with the summit you've just ascended and with generous portions of food, this pub is the perfect place to recuperate. For supplies choose from one of the town's many supermarkets.

OTHER PRACTICALITIES

Abergavenny, 5.5km (3½ miles) away, has the nearest train station, bus stop (at the bus station) and public toilets.

23 A SPOON FULL OF SUGAR

CLIMB A SWEET LITTLE PEAK FOR UNRIVALLED VIEWS OF THE BRECON BEACONS – AND BONUS WINE

WHERE	Sugar Loaf, Monmouthshire
STATS	↔ 4.75km (3 miles) ↕ 596m ↗ 266m ↻ 2 hours
START/FINISH	Sugar Loaf car park SO269166
TERRAIN	Grassy tracks take you to a bald summit
MAPS	OS Explorer (1:25,000) 13; OS Landranger (1:50,000) 161

Whenever people think of South Wales for walking, it's the Brecon Beacons that are the headliners; other ranges don't tend to get a very high billing. Yet the Black Mountains – of which the conical summit of Sugar Loaf (tinyurl.com/sugarloafwales) forms the southern terminus – are a glorious collection of tops well deserving of attention. The best thing about this particular heather- and bracken-clad moorland mound is that it's within supremely easy reach of Abergavenny, meaning that you could choose to hike to its summit straight from this market town.

The original Welsh name of this summit is Mynydd Pen-y-fal, but the Sugar Loaf moniker has been in use for centuries. The hill's pimple-like shape is the cause, given its resemblance to the cone in which sugar granules were sold in as far back as the 12th century. Views from the top of Sugar Loaf are spectacular – with the Brecon Beacons, remainder of the Black Mountains and the Usk Valley and Blorenge (page 108) all within sight. As you gaze into the distance, you may be serenaded by skylarks overhead, hear the guttural warning of a red grouse, or spot the delicately twisting form of a red kite.

But there's one other sweetener in this already sugary summit. On the southern flanks are vineyards where grapes are harvested to produce wines bearing the Sugar Loaf name (sugarloafvineyard.co.uk) – so make sure you track down a glass (or bottle) for a post-walk (or even summit) celebration.

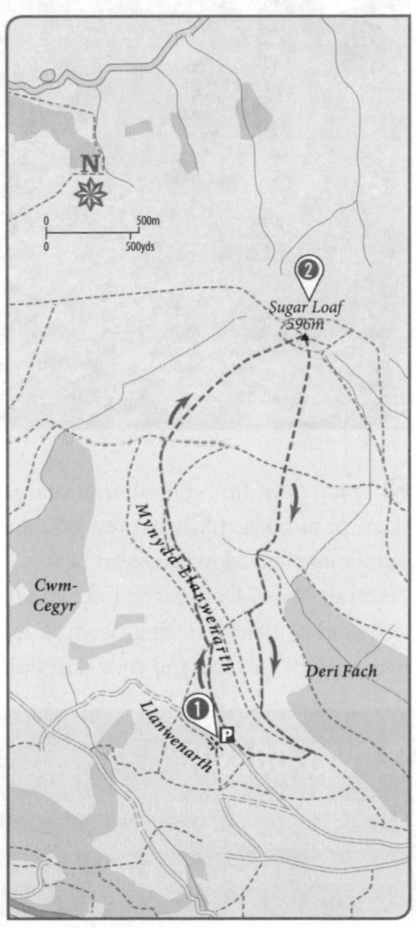

WALK THIS WAY

1 From Sugar Loaf car park on the Llanwenarth road, cross the road and take the track bearing northnorthwest to begin your ascent along Mynydd Llanwenarth. After a couple of kilometres, the path curves due northeast to tackle the summit head on.

← The fittingly white-coloured ground on the path to Sugar Loaf's sweet little summit. (Steve Pleydell/S)

❷ Enjoy views from the summit (the perfect place for a picnic) and look up to the skies for airborne birds of prey. When you've had your fill, rather than taking the same route back down, instead head south off the summit to take the path which descends above Deri Fach's oak woodland (a good place for a detour; see *Little adventurers*) before cutting down to the slopes of Mynydd Llanwenarth and the path back to the road and your start point.

SLOWLY DOES IT

If you intend to extend your little hill day to take on several summits, do take heed from overseas porters and remember it's not a race. You're much better slowing your pace so you can continue all the way to the top without stopping, rather than racing up and needing to pause multiple times.

↑ Deri Fach woodland looking mighty fine in autumn colours. (Francisco Machado)

ADDED ADVENTURE

Take a tarp (preferably green) and consider spending a night amongst the trees in one of the surrounding patches of woodland: choose from Cwm-Cegyr, Graig or Deri Fach and get pitching.

MAKE IT BIGGER

From Abergavenny you can summit not one, not two but seven hills if the mood takes you. So if you're ready to take on the 'Llanwenarth Breast', tackle Sugar Loaf then Blorenge (page 108), Ysgyryd Fawr aka The Skirrid (page 112), Deri, Ysgyryd Fach, Rholben and Mynydd Llanwenarth.

FOR LITTLE ADVENTURERS

On your way up (or down), consider taking the time to wander through Deri Fach, an ancient coppice of oak trees that were used to make fuel. Look around you to see some old charcoal-burning platforms on the forest floor.

FOR CAMPERS

Middle Ninfa Bunkhouse and Campsite (middleninfa.co.uk; from £10pn) offers the chance to stay in a 300-year-old bunkhouse as well as to pitch a tent in secluded sites. The owners also run willow coracle-building workshops and the site offers easy access to all of Abergavenny's hills.

FOR ADRENALINE LOVERS

Go climbing – inside: Cragfit Climbing Centre in Ebbw Vale is a great bad-weather option to hone your skills (cragfit.co.uk). A coffee shop caters for non-rope-loving friends or other halves.

FOR HUNGRY HIKERS

Nearby Abergavenny is home to an annual food festival (abergavennyfoodfestival.com), so you can be guaranteed of good grub. There are ample shops, cafés and pubs to buy food before or after your hike. Recommended are Cwtch Café (loveabergavenny.com/directory/cwtch-cafe) for snacks and coffee, and the quirky, cosy Hen and Chickens (tinyurl.com/henchickens) for something more substantial. There are also several supermarkets where you can get supplies.

OTHER PRACTICALITIES

There are both bus and train stations in Abergavenny from where you can start this walk. The nearest toilet is at the tourist information centre by the bus station.

Keep your eyes on the skies for red kite. (James Lowen) ↑

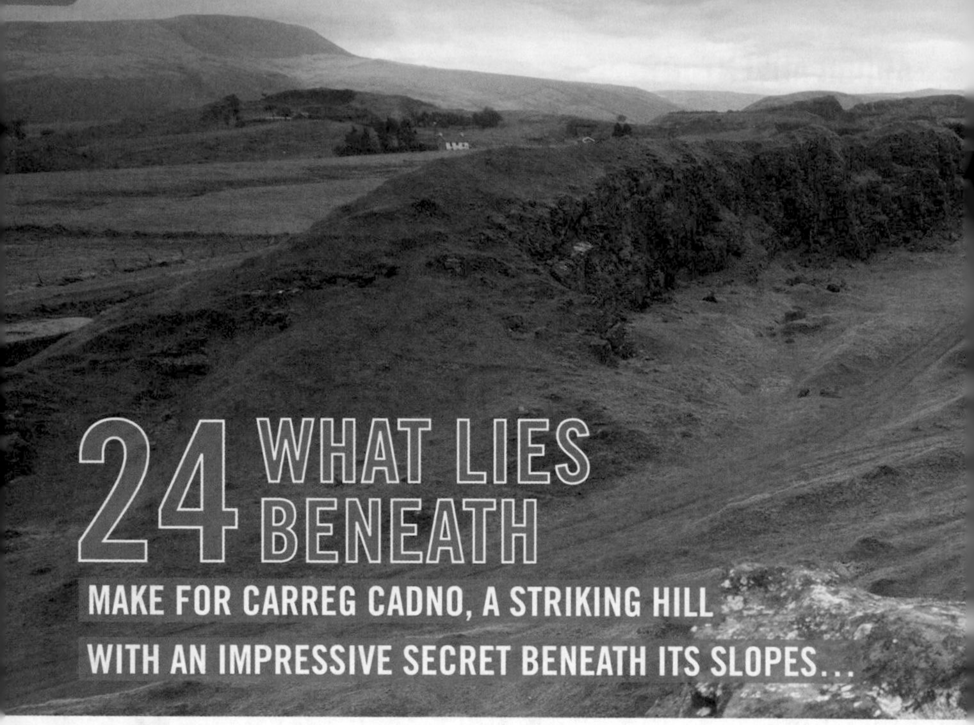

24 WHAT LIES BENEATH

MAKE FOR CARREG CADNO, A STRIKING HILL WITH AN IMPRESSIVE SECRET BENEATH ITS SLOPES…

WHERE	Carreg Cadno, Powys
STATS	↔ 5km (3 miles) ↕ 538m ↗ 188m ↻ 2 hours
START/FINISH	Penwyllt Quarry ⚲ SN855157
TERRAIN	Rough rocky, heather-covered trail with loose stones
MAPS	OS Explorer (1:25,000) 12; OS Landranger (1:50,000) 160

You don't often walk up a hill thinking about what lies beneath its slopes, but with Carreg Cadno you might be willing to make an exception. Not only does this gritstone lump offer a great vantage point over the Brecon Beacons, but it also hides Britain's deepest cave under its flanks.

The cave entrance of Ogof Ffynnon Ddu (which means 'Cave of the Black Spring') is found near Penwyllt Quarry. The cave descends to 274m and is famed for its labyrinthine structure. And while we're in the realm of impressive stats, this is also Britain's second-longest cave. (The longest – in case you're wondering as I was – being the Three Counties System in England which spans Lancashire, Cumbria and North Yorkshire.) Discovered in 1946, the cave and its mother hill are now part of the eponymous Ogof Ffynnon Ddu National Nature Reserve (tinyurl.com/ogof-nnr). The cave's limestone walls also offer a glimpse into its past importance as a former brickworks with kilns, an old tramway and quarry remains still found below ground.

Out in daylight, you start the walk from the quarry, gaining quick and easy access on the bridleway. The landscape is peaty moorland, largely dominated by heather and bilberry. There are scarce plants here, particularly wherever there is limestone: their number includes autumn gentian and mossy saxifrage.

↑ Carreg Cadno hides a special secret beneath its depressed slopes. (Steve Chatman)

Continue walking on to a hill that is as rough as it is beautiful. With a whole heap of craggy rocks sprinkled liberally all over the tufty grassland of its sprawling summit, Carreg Cadno is as much a jumble on the surface as it is on a subterranean level. So overground or underground – or a little of both? The choice is yours...

WALK THIS WAY

❶ Starting at the car park in Penwyllt Quarry follow the Beacons Way bridleway as it cuts past the quarry and heads uphill. You'll be tracking mostly northeast over rough terrain. ❷ Cross the disused tramway (a relic from

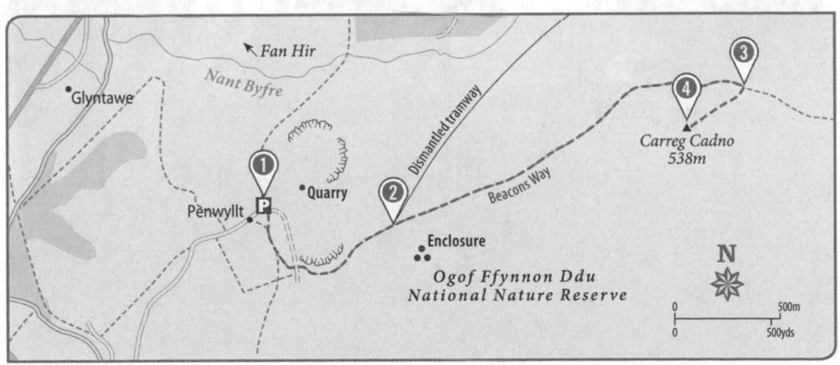

quarrying days) and continue uphill. Watch out for the many shake holes, depressions where the limestone has collapsed. Be respectful of the fenced-off limestone, which is preserved for scientific purposes. ❸ To take the summit you'll need to leave the path just before the stream and strike southwest uphill. Do so and soon you'll be the highest thing on this sprawling peak, enjoying views of wooded Fforest Fawr to the northeast and the distant Brecon Beacons to the west. ❹ Simply retrace your steps to the start.

↑ Inside one of the chambers of Ogof Ffynnon Ddu, Britain's deepest cave. (Anthony Baker/A)

ADDED ADVENTURE

Much like Snowdonia's Rhinogs to the north – a wild and often unforgiving collection of rocky peaks and very rough terrain – the summit area around Carreg Cadno feels wild and remote, despite its proximity to a town. As such, and harbouring a craggy cluster of rocks and boulders, it's the obvious choice for a night out in a bivvy. Look for a handy pocket of water for cooking and hunker down for a night out under the stars.

MAKE IT BIGGER

The Beacons Way (breconbeacons.org/beacons-way) crosses Carreg Cadno. You could easily tack a segment of this long-distance path on to this walk, whether following it east for more crumpled peaks or wending north to Fan Hir escarpment. Alternatively, shun the path and strike west to reach the peak of Carreg Goch, or southwest to the tiny but equally impressive summit of Cribarth.

FOR LITTLE ADVENTURERS

Make a list of the birds your little ones might see and get them watching the skies and moors. There could be peregrine, raven and red kite above you, plus ring ouzel, wheatear and red grouse on the fells. Underground, in the cave, there's a chance of spotting roosting bats and hibernating moths such as the herald; take a torch! If the kids are into creatures great as well as small, the National Showcave Centre at Dan yr Ogof has shire horses and a Victorian-style farm (showcaves.co.uk).

FOR CAMPERS

There's a campsite near the start in Glyntawe at the Showcaves (showcaves.co.uk/camp_site.html; from £7pn) with lots to do on site.

FOR ADRENALINE LOVERS

To check out the massive cave of Ogof Ffynnon Ddu, you will need to apply for a permit at least two weeks in advance from the OFD Cave Management Committee (ofdcmc.org.uk). Novices should definitely hire a guide. Before you go why not take a virtual journey down there so you know what to expect (ogof.net).

FOR HUNGRY HIKERS

The Gwyn Arms in Glyntawe (01639 730310) is the nearest place to grab a drink and a sit-down bite to eat; it serves classic pub grub. For supplies and snacks it is best go to one of the supermarkets nearby – either in larger Aberdare 29km (18 miles) southeast or Ystradgynlais 9.5km (6 miles) southwest.

OTHER PRACTICALITIES

The nearest train station is Neath from where you can catch the semi-regular X63 bus from Neath to Brecon. This drops you at the entrance to Dan yr Ogof caves, from where you have to walk 2km (1¼ miles) to the start. The nearest toilets are 1.5km (1 mile) west of the start, at Craig-y-Nos Country Park (breconbeacons.org/craig-y-nos-country-park), where there are tearooms in the visitor centre.

The herald – a cave-dwelling moth found under Carreg Cadno. (James Lowen) ↑

25 ANGELIC ASCENT

CLIMB A NOW-EXTINCT VOLCANO WHERE LEGEND HAS IT YOU CAN COMMUNE WITH ANGELS

WHERE	Carningli, Pembrokeshire
STATS	↔ 5.5km (3½ miles) ↕ 346m ↗ 337m ↻ 3 hours
START/FINISH	Newport car park SN052396
TERRAIN	Town streets, grassy footpaths, rugged and rocky summit
MAPS	OS Explorer (1:25,000) 35; OS Landranger (1:50,000) 157, 145

Over 400 million years ago, if you'd have journeyed to Pembrokeshire's seaside town of Newport (not to be confused with the city in southeast Wales) in search of this little striking summit you might have witnessed a volcano exploding in a cloud of crimson magma. Explosions are well and truly in the past, but catch sight of the looming peak of Mynydd Carningli silhouetted against a glowing, scarlet sunset and you might think an explosion was imminent once more.

It's these former volcanic secretions that have created a wonderfully scrambly summit that begs to be climbed. Such natural creations are reason enough to entice you here. So too are remains from both the Iron and Bronze ages that have been found on Carningli's slopes – including a massive hillfort and settlements that are thought to have been inhabited by farming communities before Roman times.

↑ Heading up to the heavenly top of Carningli. (Julian Rollins)

An even greater draw perhaps is the peak's supernatural heritage. For 'Mynydd Carningli' translates as 'mountain of angels'. The religious connotation comes from St Brynach, a Celtic saint, who is said to have climbed to the summit in the 5th or 6th century to talk with animals and birds, and to commune with the angels. Although you don't have to believe in seraphims to worship this saintly summit, go to the top and look towards the beautifully rugged Pembrokeshire coast to witness views that are truly angelic.

WALK THIS WAY

❶ Starting from the car park in Newport head south up towards Carningli, which is immediately visible. Pass the remains of 14th-century Newport Castle on your right (sadly closed to the public since 2011 due to instability of the ruins) and continue on to the footpath alongside fields until these give way to more rugged open moorland. ❷ You'll pass Carn Llwyd, old earthworks consisting of lichen-encrusted remains of a stone circle enclosure or roundhouse. Continue steadily uphill, ignoring a footpath that cuts east to west. After a steep climb you'll finally reach the rocky ramparts of Carningli's former hillfort, strewn with scree, that has never been excavated or dated and remains a great mystery to archaeologists (to learn more, see tinyurl.com/carningli). ❸ From here continue on the path bearing southwest to reach Carningli Common and the highest point of this sprawling summit at 346m. Enjoy breathtaking views of the Pembrokeshire coast and keep an eye out for overflying birds such as raven, kestrel and red kite (and perhaps the odd angel too). You'll also be able to enjoy the swathes of bilberry and heather on the moorland landscape that makes up the Common. Flora such as bogbean, and even carnivorous plants such as butterwort and sundews, add colour to the landscape. When you're done cut down across the north end of the summit, heading roughly northeast to rejoin the path you took on your way up. Then simply follow it downhill to the start. If you feel like varying your route, descend on one of plenty of other townbound paths on the hill's northern flanks – just look for the pink or green broken lines on your OS map and take your pick.

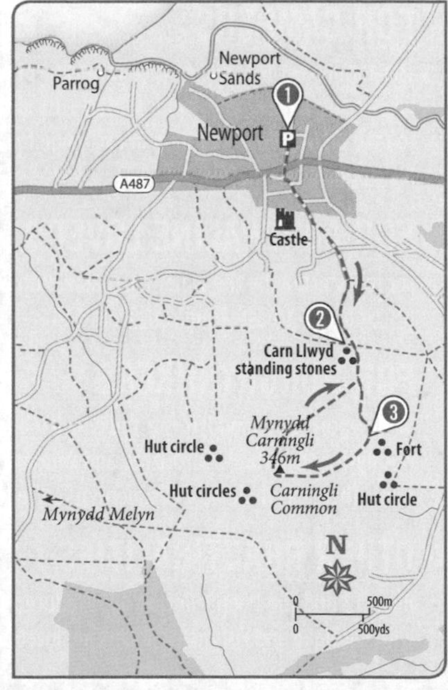

ADDED ADVENTURE

Much like the far bigger Welsh summit of Cadair Idris near Dolgellau, legend has it that a night spent on Carningli's summit will render the camper either a poet or insane. Well – there's only one way to find out…

MAKE IT BIGGER

Stick on a couple more peaks that lie to the west. The volcanic outcrops of Mynydd Melyn (307m; SN021362) and Garn Fawr (307m; SN007368) provide a suitable height complement, the latter being home to an Iron Age fort that was used as a lookout point during World War I. Then follow a combination of footpaths to pick up the Pembrokeshire Coastal Path in Fishguard, following it east to your starting point.

FOR LITTLE ADVENTURERS

The nearby beaches of Parrog and Newport Sands (parking at SN054397) are both perfect spots to end the day after climbing mini-mountains. Why not build your own sandy version of Carningli with a bucket and spade?

FOR CAMPERS

The family-run Morawelon (campsite-pembrokeshire.co.uk; Mar–Oct; from £8pppn) lies by stunning Parrog Sands within easy distance of Carningli. You can also borrow canoes to take on the nearby estuary in exchange for a donation to the RNLI (Royal National Lifeboat Institution) – win-win!

FOR ADRENALINE LOVERS

For rocky action by the water try coasteering at Abereiddy Beach with local outfit Celtic Quest (celticquestcoasteering.com; from £44).

FOR HUNGRY HIKERS

In Newport, Llys Meddyg is a funky cellar bar that is great for a post-walk, sit-down meal (llysmeddyg.com). For pizzas and burgers head to The Canteen (thecanteennewport.com). There's a whole host of supermarkets in Newport too.

OTHER PRACTICALITIES

Bus 412 and the Poppit Rocket 405 (reduced service in winter) connect Newport bus station with Cardigan and Fishguard. Toilets are located in the car park.

A rocky outcrop studs the rough plateau of Carningli. (Julian Rollins)

26 A SMALL SLICE OF WILDERNESS

DON'T BE FOOLED BY YR ARDDU'S DIMINUTIVE HEIGHT: THIS IS A WILD 'N' ROCKY RAMBLE

WHERE	Yr Arddu, Gwynedd
STATS	↔ 2.5km (1½ miles) ↕ 389m ↗ 366m ↻ 3 hours
START/FINISH	Coed Caeddafydd car park SH620467
TERRAIN	Steep slippy grass and mud path to start, then boggy ground and finally a very rough hard-to-follow (and sometimes scrambly) route to the summit
MAPS	OS Explorer (1:25,000) 17; OS Landranger (1:50,000) 115

Don't be fooled by the small stature of Yr Arddu. Wild and little visited, this boulder-strewn summit easily gives much higher peaks a good run for their money. In fact, if you look at the relationship between distance and duration of this walk, you would be forgiven for thinking that something was awry: surely it's a quicker ascent than this? But with a jumbled route consisting of rock-filled gullies, pockmarked with clumps of heather and loose piles of scree covering unexpected miniature cliff faces, plus tussocks of grass seemingly placed to trip you up when you least envisage it, Yr Arddu time seems to move at a different pace from that on other hillocks featured in this guidebook.

But there is no need to panic. On Yr Arddu, patience is the name of the game. Patience and the embrace of your inner explorer. Even though there is guidance on route-finding opposite, you will very much need to pick and choose the best path for you and not get too stressed if you have to abandon one halfway up in favour of trying another.

And should that happen, things won't be so bad anyway. There will be plenty to distract you while you reorientate. There are fantastic illustrations of volcanic activity from the epoch when the entirety of

↑ On a clear day the summit of Snowdon can be seen from the slopes of Yr Arddu. (Peter Seaton)

Snowdonia was an exploding, magma-fuelled mess. Exposed igneous tufts of rock, for example, were once deposits of volcanic ash. Once at the top enjoy the views over to Wales's mini-Matterhorn of Cnicht to the northeast. And be glad that the only eruptions tonight will be from your camp mate if you opt for too spicy an evening meal...

WALK THIS WAY

❶ In the car park face the river then turn right on to the minor road and walk through the gateposts. A few steps later you will see a footpath sign on either side. Take this, heading right, climbing over the gap in the wall. Cross the field and pass through the gate. ❷ From here the route dramatically steepens (poles are recommended) as it cuts diagonally through the trees along a narrow, muddy path. Climb over a stile at the top and continue upwards. You will likely need to use your hands in a couple of places, but keep the wall to your right as a navigational tool to keep you on the right track. ❸ As the wall turns right (south) follow it,

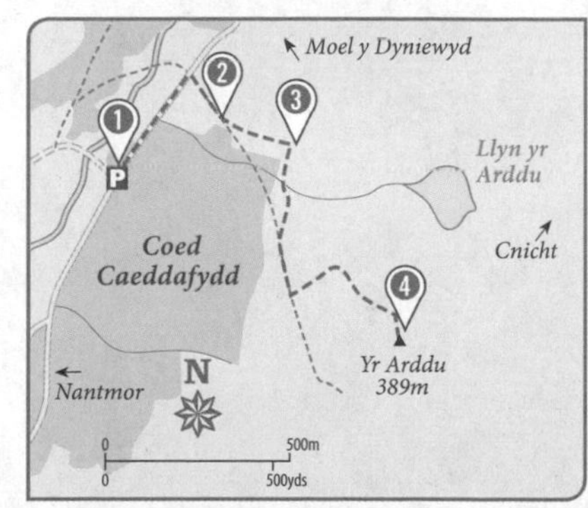

Heading for the Welsh Matterhorn of Cnicht from the flanks of Yr Arddu. (Neil S Price)

ADDED ADVENTURE

Don't leave it too late in the day to head up for a wild camp, as it can be tricky to find a suitable route. The shores of Llyn yr Arddu make for the ultimate wild camp spot – a site that feels very far removed from everyone and everything.

MAKE IT BIGGER

All the peaks in this tightly packed cluster of contours are little known and little visited. You could strike out east to make for the lumps and bumps *en route* to Cnicht – aka the Welsh Matterhorn (689m; SH645466). Or you could head west and cut back down to the valley, taking footpaths along its floor to Nantmor (SH602459), then reascend to Moel y Dyniewyd (389m; SH612477) for a second night wild camping in a place few walkers ever venture.

FOR LITTLE ADVENTURERS

This will be a tough one for very little legs so either miss it out or expect it to take a lot longer. If the weather is bad or you want something less demanding, try the footpath that runs alongside Llyn Dinas (northeast of the town of Beddgelert) or the Pass of Aberglaslyn (between Nantmor and Beddgelert) for scenic waterside strolling.

↑ Standing atop the little visited Yr Arddu. (Karl Page) ↗ Kestrel are regularly spotted in the wilder hills south of Snowdon. (James Lowen)

SOURCING WATER

Look for a fast-moving section of stream where the water is bubbling. Boiling is the best method for purification: on bringing to the boil, let it roll for at least 2 minutes and then continue boiling on a simmer heat to be sure.

then cross over a wall on your left to clamber around some large boulders. Note that it gets extremely boggy and waterlogged here. This is also where the pick 'n' mix ethos comes into play. Roughly follow the wall above the treeline for as long as you sensibly can. When you see a gully that looks right for your ascent (there are several to choose from), turn left on to it to head uphill. Keep following your nose upwards, through and over the heather-covered rocks. Gradually, the gradient will relent a little, and the route will become steadier and less steep. Keep going, gaining height all the while and you will likely emerge on to a col, between tufts of grass and a large boulder. It's worth bearing northwest a little here to find Llyn yr Arddu (a lake) to get your bearings, before cutting a route roughly south to claim the summit (389m). ❹ From here enjoy the views (and maybe pick out your wild camp spot if staying over). Then, when you are ready, retrace your steps – as best you can, and certainly carefully – all the way back to the start.

FOR CAMPERS

Nearest is the peaceful Cae Du Campsite (caeducampsite.co.uk; Mar–Oct; from £11.50pn) near Beddgelert. There is a shop and you can even buy wood-fired pizzas on Friday and Saturday nights.

FOR ADRENALINE LOVERS

Take your bicycle or your running shoes and consider starting this adventure with one or the other to pedal/run the Lôn Las Gwyrfai trail (tinyurl.com/LonGwyrfai). This is a newly established route (and one still under development) between Caernarfon and Beddgelert.

FOR HUNGRY HIKERS

There's nowhere at the start but Beddgelert has some options. A must is the ice cream at Café Glyndwr (glaslynices.co.uk). Supplies can be picked up from the village store. For a sit-down meal and a drink, Hebog Bwyty & Llety (hebog-beddgelert.co.uk) is recommended, offering an exciting, varied menu.

OTHER PRACTICALITIES

Buses run from Caernarfon to Beddgelert (87 and the Snowdon Sherpa tinyurl.com/sherpasnowdon) around four times a day. The nearest public toilets are in Nantmor car park or Beddgelert (south of the river, down the road from the post office).

27 FROM PILLAR TO POWYS

HEAD TO BREIDDEN HILL, A VOLCANIC PEAK IN POWYS, FOR SPECTACULAR 360-DEGREE VIEWS

WHERE	Breidden Hill, Powys
STATS	↔ 7km (4¼ miles) ↕ 367m ↗ 227m ↻ 3½ hours
START/FINISH	Car park near Breidden Hotel SJ301124
TERRAIN	Steep and muddy; navigation can be difficult in bad weather
MAPS	OS Explorer (1:25,000) 216; OS Landranger (1:50,000) 126

One thing you can't help but notice about the peak of Breidden Hill – aside from its domineering appearance, as perceived from the relatively flat lands below – is the giant stone pillar that stands on its summit (367m). Built between 1781 and 1782 by the 'Gentlemen of Montgomeryshire' (a local collective of men of high social standing), the monument commemorates Admiral George Rodney who led a number of successful battles for the Royal Navy during the 1700s. (He was also a slightly controversial figure, as many claimed he was motivated purely by prize money.) The pillar was built from local oaks that were also shipped along the River Severn to Bristol, where Rodney's fleet was manufactured.

But Rodney's Pillar isn't the only manmade contribution to the summit. It is also the home of what remains of an Iron Age hillfort which, legend has it, was where Welsh chieftain Caractacus made his last stand against the Romans. The third human addition (getting towards clutter, really) comes in the form of two quarries, which, to this day, are used to extract stone for road building.

The walk itself is a joy, beginning in a Forestry Commission plantation. The trees suddenly relent, offering wide views up the rounded ridge of this former volcano, and a grassy track leads you to the summit and the pillar. The western flank – being quarried away for granite and basalt – adds yet more drama to the walk with the land dropping away sharply from the summit. In spring, common redstart and tree pipit sing here, while common buzzard and sparrowhawk soar overhead in fine weather.

So whether you're interested in one or all three of the historical legacies, a walk to the summit will reward you not only with relics from the past, but also with spectacular 360-degree views of the present – across Mid-Wales into England's Shropshire Hills.

WALK THIS WAY

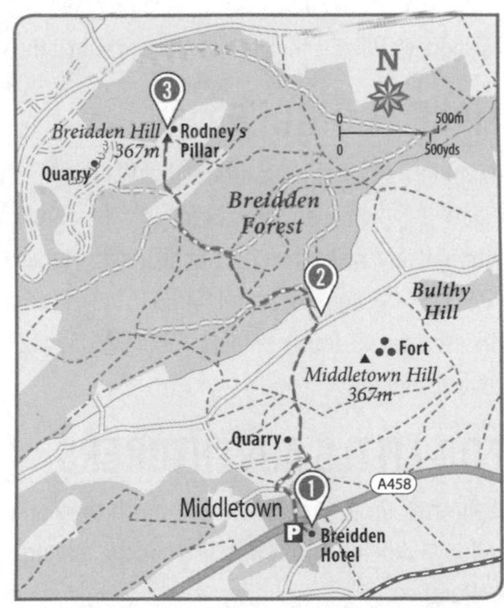

1 From Breidden Hotel cross the A458 and follow the footpath west then north towards Middletown Hill. The latter harbours remains of an ancient hillfort, which is as-yet undated, though local rumour has it down as an alternative location for Caractacus's last stand. Follow the path through the old disused quarry to the saddle between that summit and another, smaller, subsidiary top

← You'll find the unsubtle Rodney's Pillar atop Breidden Hill. (Chris Newman)

ADDED ADVENTURE

Head up here after dark to set up a discreet wild camp either in the woods on the side of the hill or next to Rodney's Pillar – the perfect place to watch the sun set or rise.

MAKE IT BIGGER

Running from north to south across Wales, Offa's Dyke Path (a National Trail) flanks the base of this hillock (nationaltrail.co.uk/offas-dyke-path). You could easily incorporate a walk along this. Alternatively, make the effort to hike to the top of the several other little bumps nearby – Bausley Hill (SJ325145), Kempster's Hill (SJ318143), Pritchard's Hill (SJ315147), Bulthy Hill (SJ308135), and the escarpment-fronted Moel y Golfa (SJ290125), which collectively make up what is known as the Long Mountain.

FOR LITTLE ADVENTURERS

If the trek up to Breidden is too much then take them instead to the first little hillock – 367m – called Middletown Hill. This also has the remains of a hillfort on its summit and makes for an easier exploration.

↑ The woodland-lined path to Breidden Hill summit. (Wichita23/D)

KEEPING WARM

When heading up to watch sunrise or sunset remember it will get cold. Take a warm jacket to throw on over all your layers as well as a hat and gloves. Consider a hot flask for the perfect way to celebrate.

(to the west) and then downhill to cross a minor road. **2** Continue up into the forestry plantation, crossing a stream where the path can be muddy. Here you join a main forestry track. Turn left on to it and follow it east until it intersects with other paths marked with footprint signs. Take the one to your right, bearing northeast, heading uphill through trees on the flank of a smaller, unnamed hillock. After just under 0.5km the path starts to descend a little, is joined by a bridleway and then reaches a junction. Turn left here and continue straight to reach another clear forestry track. Cross this and carry on to a metal gate where you turn right. Follow signposts that direct you uphill to the summit, out of the plantation, across a grass-covered plateau and then, with a final steep pull up, you reach Rodney's Pillar. **3** Enjoy the views from the top – of the River Severn, the peak of Middletown whose slopes you crossed on your way in and the woodland-covered Bulthy Hill. To the southeast you can spy The Wrekin and Long Mynd and to the northwest – providing the weather is good – you might be able to spot Cadair Idris in south Snowdonia. Once you've had your fill, simply follow your footsteps back to the start.

FOR CAMPERS

The nearest campsite is at the Royal Hill Inn (tinyurl.com/rhicampsite; from £6pppn) alongside the River Severn.

FOR ADRENALINE LOVERS

The hill rises from near the River Severn – so get yourself a packraft or canoe then start or end this walk after enjoying a watery adventure.

FOR HUNGRY HIKERS

Right by the start, The Breidden (thebreidden.co.uk) is a Chinese restaurant and pub. It offers Chinese and British food to eat in or take away as well as hot and cold drinks. For supplies pre-walk head to nearby Welshpool about 10km (6¼ miles) away where there is a range of supermarkets.

OTHER PRACTICALITIES

The nearest train station is in Welshpool, from where you take the X75 bus to the start of the walk. There are no toilets on the walk, so go in Welshpool tourist information centre before you start.

28 PRINCELY PEAK

EXPLORE THE RUINS OF A 13TH-CENTURY WELSH PRINCE'S CASTLE ATOP THE ATMOSPHERIC DINAS BRAN

WHERE	Dinas Bran, Denbighshire
STATS	↔ 2km (1¼ miles) ↕ 320m ↗ 240m ↻ 1½ hours
START/FINISH	Llangollen riverside car park ⚲ SJ215420
TERRAIN	Footpaths and grassy tracks
MAPS	OS Explorer (1:25,000) 255; OS Landranger (1:50,000) 117

Discovering ruins at the top of a hill reminds me of being a kid and finding a free toy inside your already exciting box of sugary cereal. It's an added bonus that brings an extra spring in your step. In the case of this walk, it's even better. For the ruins on top of Dinas Bran aren't those of a run-of-the-mill hillfort. Dinas Bran means 'Crow's Castle', and some of the 13th-century fortification's walls and steps remain today, providing a dramatic tableau. And the castle wasn't even the first structure housed atop this Welsh peak: in the 6th century there was an Iron Age fort.

There is much conjecture about when and for whom the castle was built. The most credible account is that it was constructed by Gruffydd Maelor II in the late 1260s. Credence is provided by Maelor's older brother founding the equally atmospheric Valle Crucis Abbey nearby. Regardless of who built the fortress, historians at least concur that both Maelors lived there for 20 or more years. Whatever its genesis, this stone-walled castle atop a conical, heather-clad slope would have loomed over the surrounding hilly landscape with an undisputed air of grandeur.

From that colourful start Castell Dinas Bran provided the backdrop for a number of other page-turning events. In 1277, it was partly burned down by the English, who then changed their tune and

↑ The remains of Dinas Bran castle look especially mystical during a misty spell. (Garry Ridsdale/A)

rebuilt it to serve as a stronghold. The castle was passed from one Earl to another. In 1402, under the leadership of Owain Glyndŵr, the self-proclaimed Prince of Wales, the Welsh nearly recaptured the castle. Later, the fortification was immortalised in paintings by Turner, poems by Wordsworth and is speculated to be the final resting place for the Holy Grail.

Finally – for anyone contemplating a last-minute bivvy among the castle's ramparts, a story called 'The Romance of Fulk Fitzwarine' tells of a self-important knight called Pain Peveril who was determined to stay the night in the ruins despite the promise of evil spirits lurking within. He persuaded 15 others to stay with him, only for a giant to appear and for battle to ensue – which Peveril and co won. I'm not trying to put you off, but it's worth considering when packing your bag…

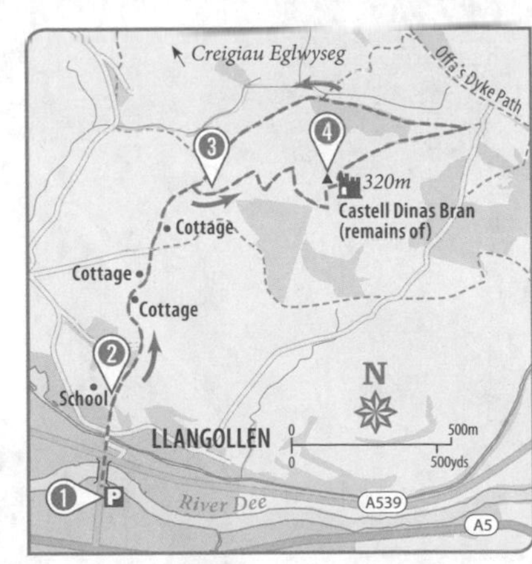

WALK THIS WAY

❶ From the town centre make your way to the bridge and cross over the River Dee, heading north. Follow the road to a footpath that runs to the right of the local school, Ysgol Dinas Bran. ❷ Continue uphill, passing some cottages until you emerge on to

The view from the summit path on Dinas Bran is as epic as the castle that would have sat on its peak. (Steve Meese/S)

the heather-clad and grassy slopes that seem to stretch impossibly steeply uphill. Fortunately, there is a stony track cleaved into the grass as well as multiple other boot-beaten ways up in the grass. Follow one of these to ascend its slopes. ❸ When the path splits take the one on your right. This climbs steeply uphill and zigzags all the way to the summit. Here you will find not only the top of the mini-mound but also the remains of Castell Dinas Bran. These consist of several crumbling stone archways, tumbledown walls and curving corridors, impressively showing how much of this hilltop the great castle covered (most of it). ❹ When you've finished exploring the ruins, enjoy the views down the Dee Valley – where both canal and River Dee snake off in different directions, cutting through the miniature urban sprawl of Llangollen, which itself is flanked by the purples or browns of the heather-covered hills. When it's time to go, it's worth varying the route back down. Head downhill (northeast) on the path that cuts down the slopes. At the bottom, where the gradient relents, the path swings back on itself to contour roughly west around the lower flanks of the hillock. Follow it all the way round the back (north) of Dinas Bran, then rejoin the path you took on your way up (at stage 3). Follow this back into town and to your start point.

↑ The crumbling arches sit above the town of Llangollen. (Phoebe Smith)

ADDED ADVENTURE

Dinas Bran is the ideal place to watch the sun set or rise through the arches of the old castle. Take your camera and head there late or early to witness it – free from other hikers. To capture the perfect sunset shot, use the specific pre-set (if your camera has it) to best replicate the orange and purple tones. Also consider taking a small tripod or using a rock or stone to eliminate camera shake and put it on self-time to stop wobbling when you release the shutter.

MAKE IT BIGGER

Head north to explore yet more signs of the life of our ancestors – including round barrows, lead-mine workings and tumuli – on the hills around the edges of Creigiau Eglwyseg 2km (1¼ miles) to the north. These are accessed via Offa's Dyke Path heading northwest from the summit of Dinas Bran, before taking the path uphill towards Eglwyseg Plantation to gain the ridge. You could then wild camp at the ominously named 'World's End' on nearby Ruabon and Eglwyseg Mountain (511m; ♀ SJ231464).

FOR LITTLE ADVENTURERS

The Llangollen Canal (🖱 tinyurl.com/canal-llangollen) runs alongside the lower (southern) flanks of this little peak. Stroll along the towpath for as long as you (and the kids) have the energy, or – for added excitement – take a horse-drawn boat (🖱 horsedrawnboats.co.uk/aqueduct-trips.aspx) along the canal all the way to the Pontcysyllte Aqueduct, a World Heritage Site (🖱 pontcysyllte-aqueduct.co.uk).

FOR CAMPERS

The nearest campsite is at Wern Isaf Farm (🖱 wernisaf.co.uk; from £20pn), just 1km (0.6 mile) from town, which nestles beneath the slopes of Dinas Bran.

FOR ADRENALINE LOVERS

There's no end of activities to try, from gorge-walking to white-water rafting on the River Dee. Particularly recommended is abseiling Eglwyseg escarpment, which overlooks Dinas Bran. ProAdventure (🖱 proadventure.org; abseiling and rock climbing from £50) offers all of these experiences from its base in Llangollen.

FOR HUNGRY HIKERS

There is a whole host of café and pub options in Llangollen. For a café try Cottage Tearooms and Bistro (🖱 cottageteabistro.com/about), which takes particular pride in its scones. For something a bit special in the evening head to The Corn Mill (🖱 brunningandprice.co.uk/cornmill), which sits right on the River Dee and even has a water wheel turning behind the bar. You can pick up supplies for your walk at the small supermarket in town.

OTHER PRACTICALITIES

Bus number 5 connects Llangollen to the nearby town of Wrexham. Public toilets are on Market Street (small fee payable).

29 SCRAMBLE THEN EGGS

CEFN Y CAPEL'S SCRAMBLES PROVIDE A PERFECT INTRODUCTION TO THE MIGHTY GLYDERS RANGE

WHERE	Cefn y Capel, Conwy
STATS	↔ 4km (2½ miles) ↕ 460m ↗ 250m ↻ 2 hours
START/FINISH	Capel Curig car park ⚲ SH720583
TERRAIN	Grassy – often boggy – path to start (and throughout) followed by scrambly sections to the summit
MAPS	OS Explorer (1:25,000) 17; OS Landranger (1:50,000) 115

Eating a fried-egg butty in Capel Curig's Pinnacle Café is something of a mandatory activity for those who love the hills. But consider this. Rather than grabbing one before heading into the mountains, why not have one for breakfast after doing a little hike on a rocky rump that rises behind it.

You couldn't get a better location than Cefn y Capel. With a path that leads straight from the café car park, it was as if nature designed it for the very purpose of a pre-breakfast yomp. Comprising the same sharp craggy rocks as found on many peaks in the infamously scrambly Glyderau (often referred to by hill-folk as The Glyders), this perfectly formed promontory may look trivial in comparison. In reality, however, it gives you a run for your money – both in terms of navigation and the chance to get your hands dirty on its ridges.

On the way up there's an abundance of route options, from grassy ramps to more rocky promontories that poke up from the ground, inviting you to test yourself. The scrambling is always short and offers a good taste of climbing on rock without being too committing. There's also plenty of escape routes, making it an ideal training ground. The top itself is a fairly flat affair (and often very boggy – so gaiters are recommended) but the views over to Moel Siabod, down to Llynnau Mymbyr and – on a good day – over to Snowdon itself more than make up for any disappointment.

↑ Breakfast beckons down in Capel Curig – the café is never far from reach on an ascent of Cefn y Capel. (Neil S Price)

Do take care on the way down; even the most experienced of hillgoers can be led astray on these escarpments if they do not concentrate (I speak of course from personal experience). This is because the rocky ridges sticking out from the grass all look very similar. This means you may unwittingly end up on this hill's more committing and higher-grade northwestern flanks, which are less fun if you're not a crag rat! One thing's for sure – you'll certainly deserve your hot breakfast butty after this.

WALK THIS WAY

❶ From the car park follow the tarmac road north towards Gelli Farm. Go past the house then pick up the faint grassy path which comes up quickly on your left. ❷ Follow this path as it weaves its way over rocks on often very wet and boggy ground. Continue up to the nose of the hill, veering north. Once the path flattens out and you begin to get views down the Ogwen Valley, turn west and get scrambling. You'll need to use your hands a few times at first, but then – if you have had enough – you can veer left for an easier and flatter (if boggier) approach. Keep left of the crags and you'll be able to make out a fairly faint path. Stay with this (as best you can) all the way to the summit. ❸ After enjoying the views, retrace your steps, making sure to stick to the southwesterly edge and not its more northeasterly edges, back to the start where that breakfast bap awaits…

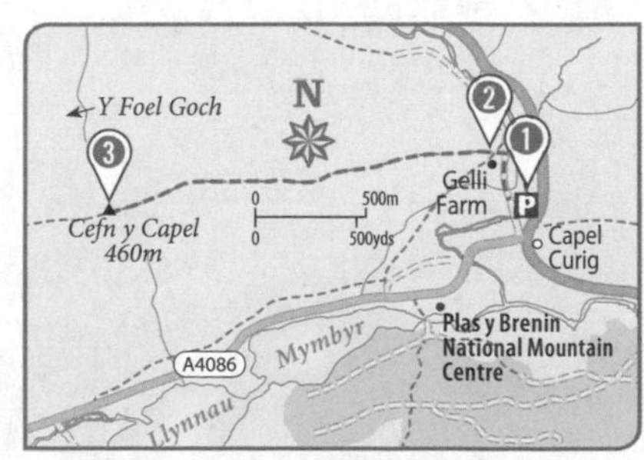

Glyder Fach – the perfect way to extend the walk from Cefn y Capel. (Phoebe Smith)

ADDED ADVENTURE

With its proximity to the car park and diminutive size, Cefn y Capel's smattering of flat ground between sections of scrambling makes it the perfect place for a bivvy camp. Arrive late but be sure to recce your route by daylight to avoid inadvertently venturing into some higher-graded climbing ground (which can be difficult to descend if you go too far).

MAKE IT BIGGER

This little peak makes the perfect start to tackling The Glyders – a wonderfully rocky ridge of mountains. Separated from other ridges by dramatic valleys, The Glyders' distinguishing feature is frequent clusters of splinter-like shards of rock – hence their name which derives from the Welsh word *gludair* meaning 'piles of stone'. Head west from Cefn y Capel summit up on to Y Foel Goch (805m; ⚲ SH677582) from where you can access the ridgeline heading west to Glyder Fach (994m; ⚲ SH656583) and the highest peak in the range, Glyder Fawr (1,001m; ⚲ SH642579).

FOR LITTLE ADVENTURERS

The National Trust visitor centre at Ogwen Cottage (tinyurl.com/ogwencottage) offers a fascinating display and interactive exhibit that explains about the area's topography and geology. There's also an opportunity to take the path behind it just a short way to get great views of The Glyders. There's even a perfect bridge from which to play Poohsticks along the river, as well as the chance to see common redstart and spotted flycatcher in summer.

FOR CAMPERS

The nearest is the riverside Dolgam Campsite (dolgam-snowdonia.co.uk/snowdonia; from £10pn), which is right on the A5 just 2.5km (1½ miles) from Capel Curig.

FOR ADRENALINE LOVERS

For something testing, at the excellent Plas y Brenin National Mountain Centre on the outskirts of Capel Curig (pyb.co.uk), you can sign up for a range of courses from scrambling to climbing, navigation to white-water rafting, and plenty more.

FOR HUNGRY HIKERS

The Pinnacle Café at Capel Curig (01690 720201) is something of an institution. It offers supplies, camping meals and a sit-down café that serves a hearty breakfast and lunches. For something later on, try Bryn Tyrch Inn (bryntyrchinn.co.uk) or Tyn-y-Coed Inn (tyn-y-coed.co.uk), both of which offer decent food and real ale, and lie within walking distance.

OTHER PRACTICALITIES

The Snowdon Sherpa bus (tinyurl.com/sherpasnowdon) runs past Capel Curig *en route* between Snowdon and Betws-y-Coed, where there is a train station. Public toilets are found in the car park at the start – though you will need change to use them as there is a nominal charge.

30 SPECIAL GEST

PORTHMADOG'S ROCKY MOEL-Y-GEST OFFERS AN EXCITING SCRAMBLE AND VIEWS DOWN THE GLASLYN ESTUARY

WHERE Moel-y-Gest, Gwynedd
STATS ↔ 4km (2½ miles) ↕ 262m ↗ 262m ↻ 2–3 hours
START/FINISH Opposite Aldi car park SH563389. If you buy from the store, you can use the car park for a limited time. Or see tinyurl.com/porthmadogpark for other options.
TERRAIN Woodland paths, rough fell paths, some scrambling near summit
MAPS OS Explorer (1:25,000) 18; OS Landranger (1:50,000) 124

It's hard to believe that any of Wales's little peaks can have a true mountain-like feel, especially those so close to the fringes of Snowdonia National Park – but Moel-y-Gest is one that unequivocally does, despite being under 300m high. Thanks to tightly knitted contours and chockstones of boulders that are seemingly sprinkled over the slopes like giant confetti, it gives the impression of being a proper peak that makes the adjacent town of Porthmadog seem a very long way away.

Requiring a bit of nous while navigating across its summit, harbouring plenty of little flat pockets perfect for an overnighter and offering the chance to get your hands on rock (and thus make the walk as scrambly as you dare), Moel-y-Gest is the mountain connoisseur's choice of small hill.

WALK THIS WAY

❶ From the car park, cross the A497 (carefully as the cars pass quickly) and turn right. Follow the pavement along until the fingerpost leads you up a footpath on your left. ❷ You'll start walking in woodland (take care after rain, in particular, as the ground can be slippy), continuing to climb upwards bearing westsouthwest. Go right through the gateposts, then over the wall at a stile. There are several path options here, but the easiest is to turn left to follow the

↑ The mini but mighty-looking Moel-y-Gest. (Peter Seaton)

wall up and out of the trees, heading roughly south. ❸ Follow the obvious path as it weaves steeply uphill and around some rocky promontories until you reach the top of the ridge. From here the views really open up down to Glaslyn Estuary at Porthmadog and out into Tremadoc Bay. ❹ Now follow the ridge bearing west. There is something of a rough path but don't worry if you sometimes lose it. Cut down into the col between an initial (smaller) 231m summit and the main peak. Then climb again over rocks; it is a bit of a scramble. Pick your way along (avoiding most scrambles if they are not your thing) and eventually you will reach the summit (262m). ❺ This is the site of an Iron Age hillfort, although it now looks more like a collection of rocks haphazardly strewn. Head to the ridge edge to look down over Black Rock Sands to the south, out to the Llŷn Peninsula over to the northwest, then back towards Snowdonia in the east to see the Moelwydians and – on a clear day – Snowdon itself. There are myriad ways off the summit, but by far the easiest is to retrace your steps. (Note: if you head nearer the north face of the peak, do be careful as the cliffs over the quarry drop off suddenly with no barriers for safety.)

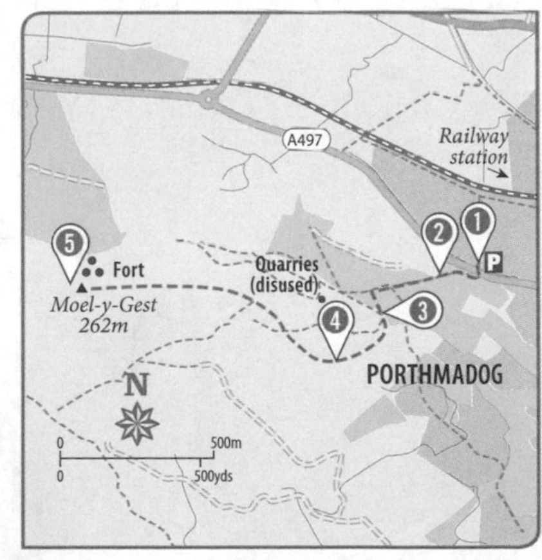

The summit ridge of Moel-y-Gest offers some scrambling and ample places to pitch a tent. (Neil S Price)

ADDED ADVENTURE

On the ridge, there are plenty of depressions hidden by boulders that make perfect bivvy and tent spots. You will need to bring water though and (as anywhere that you wild camp) make sure you carry out all rubbish with you.

MAKE IT BIGGER

You might not be able to make the walk much bigger as this is a single isolated little lump, but you can always make it harder. Up the ante by picking a more scrambly route up. Alternatively, approach it from Tremadoc Bay (there are car parks at Black Rock Sands and by the water's edge near Morfa Bychan) for a longer walk-in and a steeper approach from sea to summit.

FOR LITTLE ADVENTURERS

Lots in the area if the hill isn't enough. Nearby Black Rock Sands (tinyurl.com/blackrocksands) is good for building sandcastles. The Welsh Highland Heritage Railway Line (http://festrail.co.uk) offers the opportunity to journey through Snowdonia, starting/ending in Porthmadog, on old steam trains. There are also special events throughout the year such as the chance to meet Santa at Christmas. Choose from trips to Blaenau Ffestiniog or Caernarfon – or both.

FOR CAMPERS

A fair few sites in the area. Try Black Rock Sands to be beachside (blackrocksands.webs.com; from £10pppn) or, to be at the foot of this mini-mountain, opt for Tyddyn Adi (tyddynadi.co.uk).

FOR ADRENALINE LOVERS

Want to find your inner Bear Grylls? Dragon Raiders (dragonraiders.co.uk/bear grylls-survival-academy) offers wild-camp survival, half-day adventures and two-day expeditions – all approved by the man himself.

FOR HUNGRY HIKERS

Porthmadog offers lots of cafés, restaurants and ice-cream shops. For something a little different try The Big Rock Café (01766 512098) which offers wholefood/oriental-infused options as well as coffee, tea and bakery items to go. Hankering after some classic seaside cuisine? Allport's Fish and Chips (allportsltdfishandchips.co.uk) is the place, having won Wales and UK-wide awards in previous years. If you're after supplies for the walk, the best option is Aldi at the start.

OTHER PRACTICALITIES

Porthmadog is well served by buses from Caernarfon, Bangor and Pwllheli. Public toilets are in Porthmadog at Y Parc.

31 TINY TRYFAN

DELVE INTO DARWIN'S PAST ON THE WELSH GIANT'S GENTLER NAMESAKE WITH UNSURPASSABLE VIEWS OF SNOWDON

WHERE	Moel Tryfan, Gwynedd
STATS	↔ 0.5km (0.3 mile) ↕ 427m ↗ 127m ↻ ½ hour
START/FINISH	Moel Tryfan pull-off SH511562
TERRAIN	Grassy, steep but straightforward path directly to the summit
MAPS	OS Explorer (1:25,000) 17; OS Landranger (1:50,000) 115

I have to admit it was this peak's name – Moel Tryfan – that first attracted me to it. Its bigger, more famous namesake – Tryfan, with a capital 'T' – over in the Ogwen Valley is my favourite mountain in Britain and therefore, as it transpires, the whole world. Made up of rocky shards and splinters, buttresses and boulders, Tryfan is a scramble-only affair as well as being one of the sharpest and shapeliest peaks there is (and the sixth-highest in Wales at 918m).

Looking at the map, Moel Tryfan (Moel very aptly meaning 'bare hill', which this one is, at first glance) looks supremely unworthy of its famous cousin's moniker, possessing near-symmetrical round, looping, conical contours (although rather gouged out by quarrying beneath the hill's south and east faces). Nevertheless, heading up there one winter evening, just as the sun was beginning to set, I soon changed my tune. For sure, the ascent was nothing – simply a 'straight-up-the-slopes' deal where legs burn a little until you are distracted by hillocks of quarry debris and old buildings. Nothing sufficiently special then, to prepare me for just how incredible the view was going to be.

From the top you are greeted by surely the best and clearest view of Snowdon's summit café there is. Plastered in snow, the café's metal shutters seemed to sparkle like blinking eyes in the slumping sunlight. To the northeast the collection of peaks that make up the much-overlooked Nantlle Ridge presented themselves invitingly. Behind me the sea stretched on to the horizon, while the triple-horned peak of Yr Eifl (page 186) glowed like molars in a giant's mouth.

If such amazing views were not enough, the summit itself impresses with a small cluster of Tryfan-esque stone splinters apparently thrown on the summit like darts and sticking in the spongy grass at erratic angles. But the best bit of all is more discreet – yet will enchant everyone who takes the time and effort to check out this minuscule mountain. It is a sign that states simply that it was here, in 1842, that one Charles Darwin came to study glaciology – as this is the site where two ice sheets met 30,000 years ago, mushing together ocean debris with mountain spoil, encasing it in mud to form the Moel we see today.

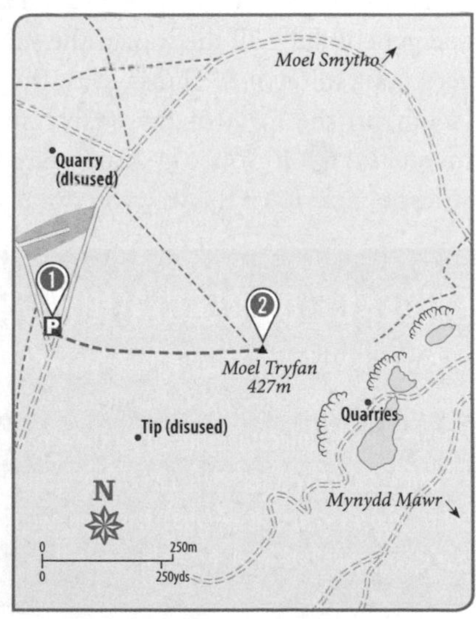

My visit to Moel Tryfan was in no way as seminal as Darwin's, but it was certainly of great personal significance. For it was this small hill that instigated my fascination with the mole (or should it be moel?) hills that dot our beautiful island.

← Looking down into the quarry from the edge of Moel Tryfan, the 726m peak of Moel Eilio in the distance. (Phoebe Smith)

WALK THIS WAY

1 From the pull-in, just beyond the houses, simply face the hill – due east – and get climbing all the way to the summit. It's a hole-ridden trek, following a very faint track in the grass, with the only other views coming to your right (south) in the form of the quarry spoils that seemingly make up an entire mountain! 2 If you can tear yourself away from the views, simply head straight back down the way you came.

EVIDENCE OF GLACIATION

It's easy to see whether or not a place has been formed as a result of glaciers. U-shaped, trough-like valleys with steep sides and flat bottoms (as opposed to sheer-sided V-shaped ones with pointed bottoms) are an indication that an ice sheet has carved through the landscape. Anything labelled as a 'cwm' – basically a rounded, calved-out cirque – is also indicative of this. Look out also for rocky debris (known as moraines) which has been swept along to a new location by the glacier and retains its current position long after the ice has melted.

↑ The summit rocks where Darwin sketched out his theories about glaciers. (Neil S Price)

ADDED ADVENTURE

To spend the night tucked into the craggy rocks here would be perfect, but remember you are very close to people's houses. If you are considering camping, it is best to leave the car further down in the village of Rhosgadfan, at the foot of the hill, and head up late on. Tuck yourself into the rocks as it can get very windy up here – the sunset and sunrise, however, should more than make up for any hardship suffered.

MAKE IT BIGGER

Start a little further north and you can tack on another bump called Moel Smytho (343m). Then, after summiting Moel Tryfan, the obvious way to extend the walk is to take your time to carefully explore the spoils from the quarrying past. There is a network of trails that will take you down to the northern side but do be careful near the edges as these are unstable and unfenced. From the bottom of the quarry you can pick up pathways to Mynydd Mawr (698m) to the southeast and Craig Cwmbychan (592m) to the east, before descending into Beddgelert Forest and heading back via the collection of footpaths in the Nantlle Valley to your start around 6km (3¾ miles) away.

FOR LITTLE ADVENTURERS

The rocks up here make for the perfect sheltered picnic spot at sunrise or sunset. So on the shortest or longest day head up here in the evening to make a special event of the meal in this, your outdoors dining room.

FOR CAMPERS

Nearest is Snowdonia Parc campsite (snowdonia-park.co.uk; from £10pn), which comes complete with its own real-ale pub and on-site micro-brewery – cheers!

FOR ADRENALINE LOVERS

Maybe not high adrenaline, but to really push yourself instead of calling it a day after the *Make it bigger* suggestions – carry on to walk the Nantlle Ridge (and bung in a wild camp). Then loop around the Moelwyns, add a second wild night out, then finish with an ascent of Snowdon before heading back to your start. A hill walk of truly marathon proportions (at least 40km/24¾ miles) – depending on your chosen route.

FOR HUNGRY HIKERS

There's nowhere in the nearest village of Rhosgadfan. The micro-brewery and pub at Snowdonia Parc (see *For campers*) is the best and nearest place to grab a bite and drink (open to non-residents). Collect pre-trip supplies from nearby Caernarfon or Bangor.

OTHER PRACTICALITIES

Sporadic buses from Caernarfon (number 1F) stop in Rhosgadfan (near the start). No public toilets are available: it is best to go in Caernarfon before your walk.

32 SNOWDONIA'S SECRET SCRAMBLE

THE OVERLOOKED MOELWYNIONS OFFER A CRAGGY AND SCRAMBLY ADVENTURE ATOP CARNEDD Y CRIBAU

WHERE	Carnedd y Cribau, Gwynedd
STATS	↔ 6km (4 miles) ↕ 591m ↗ 551m ↻ 3–4 hours
START/FINISH	Layby parking at Hafod Rhisgl ⚲ SH656528
TERRAIN	Steep pull up Bwlch y Rhediad, then rocky and rough ground to summit
MAPS	OS Explorer (1:25,000) 17; OS Landranger (1:50,000) 115

Perched on the edge of Snowdonia's little-explored Moelwynion range, Carnedd y Cribau escapes a lot of footfall thanks to a trio of well-known near-neighbours. There's the Snowdon massif almost directly opposite, the back of the Glyders within easy access and, just a short drive away, you can start hitting the Carneddau.

Stick with the well-trodden paths, however, and you'll be missing a treat. At the centre of a craggy collection of clusters to the east of Wales's highest is the sub-600m peak of Carnedd y Cribau. It may not have that much height compared with its neighbours but the ascent demands an adventurous attitude and provides a wonderfully scrambly summit worthy of exploration. The terrain is a glorious mix of grass and rock, jumbled together in a haphazard fashion that makes Carnedd y Cribau feel considerably wilder than its more famous hilly cousins. Moreover, as is the case with many little peaks, it offers one of the best views going of Wales's highest peak with nothing standing in the way between them. So when the crowds are descending on Snowdon, it's time to head east…

WALK THIS WAY

❶ From the layby at Hafod Rhisgl on the minor road west of the A498, pick up the footpath that heads southeast directly uphill. ❷ Be careful crossing the A498, then pick up the footpath on the other side of the road. Continue upwards on a steep path that gains height efficiently, passing through thick, mixed woodland that temporarily swallows up the daylight, before thrusting

↑ Carnedd y Cribau as seen from across Llyn Llydaw. (David Hughes/D)

you out on to tussocky ground of the rough heather, grass and rocky hillside, until you arrive at Bwlch y Rhediad – the shoulder of land between Carnedd y Cribau and the neighbouring peak of Moel Meirch (607m). ❸ From here any paths are pretty faint, so it's best to turn left off your present path and follow the nose of the ridgeline where it's flattest and least rocky, heading northnorthwest. Keep left of the ridge to pick your way up to the summit, enjoying the excitement that inevitably grows when the surrounds become more exposed and rocks protrude from the ground thick and fast. There will be some scrambling required – this is definitely a pick your-own-way adventure – but eventually you will reach the summit. Do be sure to take care after heavy rain or if it's frosty as these rocks can be very slippy. ❹ Take some time to appreciate the views overlooking the Vale of Conwy to the east and Gwynedd to the west and south. Enjoy the vista of Snowdon with the sprawling mass of spurs and shoulders that make for different routes to the summit. Peer north to spy the even rockier tops of the Glyders, and don't forget to look down to the east for a picture-perfect panorama of Llynau Diwaunedd and its neighbouring forest. And should a common buzzard soar overhead, watch its progress and imagine sailing free. When you are ready simply retrace your steps back to the beginning.

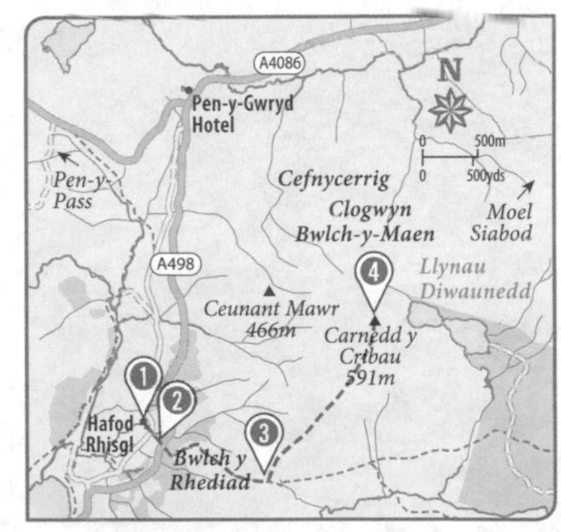

Walkers descend Snowdon with Carnedd y Cribau in the distance. (Phoebe Smith)

ADDED ADVENTURE

This neglected corner of Snowdonia is ripe for a wild camp. Look for a summit spot or, in inclement weather, try the woodland near Llynau Diwaunedd, accessed by descending east from the col (where you turned left at stage 3) and heading downhill on the path for 2km.

MAKE IT BIGGER

You can combine this peak with an ascent of Moel Siabod (872m), about 4km northeast, or continue south to tackle the rest (or at least some) of the more modest Moelwynions: Moel Meirch, Moel Fleiddiay, Moel Lledr, Moel Druman, and Moel Dyrnogydd.

FOR LITTLE ADVENTURERS

This is a fairly tough walk on steep and scrambly ground. For little legs you could approach from the Dolwyddan (east) side of the hill, taking the path up to the col at stage 3 from Blaenau Dolwyddan and the path that runs from Coed Mawr farm (SH697513).

FOR CAMPERS

The campsite at Llyn Gwynant (gwynant.com; from £9pn) offers idyllically situated pitches next to the eponymous lake and in the shadow of Snowdon itself. Note, however, that there is a 'family festival' atmosphere during holiday periods.

FOR ADRENALINE LOVERS

Take your swimsuit and towel (possibly a wetsuit in cold weather) to take a dip in Llynau Diwaunedd (SH686536) on the east side of the hill.

FOR HUNGRY HIKERS

The nearest place to grab a bite pre- or post-walk is in Capel Curig at the Pinnacle Café (01690 720201). Other nearby options are Pen-y-Pass café (01690 710426; when train operational, usually Easter–Sep) at the car park of the same name (SH647555) and Mallory's Café & Bar inside the youth hostel across the road (yha.org.uk/hostel/snowdon-pen-y-pass).

OTHER PRACTICALITIES

Connecting to trains and other local buses, the Snowdon Sherpa bus (tinyurl.com/sherpasnowdon) runs from Betws-y-Coed and Llanberis up to Pen-y-Pass car park which is about 3km from the lower flanks of the hill. If arriving by bus it is much easier to start the walk from the northwest end across the road from Pen-y-Gwryd Hotel (pyg.co.uk) at the junction of the A4086 and A498. From here, aim for the subsidiary bump of Cefnycerrig then ascend by heading southeast to the summit. The nearest public toilets are in Pen-y-Pass car park.

Wild camping on Moel Siabod – the perfect way to make this walk bigger. (Ian Moore)

33 LIMESTONE LOVELY

BAG BRYN ALYN, HOME OF A DRAMATIC LIMESTONE CLIFF IN THE RURAL HEART OF DENBIGHSHIRE

WHERE	Bryn Alyn, Denbighshire
STATS	↔ 2.6km (1½ miles) ↕ 403m ↗ 116m ↻ 1½ hours
START/FINISH	Layby 0.4km south of Llanferres ⚲ SJ187599
TERRAIN	Farm tracks, open moorland, rough mud and grassy paths
MAPS	OS Explorer (1:25,000) 265; OS Landranger (1:50,000) 117

Bryn Alyn sits meekly east of the A494, a major road cutting through North Wales. It would be easy to keep your foot to the floor, and speed past it. But don't. This little lump hides a secret on its summit – one of the largest limestone pavements in Wales.

As with other limestone lovelies, Bryn Alyn started life underwater more than 350 million years ago, its slopes made up of the remains of animal and plant matter (particularly shells). Compressed, fractured and uplifted, the composite rock was subsequently torn open and exposed by ice years later. Over time the limestone was selectively eroded by rain, creating fissures and cracks in its weakest points. The result is the impressive limestone pavement that you can now see on Bryn Alyn's little top, stretching unexpectedly amidst the surrounding grass, tracts of gorse and the odd scattering of trees. Then there's the views. The hill offers a panorama over the patchwork of fields and hedges that lies in front of the wave-like sprawl of the surrounding Clwydian hills. There's even a secret cave to explore too (see *Added adventure*). So what are you waiting for? Take your foot off the accelerator and get walking…

↑ Classic Clwydian views from Bryn Alyn. (Henry Ciechanowicz)

WALK THIS WAY

❶ There's a stile at the end of the layby. Climb over it and follow the track southeast, keeping the hedge to your right. Cross the bridge and continue on the path over stepping stones and past some houses until you come to a minor road. ❷ Turn briefly right on to the road then immediately left off it and over a stile on to a path. Follow this uphill, over a stile until you reach a wall. You should be able to see the summit of Bryn Alyn from here. Head up towards it. ❸ At the summit check out the limestone pavement. This resembles a sort of rocky jigsaw as the smooth, exposed blocks known as clints protrude from the cracks and fissures between them (called grykes). It's here that you can really picture the story of the hill's origin, when the world would have looked very different. Also enjoy the views of the

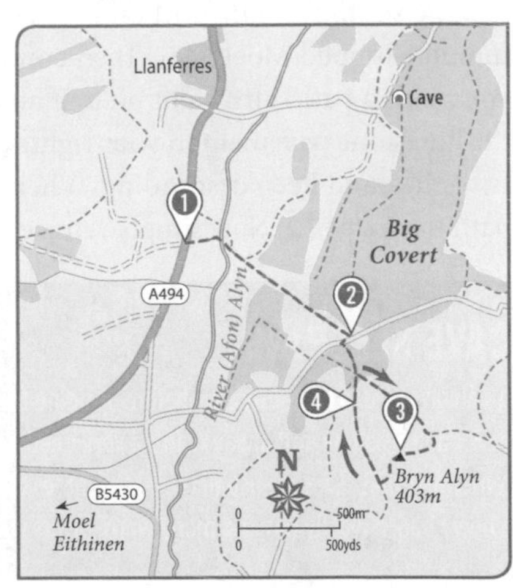

here and now, of course: you should be able to see Moel Famau – the highest hill in the Clwydian range at 555m, which sits bang on the border between the counties of Denbighshire and Flintshire – along with other Clwydian bumps looking south from the fort on Foel Fenlli, to Moel Eithinen directly west, and tumulus-topped Moel Gyw. Then continue southwest over the summit. When you reach a path, turn right on to it and follow it north as it descends, keeping the limestone pavement to your right. **4** Go through the gap in the wall, cross two stiles, and keep descending. When you reach a path, turn left to rejoin the path from stage 2. Now simply retrace your steps to the start.

CAVE SLEEPING

It's always best to recce any cave before deciding to spend the night there. Always approach with care – never do this alone and always carry a very good headtorch. If deciding to spend extended time there, remember that caves are usually several degrees colder than the area outside them and do get damp so a bivvy bag, a woolly hat and many warm layers will be necessary.

↑ Limestone rocks line the summit. (Lucas Lukomski)

ADDED ADVENTURE

After summiting Bryn Alyn head north into Big Covert woodland above Llanferres. At ⚲ SJ197605 (and marked on the OS map) you'll find the entrance to Maeshafn cave. Evidence of Bronze Age people has been found here including six burials and some artefacts. This could make for an interesting place to spend an evening.

MAKE IT BIGGER

After Bryn Alyn, consider crossing the A494 at the start/end point and heading west to add a few more Clwydian peaks to your stroll. Candidates are Foel Fenlli and Moel Eithinen then, heading south, Moel Gyw, Moel Llanfair and Moel y Plas.

FOR LITTLE ADVENTURERS

Nearby Loggerheads Country Park (tinyurl.com/loggerheadscp) is the place to take little ones. There are short, well-marked walks by the river and up to some limestone cliffs. In spring and early summer, look for common redstarts and pied flycatchers in the woodlands, dipper and grey wagtail bobbing along the rocky river, and grizzled skipper (a tiny, pugnacious butterfly) in the grasslands. Hebridean sheep often graze the wooded glade behind the cliffs.

FOR CAMPERS

As with Moel Arthur (see overleaf) most sites nearby only take caravans but not tents. The nearest that does is Fron Farm, just north of Mold (fronfarmcaravanpark.co.uk; from £12pn).

FOR ADRENALINE LOVERS

Abseil Devil's Gorge – a popular 36m (120ft) overhang in Loggerheads Country Park. Try local outfit abseiluk.com, which charges £40 for a half-day experience.

FOR HUNGRY HIKERS

For a snack or light lunch there's Caffi Florence (caffiflorence.co.uk), a co-operative in nearby Loggerheads Country Park serving homemade food from locally sourced ethical suppliers. If you're hankering for some proper pub grub, try We Three Loggerheads, a restored 17th-century coaching inn (we-three-loggerheads.co.uk) in Loggerheads, or, in Llanferres, The Druid Inn (thedruidinn.com). For snacks or walking supplies, your best bet is Mold.

OTHER PRACTICALITIES

The X1, 1 and 2 buses run regularly between Chester, Mold and Ruthin, with a stop in Llanferres less than 0.5km from the start point. The nearest toilets are inside Loggerheads Country Park, next to the tea gardens.

Pied flycatcher, a summer migrant found in the woods near Bryn Alyn. (Martin Fowler/S) →

34 ARTHUR GOOD AS THE REST

TAKE THE CLWYDIAN PATH LESS TRAVELLED TO EXPLORE MOEL ARTHUR RATHER THAN ITS SISTER PEAK

WHERE	Moel Arthur, Denbighshire/Flintshire
STATS	↔ 2.5km (1¼ miles) ↕ 456m ↗ 246m ↻ 1 hour
START/FINISH	Fron Dyffryn car park ⚲ SJ138668
TERRAIN	Grassy hill paths
MAPS	OS Explorer (1:25,000) 265; OS Landranger (1:50,000) 116

Stretching along the hinterland of North Wales – well away from the heady heights of Snowdonia – are the Clwydians, a collection of rounded lumps and bumps that offer easier walking without compromising on views. They provide historical interest too, with their proliferation of hillfort remains. Though most people think of battles when they picture forts, the reality is that the Celts who lived in these hills were likely farmers and (wood/metal) craftworkers who used these sites first and foremost as a place to live.

The fort on top of Moel Arthur is one of the most easily seen and certainly worth some attention. This is all the more so given that most walkers gravitate instead to Arthur's sister peak of Moel Famau (moelfamau.co.uk) thanks to its proximity to a well-served car park with multiple facilities and the in-your-face Jubilee Tower, built in 1810 to commemorate the golden jubilee of King George III. In contrast, Moel Arthur requires both effort and imagination – both laudable and rewarding enterprises.

Though there is a quicker way to get to the summit of this pinch of a peak, it's best ascended from a little further away: this helps give the fullest sense of scale and shows the earthworks at their

↑ Moel Arthur as seen from nearby Moel Llys-y-coed. (Neil Thomason)

most prominent. When you eventually reach the summit proper take the time to imagine a tableau of wooden roundhouses that would have once covered the place, with families busily living and working inside.

Although the hillfort was built 25,000 years ago, reflect too on Arthur's more recent history. In the 1960s, some flat axes were discovered here suggesting that it was still being used just 400 years ago. And it's not just axes that were found here. In 1888, the hill was the site for what was known as the Cilcain Gold Rush. Victorians were certain that the gorse- and heather-topped flanks of Moel Arthur concealed metal nuggets that would make them rich. Some quarried the slopes for many years but nobody made any significant fortune. Today enjoy the easy path up Moel Arthur's perfectly rounded summit, listening for the distinctive call of red grouse, content in the knowledge that the real treasure lies in the walking itself.

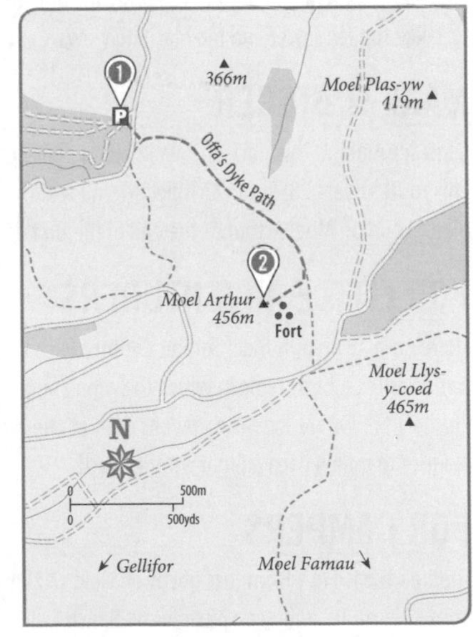

ADDED ADVENTURE

Moel Arthur is not the only Clwydian hill hosting the remains of a fort. Carry on south along the ridge to enter Moel Famau Country Park (tinyurl.com/mfwales) for the eponymous peak complete with the fort-like Jubilee Tower and far-reaching views.

MAKE IT BIGGER

Consider making this part of a walk along Offa's Dyke Path (nationaltrail.co.uk/offas-dyke-path). This route covers 285km (177 miles) from Prestatyn in the north to Chepstow in the south. You could plan to end on Moel Arthur at the end of the first day of walking for a perfect sunset…

FOR LITTLE ADVENTURERS

There's a play area in Moel Famau Country Park that offers a giant hawk's nest to climb into, a cedar tree to enter, a bird cradle in which to swing and plenty more. Wildlife sculptures line the short Animal Puzzle Trail, where kids use crayons (ask at the catering van if you haven't brought any) and brass plaques to match each animal with its tracks.

FOR CAMPERS

The nearest is Fron Farm just north of Mold, 7.2km (4½ miles) away (fronfarmcaravanpark.co.uk; from £12pn). Try and get a pitch in the Ranch Field for the best sunset views of the Clwydians.

↑ Approaching the summit cairn which would have once been the heart of a thriving hill settlement. (Phoebe Smith)

SPOTTING SIGNS

Hillforts are not always obvious. Signs to look out for include depressions in the ground that either run in dye straight lines or perfect circles – especially on hills. Also look for old wall lines that seem to make no sense and, finally, try heading to an adjacent hill for a greater sense of perspective.

WALK THIS WAY

❶ From the car park carefully cross the road and head uphill southeast along the obvious path in front of you. You'll weave through heather that glows like a purple haze in summer then, come autumn, deepens the hills' hew to an earthier russet-brown. As you walk, look out for depressions in the ground where features such as guard towers and animal pens would have stood. Also try to discern patches in the gorse that denote wall lines that would have separated different parts of the hillfort. After about a kilometre you'll reach the summit. ❷ Stand here and look carefully around you for the telltale signs of ramparts and walls that would have sat here thousands of years ago. Then look further away to the west to take in views of Snowdonia on the horizon and the rest of the Clwydians stretching off to the south. To get back to your car, simply retrace your steps.

FOR ADRENALINE LOVERS

Combine peaks with pedals: there's a blue graded (moderate) 12km-long mountain-bike trail – perfect for those getting into the activity – that cuts through Moel Famau Country Park. You'll need to take your own bike to access them, otherwise you could rent an e-bike from ebikehirenorthwales.co.uk in nearby Eyrys (from £20/half day) to make tackling the undulations a little less stressful.

FOR HUNGRY HIKERS

The friendly White Horse Restaurant (whitehorserestaurant.co.uk) just outside Gellifor, 2.8km (1¾ miles) away, is a good place for a sit-down meal. It is best to pick up pre-walk supplies in either Ruthin or Mold (both of which also have supermarkets and cafés).

OTHER PRACTICALITIES

Bus 76 from Denbigh stops in nearby Llangwyfan, a 3km (1¾-mile) walk away. Otherwise Bus 14 between Denbigh and Mold stops at Moel Famau Country Park. The nearest toilets are here too, in the Forestry Commission car park.

Black grouse are often spotted (and heard) in the Clwydians. (Sergey Uryadnikov/S) ↑

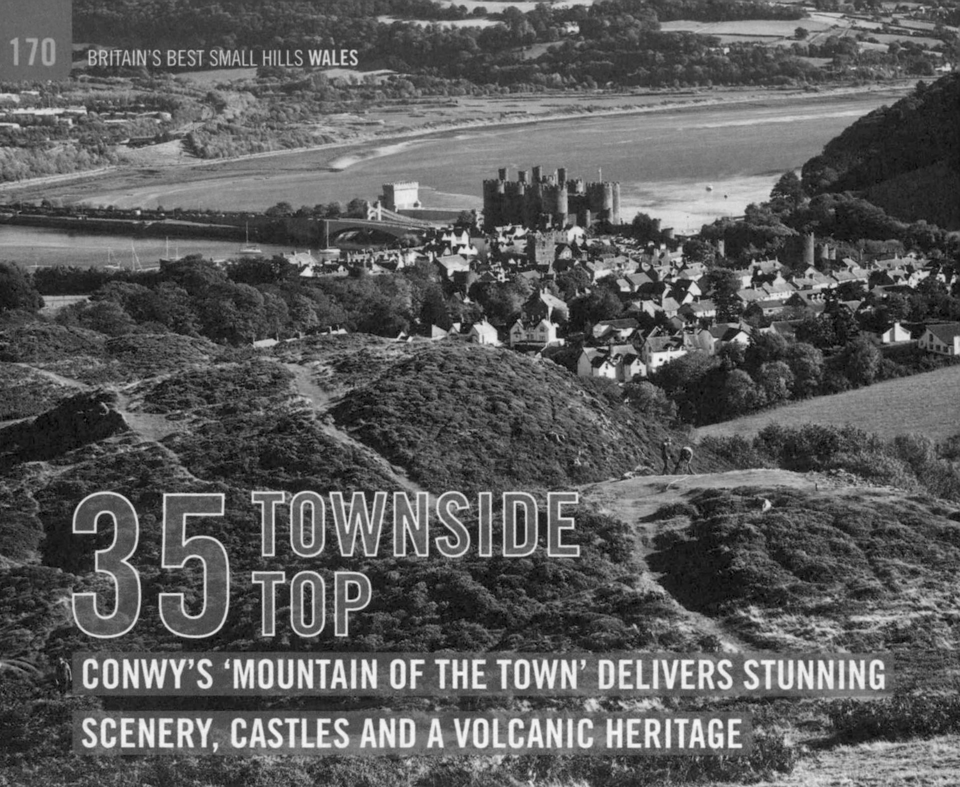

35 TOWNSIDE TOP

CONWY'S 'MOUNTAIN OF THE TOWN' DELIVERS STUNNING SCENERY, CASTLES AND A VOLCANIC HERITAGE

WHERE	Mynydd y Dref, Conwy
STATS	↔ 4km (2½ miles) ↕ 244m ↗ 64m ↻ 2 hours
START/FINISH	Sychnant Pass car park ⚲ SH750769
TERRAIN	Tarmac to start then grassy paths to rocky summit
MAPS	OS Explorer (1:25,000) 17; OS Landranger (1:50,000) 115

There are not many summits that you can access directly from a town (although granted a fair number feature in this book), and even fewer that you can reach from an urban area that offers so much in the way of other attractions too. Mynydd y Dref (which literally means 'mountain of the town' but is known in English as Conwy Mountain) delivers on both points.

Rising above one of North Wales's most famous castle towns and offering fine views over the Conwy estuary, this peak is also the site of a castle. Castell Caer Seion is an Iron Age hillfort: many stone circles remain visible on the extensive summit ridge of Mynydd y Dref. It's also home to a series of what look like shards of rock arranged in piles, but are actually Neolithic burial cairns thought to be located high on mountains to honour people of social significance. Dredging further back into the hill's history – well, much further back actually, around 450 million years ago – Mynydd y Dref was actually part of a volcano, which accounts for its strikingly conical and rocky profile.

You can easily approach Mynydd y Dref from Conwy town itself, but a better route starts at the Sychnant Pass. This road is itself a pleasure to drive on, twisting and turning through beautiful Welsh countryside. The vehicular approach means that you start high – so can use the time you've saved

↑ Looking down to Conwy, the town above which Mynydd y Dref rises. (Gail Johnson/D)

ascending to explore other little hillocks nearby and to admire views over to the lower Carneddau, out to Colwyn Bay and along the coast.

While you're up here be sure to keep your eyes out for Carneddau ponies, a special breed that don't actually belong to anyone in particular and are left to roam the slopes, where they munch grass amongst the heather. There are smaller creatures too. In mid-summer, keep your eyes peeled for moths such as garden tiger; this scarlet, white and black beauty is so striking that it makes most butterflies look dull. Birdwise, listen for choughs calling their name as they flap, wrinkle-winged, overhead. Also of airborne interest are dragonflies such as keeled skimmer, black darter and four-spotted chaser.

WALK THIS WAY

❶ Use the car park on the dramatically steep Sychnant Pass, by Pensychnant Nature Conservation Centre (🖉 pensychnant.co.uk). Cross the road and take the well-marked North Wales Path (which runs from Bangor in the west to Prestatyn to the east) that starts on tarmac but soon becomes rougher as it swings around the corner to the right, changing from northwest to northeast in orientation. ❷ Follow this path, turning right through the gateposts, and steadily climb uphill. At the junction of paths leave the North Wales Path to take the higher (non-waymarked) footpath over rising grassy folds interspersed with small bogs and large rocks. You will gain height on to the Mynydd y Dref ridge, climbing over increasingly rocky ground until you reach what is left of the Castell Caer Seion walls. Continue to gain the summit proper. ❸ Here you'll get exquisite views down the Conwy Valley, over to the Carneddau mountain range and out to Llandudno and the Great Orme (page 178). Enjoy them for as long as you like before heading back to your car. You can retrace your steps or vary the route by cutting downhill (south) sooner to pick up the North Wales Path, which you left in stage 2.

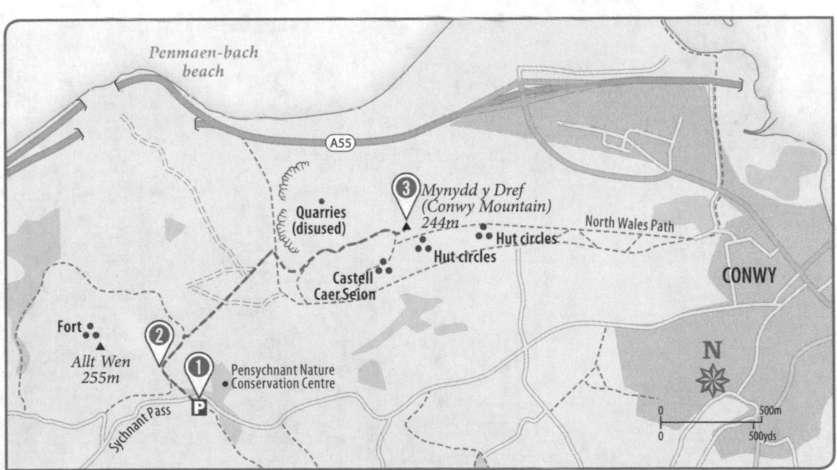

Funny to find wild ponies so close to town, but the Carneddau breed call these slopes home. (Neil S Price)

ADDED ADVENTURE

The grassy folds, looking out to sea, make for perfect bivvy spots. Simply take one of the many faint paths rather than the waymarked one to the summit. For those who don't want to camp it's worth sitting out on the top of this peak to watch the sun set.

MAKE IT BIGGER

Start your walk down on Penmaen-bach beach from the car park at Conwy Morfa (SH761786) then pick up the path heading steeply uphill (south) to gain the summit. End by heading down to Conwy on the North Wales Path before looping west along the Wales Coast Path to your start. An epic day out.

FOR LITTLE ADVENTURERS

Conwy has lots to entertain little ones, from striding around the castle itself (tinyurl.com/castleconwy) and its walls, to visiting Britain's smallest house on the seafront (thesmallesthouse.co.uk).

FOR CAMPERS

The nearest one that accepts tents is Cafn Cae Camping Site in Rowen (campinginnorthwales.co.uk; from £14pn). Rents tents and offers glamping options too.

FOR ADRENALINE LOVERS

Not quite in Conwy itself, but nearby in Dolgarrog is Surf Snowdonia (surfsnowdonia.com; from £30 including surfboard hire) where you can take to an inland 'surf lagoon', either cutting your teeth at the watersport or improving your existing technique.

FOR HUNGRY HIKERS

Conwy is the place to pick up snacks pre-walk or reward yourself with a pub meal afterwards. For a snack with some reading on the side try L's Coffee and Books (7 High St; 01492 596661). For a take-away sandwich head to Edwards of Conwy (edwardsofconwy.co.uk). Beer fans should make for The Albion (albionalehouse.weebly.com) which *The Guardian* newspaper named as one of the world's best pubs. The nearest supermarket for supplies is in Llandudno Junction.

OTHER PRACTICALITIES

Buses link Conwy with Llandudno and Colwyn Bay where trains provide onwards travel (traveline-cymru.org.uk). The nearest public toilets are in Conwy, close to the information centre on Rose Hill Street.

36 TRUNK-ROAD TOP

SUPREMELY ACCESSIBLE BRYN EURYN HOLDS A TRIO OF DELIGHTS IN LESS THAN A MILE'S WALK

WHERE	Bryn Euryn, Conwy
STATS	↔ 1.5km (1 mile) ↕ 131m ↗ 91m ↻ 1 hour
START/FINISH	Bryn Euryn nature reserve car park ♀ SH833801
TERRAIN	Footpaths, grassy tracks and woodland trails, some of which are steep and slippery – especially after rain
MAPS	OS Explorer (1:25,000) 17; OS Landranger (1:50,000) 115

It sounds almost too good to be true. A hill that's not only easy to climb (being just 131m high) but also offers a quartet of fabulous experiences, namely opportunities: to spot an abundance of butterflies and a profusion of interesting plants; to walk unbounded around the ruins of an old mansion; to discern the impressions of an old Iron Age hillfort on its summit; and to enjoy incredible views over towards Snowdonia (with all its big hitters). Yet it's all here on Bryn Euryn. And not only that: it's all easily accessible from the wonderful little seaside town of Rhos-on-Sea, just minutes from the dual carriageway that hems North Wales (and within easy reach of a bus stop to boot).

But let's talk the various plus points for a second. First, wildlife. Some 26 species of butterfly have been recorded in Bryn Euryn local nature reserve, including grayling and wall brown, which both frequent rocky areas. There are butterfly lookalikes too – colourful moths such as the six-spot burnet. And there are some very special plants, from hart's-tongue fern in the damp woodland to pyramidal orchids in the grassland, and even the rare Nottingham catchfly amidst the limestone rocks.

↑ The trig point on Bryn Euryn – once a key marker in WWII. (Mike Spence/A)

Then there's the mansion. An impressive chimney stack and several door arches hint at the former glory of a grand, 14th-century home called Llys Euryn. Even older is the Iron Age hillfort. Excavations in 1997 revealed a huge 3m-high wall that would have been cleaved out of the same limestone from which Bryn Euryn's summit itself is made. Archaeologists date the fort to the 6th century due to its pre-Norman (rounded) layout. From the peak, you can make out the depressions in the ground where the wall once stood.

Talking about the summit, the views from there are spectacular – from mountains to sea and back again. In fact they are so good that this pimple-like peak was pressed into military service during World War II. Bryn Euryn was adopted by the Home Guard as a lookout and even utilised by the RAF as a radar post to detect German bombers that were flying across the sea to nearby Liverpool.

All this in just under 100m of ascent.When you head back after ticking off the trig pillar you'll wonder why Bryn Euryn is not teeming with people. So go and enjoy it – just keep it to yourself.

WALK THIS WAY

❶ From the car park head back towards the road you drove up (Tan y Bryn Road) and take the footpath on your left, which ascends behind the parking area, heading northwest. ❷ As the footpath turns left the remains of Llys Euryn mansion will be directly in front of you. Take some time to explore the ruins before turning left on to the footpath and following it southwest. You'll be roughly following signposts for the green-marked Summit Trail, though Bryn Euryn is the kind of peak where you can play a bit free and easy, picking your own way up – especially on the northwestern side. ❸ Where the path splits (and the red markers for the Woodland Trail veer off to your right) continue ascending on to open hillside. Pick your way south through pockets of trees that then give way to open grassy hillside paths that lead to the summit. Here the trees recede and you're suddenly treated to far-reaching views in all directions. ❹ Enjoy the views down to Rhos-on-Sea and all along the northern Welsh coastline and beyond. Unfortunately offshore wind turbines now interupt the sea view, but you can turn your back on them to stare south towards Snowdonia. From here, take the path northeast off the summit. Follow this through the trees and downhill. When the trail intersects with another path turn right to follow the latter as it zigzags down on to a much wider track that will take you back to the start.

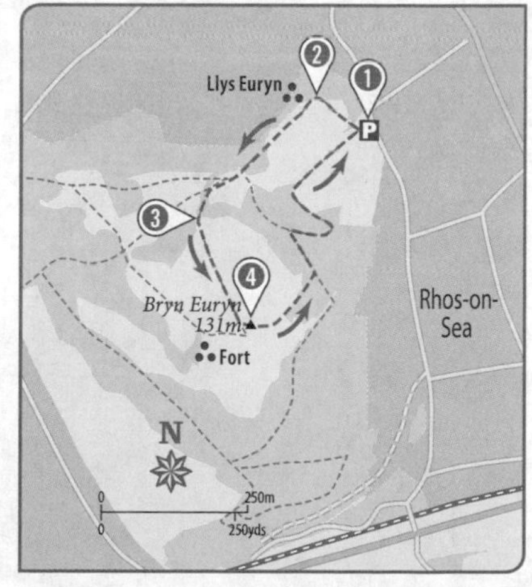

ADDED ADVENTURE

Take a hammock and wild camp in the woodland below the summit on the hill's east or southeast side. Very sadly, you may see from the rubbish left lying around that you are far from the only person coming up here after hours. Accordingly, it's best to leave any sleep out for a weekday night rather than a Friday or Saturday. Moreover, please be a responsible wild sleeper – taking all your rubbish out with you (and as much of other people's as you can carry).

MAKE IT BIGGER

Combine a stroll up to Bryn Euryn's summit with a meander along the Rhos-on-Sea Heritage Trail (tinyurl.com/rhosheritage) which starts at St Trillo's Chapel – thought to be the smallest in Britain – and takes in 25 historic sites along a 3-hour route.

FOR LITTLE ADVENTURERS

With the old manor to play in and a field at the start perfect for ball games, not to mention the (easily gained) summit, there is plenty here to keep kids occupied. Otherwise the sandy beach at nearby Rhos-on-Sea provides the perfect end to the day.

Looking down over Rhos-on-Sea, Colwyn Bay and beyond. Some of the pier at Colwyn Bay was sadly lost during storms in early 2017. (Jay Adamson Photography)

FOR CAMPERS

The nearest is Dinarth Hall Camping (dinarthhall.co.uk; from £8pn), which is within walking distance or (for tired limbs) a short bus ride away.

FOR ADRENALINE LOVERS

There's nothing on the hill but, nearby in Colwyn Bay, you could sign up for a taster day with Colwyn Bay Watersports (colwynbaywatersports.co.uk), getting the chance to try sailing, windsurfing or powerboating from £35.

FOR HUNGRY HIKERS

Rhos-on-Sea is the place to pick up meals, snacks and supplies pre-walk. For the best ice cream in town try Ninos, which faces the promenade. For post-walk fish and chips it's got to be The Galleon on Colwyn Avenue (01492 544638).

OTHER PRACTICALITIES

Buses (numbers 14 and 15) from Colwyn Bay (where there is a train station) will drop you off on the Llandudno road (B5115) near the nature reserve (traveline-cymru.org.uk). There are no public toilets on site; the nearest are on Rhos-on-Sea promenade, opposite the Cayley Arms pub.

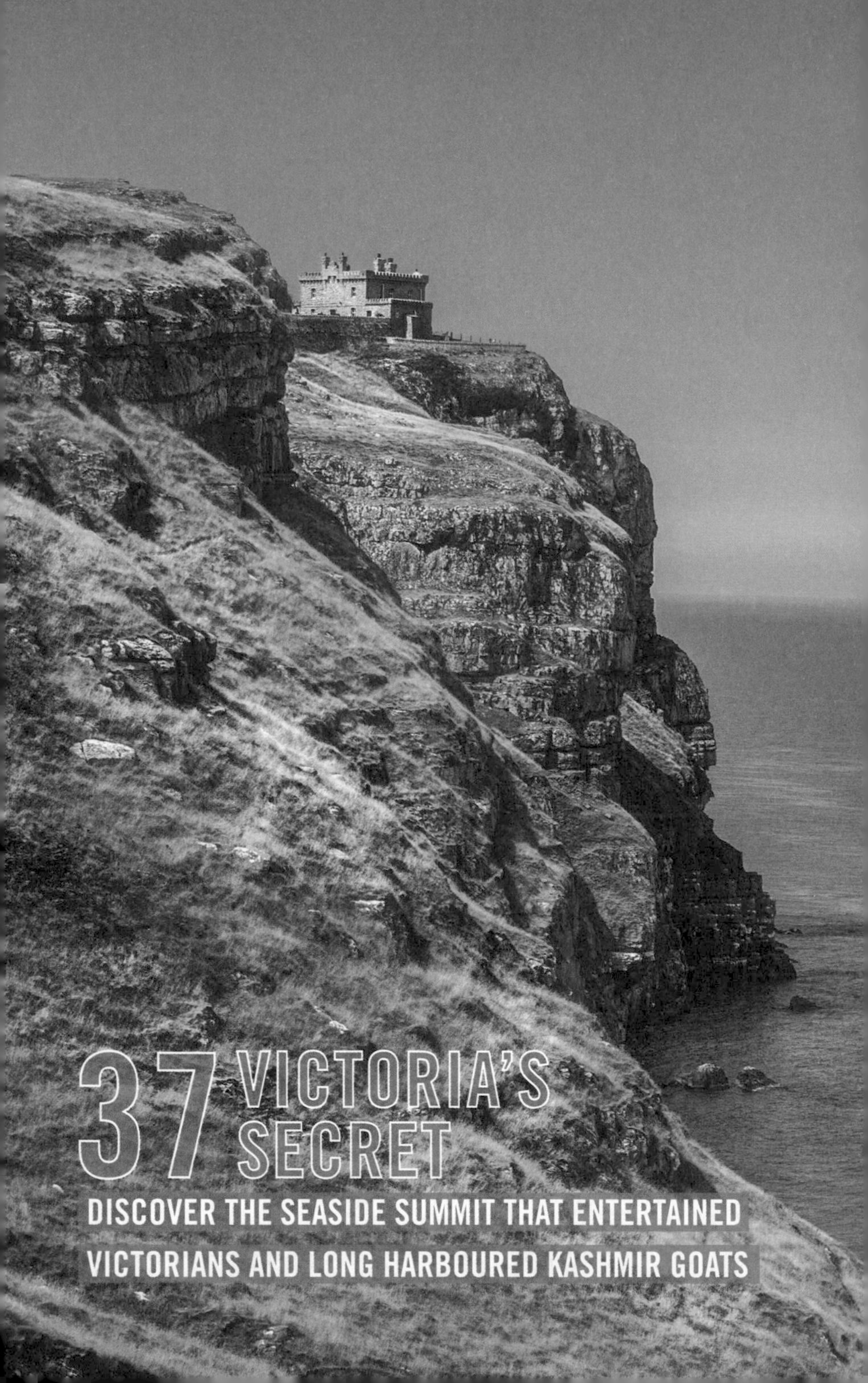

37 VICTORIA'S SECRET

DISCOVER THE SEASIDE SUMMIT THAT ENTERTAINED VICTORIANS AND LONG HARBOURED KASHMIR GOATS

WHERE	The Great Orme, Conwy
STATS	↔ 5km (3 miles) ↕ 203m ↗ 207m ↻ 2½ hours
START/FINISH	West Shore car park SH773815
TERRAIN	Well-marked and waymarked footpaths to summit
MAPS	OS Explorer (1:25,000) 17; OS Landranger (1:50,000) 115

For this peak, the clue's in the name. The Great Orme really is a fabulous little limestone lump, very much worthy of your attention. The other part of its name is thought to come from the Old Norse *orm*, meaning 'sea serpent'. Indeed, its form, jutting out on to the headland at the end of Llandudno's promenade, could be said to resemble such a reptile – perhaps with its tail comprising the similarly named Little Orme, which forms the eastern border to the interpolating Llandudno Bay.

Once popular with Victorian tourists, the Great Orme's slopes are littered with entertaining excursions. There are trams (built in 1902) and cable cars (from around 1969), a copper mine (established in the Bronze Age and functional until 600BC), the 6th-century chapel of St Tudno (with its accompanying well), some stone circles, a dry ski-slope and toboggan run – plus the Summit Complex restaurant and gift shop.

But forget all the manmade attractions and even the road to its top (!). The most rewarding form of visit is to grab some walking shoes and head up along one of the many paths from town. Arriving on foot means that the views out to Snowdonia, along the North Wales coast, island of Anglesey and beyond will feel all the more deserved.

If you do decide to venture further than the summit, keep a lookout for the wild herd of Kashmir goats that roam the hill. These have something of a regal background. The first herd was presented to

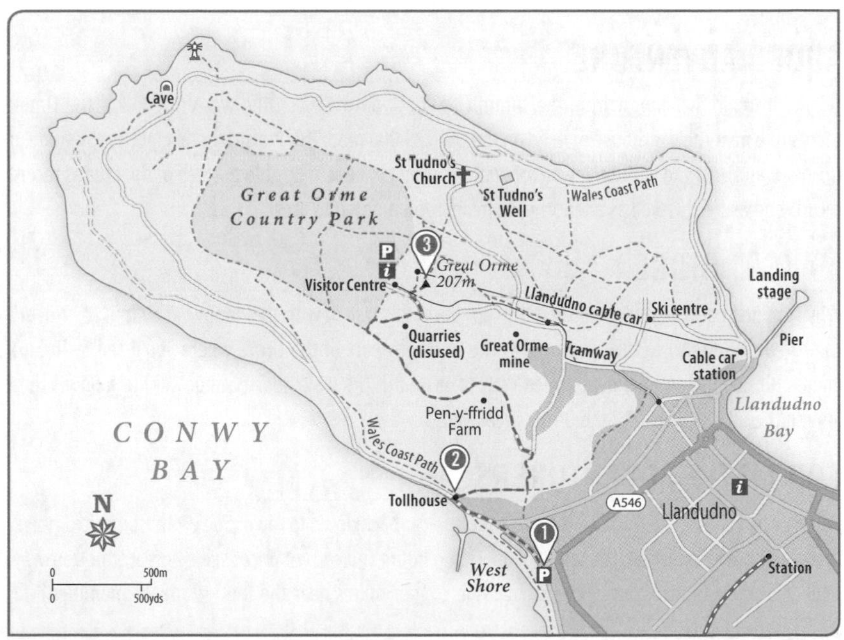

← The Great Orme is replete with trappings from the Victorian era. (Marbury/S)

King George IV back in the late 19th century and used to live in Windsor Great Park, before – during Queen Victoria's reign – Major General Sir Savage Mostyn of Gloddaeth Hall was given two and took them to graze on the Orme due to their ability to forage on very steep ground. Even now they keep their links to nobility. Ever since Queen Victoria presented one to them in 1844, the British Army's Royal Welsh regiment has usually selected one of these to be lance corporal. Atten-shun!

There are plenty of other natural highlights atop this limestone plateau, where heather dovetails with seacliffs. The star bird is chough, a red-billed ragamuffin of a crow. Cliff-nesting seabirds include

ADDED ADVENTURE

For the intrepid, head west from the summit to check out caves on the western edge of the Orme; there's one near the lighthouse marked on the OS 1:25,000 map. This is also a good place to spy some of the headland's myriad birdlife. A word of warning: don't expect to be able to sleep in the cave as recent security measures (as well as a fence) have been implemented to prevent this.

MAKE IT BIGGER

Why stop just because you've reached the top? Loop this trail in with the Happy Valley Trail (tinyurl.com/greatormetrails) to take you over to the northern part of the Orme where you'll see St Tudno's Church. Or use the recently established Wales Coast Path (walescoastpath.gov.uk) to follow a loop around the whole plateau of the Orme. Great, huh?

FOR LITTLE ADVENTURERS

When finished, as a reward, take the tram or cable car back down to town. See thesummitcomplex.co.uk for more information. For seasonal operating hours and current prices see greatormetramway.co.uk. Or take a guided tour of the Bronze Age copper mines near the top (greatormemines.info; 15 Mar–31 Oct).

↑ Looking down to the West Shore from the Great Orme – this route is the best way to the top. (EddieCloud/S)

three types of auk: razorbill, guillemot and black guillemot. Peregrines saunter around, well fed on local pigeons. In summer there are two dwarf butterflies – unique local variants of silver-studded blue and grayling – whilst rare plants (if you can find them) include dark red helleborine (a sumptuous orchid), some unusual ferns and wild cotoneaster (aka Great Orme berry). Offshore, grey seal and harbour porpoise are often seen.

WALK THIS WAY

❶ There are several routes to the top, but the best for hill lovers is the steepest – the 'Zig Zag Trail' that leaves from Llandudno's often-neglected West Shore Beach. From the car park walk northwest along the seafront heading towards the Great Orme until you reach the tollhouse. ❷ Go through the gate and turn right on to the footpath. You'll soon see a waymarker to confirm you're on the correct track. The trail becomes stepped as it ascends steeply. Follow the waymarker posts to take you around the farm. When the path splits, take the left fork to head out on to the open slopes. Continue along the path, cutting through cliffs, after which the views really open out. You'll then pass between a disused quarry and the cliff edge before the path dog-legs right to lead you up to the summit (207m). ❸ A trig pillar marks the top. From here you can simply retrace your steps back to the start, choose to explore the summit further or take one of the other paths down to Llandudno promenade to the east and make your own way back to the West Shore.

FOR CAMPERS

Nearest is Dinarth Hall Camping (🖱 dinarthhall.co.uk; from £8pn) within walking distance from Llandudno (or a short bus ride, for weary legs).

FOR ADRENALINE LOVERS

Snowsport lovers will be in their element. The Great Orme is home to a dry ski-slope as well as the longest toboggan run in Britain (750m) and you can even go tubing (🖱 jnlllandudno.co.uk; from £5).

FOR HUNGRY HIKERS

The Summit Complex (🖱 thesummitcomplex.co.uk) on the top is a great place to reward your efforts with a cup of tea, coffee or sit-down meal. To grab supplies pre-walk Llandudno has a couple of supermarkets including a Sainsbury's Extra on Mostyn Street.

OTHER PRACTICALITIES

Nearest train station is in Llandudno Junction. Coasthopper buses connect Llandudno with the rest of North Wales (🖱 traveline-cymru.org.uk). Public toilets can be found in the main parking area by the Summit Complex.

38 CLANDESTINE CARNEDDAU

SHUN THE WELL-KNOWN NAMES TO TASTE WILDERNESS ON FOEL-GANOL, A DIMINUTIVE SNOWDONIAN OUTLIER

WHERE	Foel-ganol, Gwynedd
STATS	↔ 4.5km (2¾ miles) ↕ 536m ↗ 336m ↻ 3 hours
START/FINISH	Upper (eastern) car park above Coedydd Aber National Nature Reserve ⚲ SH675716
TERRAIN	Rough paths and fell tracks that can be difficult to navigate in bad weather
MAPS	OS Explorer (1:25,000) 17; OS Landranger (1:50,000) 115

If you were to do some research on the Carneddau range, you would quickly find some obvious big hitters – from the guardian-like Pen yr Ole Wen, which sits at the head of the Ogwen Valley, to Carnedd Dafydd, the fourth-highest peak in Wales, with a swooping curve of a ridge that leads to a rocky spur of a summit. You would have to read a long way down any list of Carneddau hills, well beyond the well-known names, to find mention of Foel-ganol.

Most walkers omit this peak from their hilltop list-ticking exploits. Such an approach might be understandable: Foel-ganol rises to a modest height of just 536m, and lies on the distant western fringes of the Carneddau range, beyond the interest threshold of most visitors who have already looped back to their car on the eastern or southern side.

Yet for those just starting out into wilder hills, this little peak offers a supreme sampler of the Carneddau's greatest hits. There are prehistoric huts (for which the range as a whole is renowned),

↑ Winter makes the diminutive Foel-ganol look suitably muscular. (Steve Lewis ARPS/A)

a muscular ridge (again, a trademark of Foel-ganol's hillier brethren) and the chance to spy one of the wild Carneddau ponies that roam amidst this mountainous landscape.

With their short, stocky build, thick coat and mane, and typically red, black or grey colouration, these distinctive equines are not only important for the ecosystem (grazing the land to provide ideal habitat for the chough, a rare crow), but are also a unique breed – having been isolated up above the 600m contour for hundreds of years. Indeed, a study by Aberystwyth University in 2013 showed that, although the Carneddau's horses are related to the Welsh pony, they are genetically unique from other feral breeds that wander Britain.

We are fortunate to still have them. They were nearly wiped out by Henry VIII who ordered a cull on grounds that they couldn't carry a knight in full armour. The horses would have been lost had it not been for a collective of hill farmers who strived to protect them. And the best bit? You can enjoy seeing these rare quadrupeds and all of the other delights of the Carnedds within a mere half-day stroll.

WALK THIS WAY

❶ Starting at the car park take the wide bridleway (actually the 96km/60-mile North Wales Path that runs from Bangor to Prestatyn) as it ascends, skirting the lower (northern) flanks of the hill. The going is straightforward over rocky grassland interspersed with clumps of heather – a landscape typical of the vast, high moorland that is the Carneddau range. ❷ Continue along the North Wales Path as it heads east, ignoring two paths that cross at right angles. Continuing on the bridleway, keep your eyes peeled for a number of features – from cairns to burnt mounds. Typically crescent-shaped, the latter are remains of rocks that were heated in fires and then used for cooking, bathing and

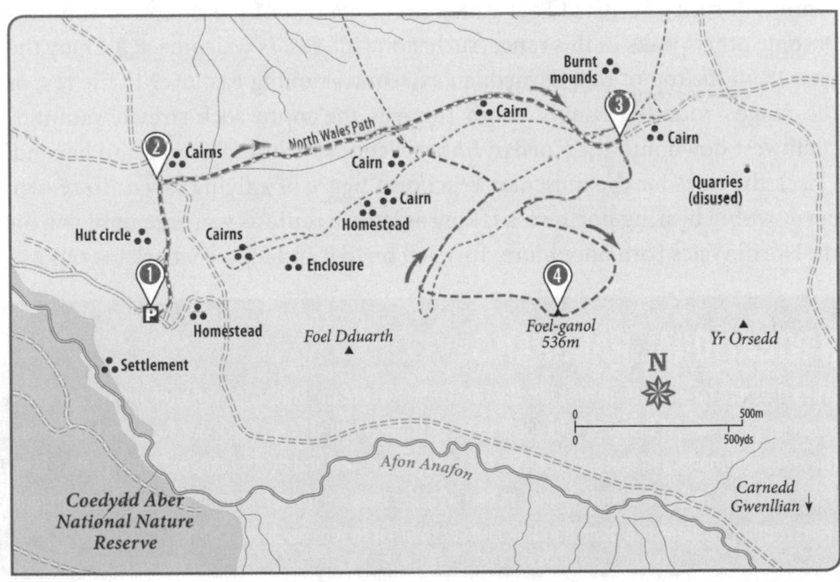

craftwork such as making leather or dye. What you see on the ground is a mound of shattered stone and charcoal that would have broken through thermal shock when doused in cold water. Most of these mounds lie uphill from the path you walk along. **3** After the burnt mounds, the North Wales Path veers southeast then switches northeast. At the latter point, leave the main drag to pick out the much fainter trail that cuts first south then southwest, before switching southeast. This makes for a big zigzag that leads up to the summit of rock-encrusted Foel-ganol. In the context of the smoother summits of some other peaks in this range, such stone interest is welcome. **4** Enjoy the view from the top of this Carneddau extremity, looking east over to the rest of the range's rounded rumps, south towards the more rock-strewn summits, southwest down into the Coedydd Aber National Nature Reserve and beyond. Check the skies for the muscular, cruciform figure of a flying raven. To return, cut downhill bearing northwest, taking as steep a route as you dare until you hit the North Wales Path once more. Turn left on to it and follow it back to your car.

NAVIGATIONAL HANDRAILS

When trying to navigate in an area like the Carneddau, where the landscape is flatter and there's fewer prominent features, it helps to look for 'handrails' to help you stay on track in case a mist descends. These are landmarks and features that don't change, ie: streams and rivers, walls or defined paths. Even if following one makes the route longer, in bad weather they are the safest option. As soon as the cloud starts coming in, identify a good handrail and stick with it to see you down safely.

↑ The view from Foel-ganol over to the other Carneddau peaks of Drum, Foel-fras and Llwytmor. (Jennifer Vidal)

ADDED ADVENTURE

The Carnedds offer a truly wild place to spend the night, whether high on the summits in a tent or nestling among old hut circles alongside the River (Afon) Aber below the car park. So take a bivvy or a hammock and tuck yourself in.

MAKE IT BIGGER

From Foel-ganol, you might decide to continue east then south along the Carneddau ridge to take in the summits of Drum, Foel Fras and Carnedd Gwenllian (formerly Carnedd Uchaf). Then either loop back down northwest to your start point via Yr Aryg, Bera Back and Drosgl or – if you're feeling especially fit – continue to take in Foel Grach, Carnedd Llewelyn and Carnedd Dafydd (which adds an extra 10km/6¼ miles). Throw in an overnight camp and you've got the perfect wild weekend.

FOR LITTLE ADVENTURERS

These hills are renowned for having a wild herd of Carneddau ponies. You don't need to get up high to see them, so stick to the lower riverside path on the southern flanks of Foel-ganol and keep eyes peeled.

FOR CAMPERS

Nearest to the start of the walk is the small but perfectly formed Platt's Farm Campsite and Bunkhouse (🖰 plattsfarm.com; from £8pn), which offers pitches set within a Grade II-listed Victorian farm (and ideally placed between the mountains and the sea) and, to amuse the kids, has chickens and ducks running around freely. There's even a bunkhouse for those wanting a break from canvas.

FOR ADRENALINE LOVERS

Go in winter. The Carneddau is already one of Snowdonia's quieter ranges; add fresh snow or frost and there are even fewer people. The range can be tricky to navigate, however, due to its sprawling, often featureless, moorland so you'll need to know what you're doing, especially if the mist descends. Even so, the good news is that a big freeze firms up all the nasty ankle-sucking bogs for which these hills are renowned.

FOR HUNGRY HIKERS

It is best to pick up supplies *en route* in Conwy or Llandudno Junction. Close to the start and good for a pre- or post-walk treat is the community-run Yr Hen Felin café in Abergwyngregyn (🖰 abergwyngregyn.org.uk/yr-hen-felin/cafe; ⏲ 10.00–16.00). The nearest pub is The Village Inn in Llanfairfechan (🖰 thevillageinn.wix.com/mainmenu), which serves typical fare.

OTHER PRACTICALITIES

There is no public transport to the start of the walk. The best is the number 5 bus, which goes from Bangor to Abergwyngregyn, from where you'll need to walk approximately 3km (1¾ miles) southeast to the start point. The nearest public toilets are at the lower (western) car park at Bont Newydd where there are also picnic tables and trails along the River (Afon) Rhaeadr.

39 A WALK TO RIVAL ALL

TACKLE THE THREE SUMMITS OF YR EIFL TO DISCOVER THE BEST-PRESERVED HILLFORT IN BRITAIN

WHERE	Yr Eifl, Gwynedd
STATS	↔ 6km (3¾ miles) ↕ 564m ↗ 94m ↻ 2 hours
START/FINISH	Porth-y-Nant upper car park ⚲ SH353439
TERRAIN	Clear bridleways throughout, with scree and loose rocks on all three summits, which can be very slippery
MAPS	OS Explorer (1:25,000) 254; OS Landranger (1:50,000) 123

Guarding Wales's spectacular Llŷn Peninsula like a giant trident is the trio of summits that make up Yr Eifl. Pronounced 'earr eye-vul' (and sometimes Anglicised to 'The Rivals') the name comes from the Welsh word for fork – *geifl* – and driving towards it along the road it's easy to see why: three peaks rise like prongs above the sea.

The smallest summit, Garn For, is home to a quarry from which granite was used to make curling stones for the 2006 Winter Olympics. The highest summit, Garn Ganol, gives 360-degree views of the peninsula, Snowdonia, Anglesey and even the Lake District and Ireland on a clear day. And on top of the final summit is Tre'r Ceiri ('town of the giants') – one of Britain's best-preserved Iron Age hillforts, perfect for exploring. All the while, choughs (the charismatic crow of western Britain's wilds) float around the crags or probe the heathery ground for insects.

Yr Eifl's proximity to Snowdonia National Park means that it stays crowd-free year-round. Whilst the highest point of this walk is only 564m, this pocket-sized mountain is absolutely perfect for a quick foray – whether you walk up one, two or all three of its tops!

↑ The approach to the triple crowned Yr Eifl. (Joana Kruse/A)

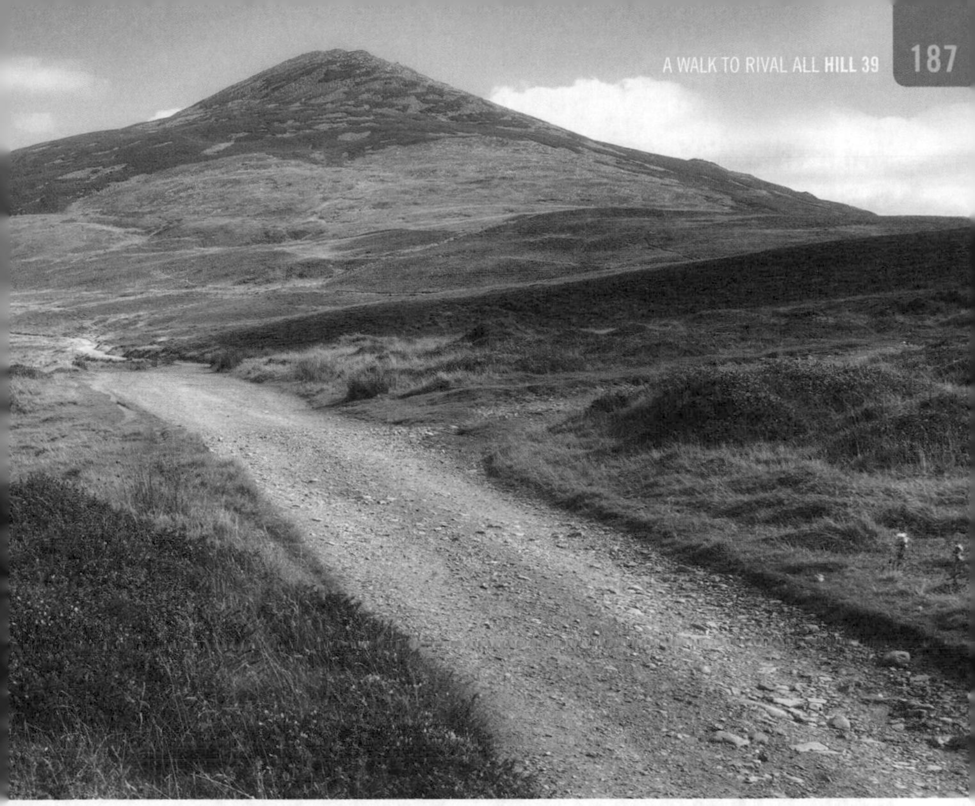

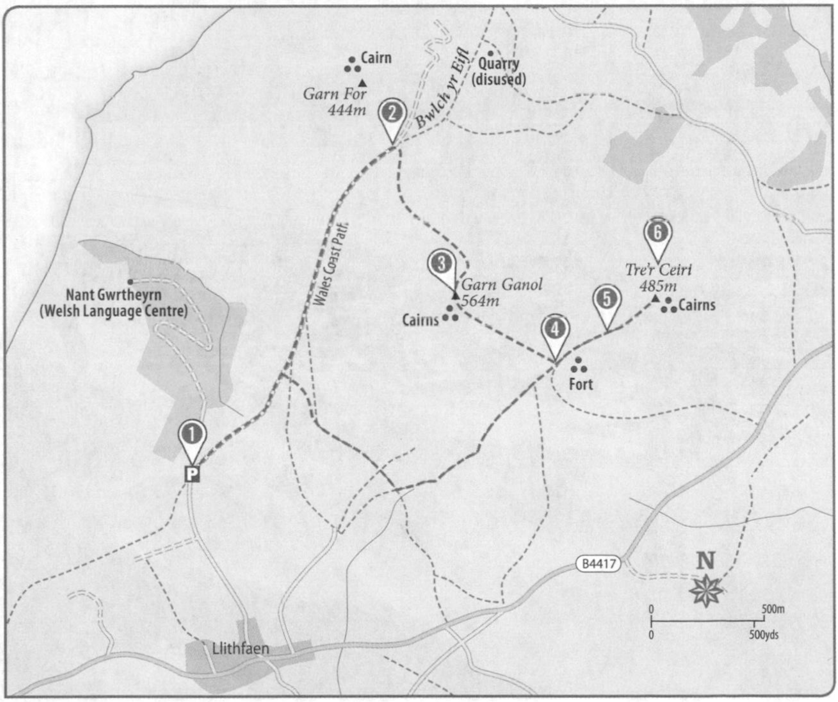
Cairn
Quarry (disused)
Garn For 444m
Bwlch yr Eifl
Wales Coast Path
Garn Ganol 564m
Cairns
Tre'r Ceiri 485m
Cairns
Nant Gwrtheyrn (Welsh Language Centre)
Fort
B4417
N
0
500m
0
500yds
Llithfaen
1
2
3
4
5
6
P

WALK THIS WAY

❶ Starting at the car park follow the obvious bridleway northeast, heading towards the col between Yr Eifl's smallest and largest peaks. Soon, on your left, you'll see the smallest and northernmost peak of the three – Garn For – and the scars on its slopes from quarrying. The path to its top is very faint and rocky so take care if you decide to tackle it. ❷ From here continue a little further along the Wales Coast Path (walescoastpath.gov.uk) towards Bwlch yr Eifl (the col between Garn For and Garn Ganol) until you see a clear and wide path on your right (not marked on the OS map). Take this southeast as it ascends Yr Eifl's highest peak, Garn Ganol. Take time to enjoy the ever-expanding views as you stroll, first on grassy ground then, as you get higher, on rocky splinters. This eventually becomes a thin path on loose scree and large rocks. It remains fairly easy to spot, though the going is slippery if it has been raining. It's not long though before the ascent relents and you're on the summit plateau. Once here bear south to touch the trig point. ❸ On a clear day from Yr Eifl's summit cairn, you can see the whole of the Llŷn Peninsula stretching out to the sea like

↑ Tackle Yr Eifl in winter for a more dramatic approach to Tre'r Ceiri. (Phoebe Smith)

a giant finger. Piles of stones create a handy windbreak around the marker stone. Here you can eat a snack while enjoying views of Snowdonia, Cardigan Bay, Anglesey and beyond. After taking in the fantastic panoramic vista, leave the cairn and make your way eastsoutheast off the summit via a rough path. The descent through rocks and heather is littered with holes – so take care. The gradient will level out before a short climb up to Tre'r Ceiri – Yr Eifl's final summit. **4** Here you'll come to an interpretation board that explains the origin of the hillfort that adorns its peak. Dating back to 100BC this is one of Britain's best-preserved occupied hillforts: it enclosed over 150 stone houses. In some places the fort still stands at its original height, and recent excavation revealed that it surrounds an early Bronze Age cairn. You'll see both of the main entrances and the paths that lead up to the cairn itself – follow one of them inside. The latter passes terraced enclosures that are thought to have been used for cattle and growing crops. A spring immediately outside is likely to have provided the community with water. Archaeologists think that the original Iron Age fort housed about 100 people in 20 houses – but that, during the Roman period,

the population grew to nearly 400. Interesting finds have been made here over the years, from iron tools and pottery to glass beads and even an elaborately decorated gold-plated brooch. **5** Enter the ruins through the opening in the wall and follow one of several obvious paths to the summit cairn. From here you can enjoy a view back to Yr Eifl's highest summit as well as taking in the extent of the Iron Age remains that surround you. **6** If you fancy exploring, there are many paths that will take you to some of the stone huts. Otherwise take the track heading southwest out of a second opening in the wall and take a path through the grass in the same direction. Continue on the path to a fence and over the stile still heading southwest. There are several path options along the way heading in the same general direction until you come to something of a crossroads of possible routes. At this point you'll be able to spot the woods next to the car park where you started, so make your way along one of the paths heading northwest until you eventually hit the bridleway you walked up at the beginning. Turn left on to it and return to the start.

ADDED ADVENTURE

Go in winter – the perfect time to tackle this mini-mountain with a bivvy bag in tow. Tre'r Ceiri offers a whole network of walls and ramps in which to hunker down and shelter from the wind. In the morning you can see the sunrise from the summit of Garn Ganol illuminating the peninsula.

MAKE IT BIGGER

Yr Eifl sits just a few kilometres from the start (or indeed the end depending on your direction) of the 146km (91 miles) Llŷn Coastal Path (itself part of the Wales Coast Path), a route from Caernarfon to Porthmadog that is based on an old pilgrim trail to Bardsey Island, aka the Isle of 20,000 Saints. An ascent of this triple summit makes a very fitting jumping-off point for those wanting to undertake a long-distance trail. And if you start the trail and need a break – there's the Llŷn Coast Bus (Mar–Oct four days a week; see tinyurl.com/llynbus).

FOR LITTLE ADVENTURERS

The Llŷn Peninsula is home to some excellent beaches perfect for sandcastle building not far from the car parks. Recommended is the National Trust-owned Porthor beach (nationaltrust.org.uk/features/porthor), aka Poerth Oer, named after its 'whistling sands' that squeak as you pad along (a result of the interplay between the granules' shape, your weight and warm air). It's also a good place for watersports enthusiasts with sailing, surfing and diving available. Traeth Penllech is a pet-friendly stretch of white sand that offers great rockpooling (head to the right as you walk down to it). Just be aware that at high tide you can be cut off quickly.

A charismatic chough. (Iain H. Leach) →

FOR CAMPERS

For those who want to stay nearby and don't fancy going wild, Aberafon (maelor.demon.co.uk/aberafon.html) offers incredible sea views and is less than 10km (6 miles) away.

FOR ADRENALINE LOVERS

If you've got a head for heights, nearby Gaia Adventures (gaiaadventures.co.uk) offers cliff camping. You can spend the night suspended above the sea on nearby Anglesey or above the river in Betws-y-Coed. It's one extreme sleep you won't forget, whether before or after this three-summit peak.

FOR HUNGRY HIKERS

Ty Coch Inn (tycoch.co.uk) is 9.6km (6 miles) west along the coast in the tiny fishing village of Porthdinllaen near Morfa. It offers filling food and great views to boot. The best thing about this inn, boldly considered by one travel website to be among the world's best beach bars, is that only those willing to put in some effort can reach it as vehicle access is restricted to residents only. You can park at the golf club (SH281408) from where a bracing 20-minute walk stands between you and your pint. Bear in mind that high tide can stop you reaching the inn via the beach and that opening hours vary out of season so do call ahead. The nearest place to the hill itself to grab a cuppa/cake is Caffi Meinir in Llithfaen (nantgwrtheyrn.org/days-out/cafe), which offers views over the bay towards Anglesey. Best to pick up snacks at Caernarfon, 45km (28 miles) away along the coast to the north.

OTHER PRACTICALITIES

The nearest town is Llithfaen, just 1km from the start of the walk, which is served by sporadic buses numbers 14 and 27 from and to Pwllheli and Nerfyn. There are limited supplies and no public toilets.

Looking towards the smaller of Yr Eifl's three peaks from the North Wales Path. (Paddy Dillon) ↑

40 PEAK AT THE END OF THE WORLD

ANGLESEY'S ROCKY PEAK BLENDS AMPLE HISTORICAL LEGACIES WITH A CLIMBER'S NIRVANA AND ABUNDANT BIRDLIFE

WHERE	Holyhead Mountain, Anglesey
STATS	↔ 3km (1¾ miles) ↕ 220m ↗ 162m ↻ 1½ hours
START/FINISH	Porth Namarch car park SH225832
TERRAIN	Rough footpaths and heather and rocky trails
MAPS	OS Explorer (1:25,000) 262; OS Landranger (1:50,000) 114

There's nothing quite as exciting as climbing the highest point on an island – except, of course, climbing the highest point on an island that's also home to a Roman watchtower, spoils from the Iron, Bronze, Neolithic and Stone ages, a lighthouse, a huge number of seabirds nesting along the cliffs, and a quarrying site from which rocks were hewn that now form the longest breakwater in Britain, over in the island's main town of Holyhead. Welcome to Holyhead Mountain (a mountain in name but a small hill in stature) on the Isle of Anglesey, just off the northwest coast of Wales.

As if that isn't enough, this mini-mountain is also home to an old magazine store (for dynamite used in the quarry), a former foghorn station (now an artist's studio that is sometimes open to the public for exhibitions; see northstackstudio.co.uk) and a Victorian folly that has morphed into a birdwatching lookout run by the RSPB. From here, you can get fine views of the nesting seabirds, which include Atlantic puffin and guillemot, plus chough (acrobatic crows). Peer down into the waters below and you may spot a grey seal bobbing around.

Need any more reasons to walk Holyhead Mountain? Well, I'll give you one anyway... this peak is also renowned for its cliffside rock-climbing routes. So whether you are an adrenaline junkie, birdwatcher, history buff or hillwalker – all your coastal kicks are available here at this peak that marks the end of Wales's northerly outpost.

↑ Looking over Anglesey's distinctively white Holyhead Mountain. (Gail Johnson/S)

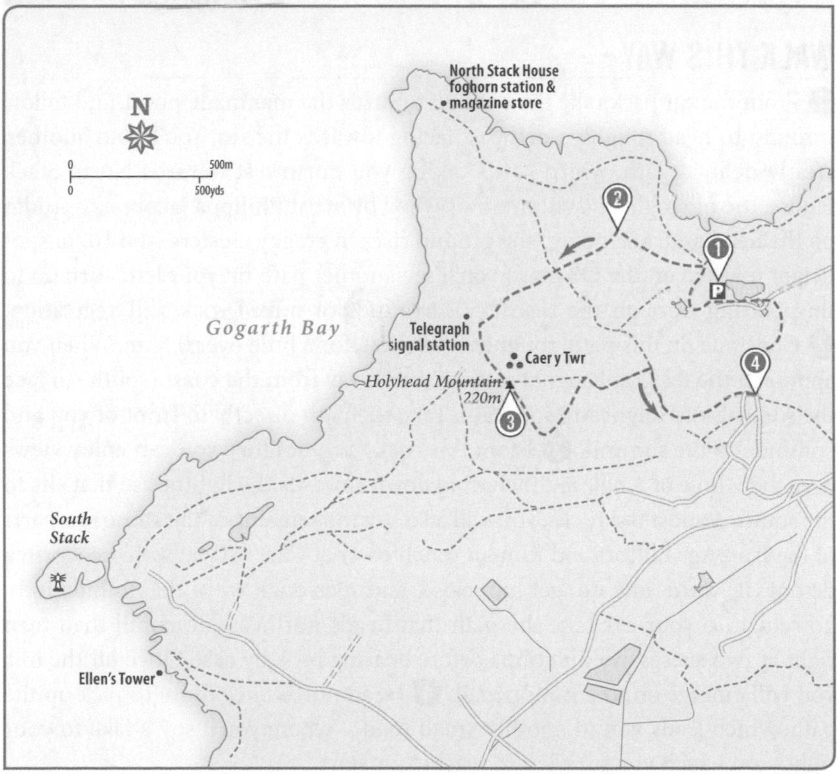

North Stack House foghorn station & magazine store

N

0 500m

0 500yds

Gogarth Bay

Telegraph signal station

Caer y Twr

Holyhead Mountain 220m

South Stack

Ellen's Tower

WALK THIS WAY

❶ From the car park take the path up towards the manmade pond, and follow it round to head roughly northeast facing towards the sea. You'll join another, clearly defined path, which starts taking you northwest towards North Stack House, the old foghorn station now owned by artist Philippa Jacobs as a studio on the headland. Just before the ground rises in craggy clusters (the 107m spot height marked on the OS map) you'll see another path on your left. Turn on to this, cutting through the tussocky surrounds of mixed rock and vegetation. ❷ Continue on this path, roughly southwest, for a little over 0.5km. When you approach the telegraph signal station, turn away from the coast (south) to face the summit of Holyhead Mountain. Take the path directly in front of you and continue to the summit. ❸ From this rocky promontory you can enjoy views over the whole of Anglesey, including down towards the lighthouse that sits to the south. Amidst the rocks, you will also spy the remains of the stone ramparts of the Iron Age hillfort and Roman watchtower at Caer y Twr. Both are worth a detour if you'd like to get up close and personal with the foundations. To return to your car take the path that heads northeast downhill then turn right at two successive junctions before bearing broadly east. Once off the hill, you will emerge on to a minor road. ❹ Head north once more to pick up the path, which leads you to another small road – where you'll spy a lake to your right – on which you turn left to reach your start.

↑ Take the path leading to the craggy summit of Holyhead – and maybe bring your climbing gear. (Mike-Hawkes/angleseydigital)

ADDED ADVENTURE

Next to the old foghorn station there's an ornate magazine store that makes a good spot for an impromptu bivvy. Remember to arrive late and leave early and take out all your rubbish with you.

MAKE IT BIGGER

Don't just stop at the summit; head down to the fog signal station/artist's studio to gaze out to the seemingly endless sea as though perched on the end of the world. Then check out the whitewashed Twr Ellin (Ellen's Tower) on the west coast (now used by the RSPB as a watchpoint) before looping back to your start point.

FOR LITTLE ADVENTURERS

From hillforts to towers plus birds to spot (go to RSPB South Stack; tinyurl.com/southstackrspb), there's a lot to distract kids on and around this walk. But if they are getting restless take them further down the coast to Newborough (43.3km/27 miles away) from where you can walk to Llandwyn Island, legendary home to St Dwynwen – Wales's own Valentine's Day saint – who, legend has it, cast herself out to live on this spit of land as a nun after the man she loved was turned into a block of ice. She prayed and was granted three things: that her former lover be thawed, that she would never marry and that God would look after all lovers.

FOR CAMPERS

There's not masses of choice but Ty'n Rhos (tinyurl.com/tynros), which is mainly a caravan park, also offers space for tents near to the walk.

FOR ADRENALINE LOVERS

If you ever wanted to try climbing on quartzite then Holyhead Mountain is the place to do it: there's said to be 123 short routes to try, so get your gear and hire a guide if needed. Full information can be found on The Crag Collective (tinyurl.com/holyheadcrag); most Snowdonia-based climbing guides will be able to take you here.

FOR HUNGRY HIKERS

Groceries and baked goods can be picked up easily in nearby Moelfre at Rhew Fecws village shop. The nearest pub is The White Eagle (white-eagle.co.uk) at Rhoscolyn, which serves locally sourced gastro-pub grub, and offers an outside terrace with nice views.

OTHER PRACTICALITIES

You can reach Holyhead by train, from where sporadic buses (22 and 22A) head to Llaingoch. From here you would have to walk just over 1km (½ mile) to the start. The nearest toilets are at RSPB South Stack reserve.

Puffins nest around this little mountain so keep your eyes peeled. (johnbraid/S) →

↑ **Proof that little peaks can outperform the biggest on the small summit of Ben A'an (461m). (David Robertson/A)**

SCOTLAND

41 SMOKE ME A KIPPFORD

GET COASTAL KICKS, WILD WOODLAND AND CRACKING VIEWS WITH THIS EASY DUMFRIES ASCENT

WHERE	The Muckle, Dumfries and Galloway
STATS	↔ 5km (3 miles) ↕ 120m ↗ 110m ↻ 1½ hours
START/FINISH	Kippford car park NX837553
TERRAIN	A minor road then clearly marked woodland paths
MAPS	OS Explorer (1:25,000) 312, 313; OS Landranger (1:50,000) 84

When you think of a little hill in Scotland, you tend to think of the lowland humps that fringe larger hills close to the Highlands and that missed the explosive action that blessed their northern cousins with additional height. But look a little closer to the water, and – dare I say it – to the border with England and you can find some very agreeable mini-peaks that offer plenty of views for much less sweat.

A case in point is the little-visited seaside area of Kippford (and neighbouring Rockcliffe) on the Solway Firth – the watery crooked finger that cleaves between England and Scotland. From the viewpoint of the resonantly named Muckle (aka Mark Hill), you can peer south into the Lake District and even see the Isle of Man – all from its positively petite 120m summit. Minimum effort with maximum views: surely that's what good small hills are all about.

And there's more than views to enjoy as well. Without climbing the peak at all, you can explore the Mote of Mark, a 6th-century fort. Perfect for little or tired legs! Then there's wildflower meadows that glow with colour and buzz with winged insects such as ringlet (a butterfly) in summer. Wading birds such as oystercatcher and ringed plover probe the Firth mud at low tide (they breed on nearby Rough Island). In winter, ducks such as wigeon whistle around the tidal waters as well. Add to that the very handy pubs in Kippford and tea shop in Rockcliffe and you're never too far from refreshments. A coastal walk that offers nourishment, both practically and spiritually.

↑ Rockcliffe and the Solway Firth – an often overlooked outdoors beauty. (James Johnstone)

WALK THIS WAY

1 From the car park at Kippford head south along the road, skirting the estuary, until it ends. Here you continue on a footpath, moving slightly further from the shoreline. Soon you'll enter Mark Hill Forest (scotland.forestry.gov.uk/visit/mark-hill), which coats the lumps and bumps between Kippford and the nearby town of Rockcliffe. Turn left (almost back on yourself) on what is marked as part of the Woodpecker Trail. (Keep an eye out for the eponymous headbanging birds.)

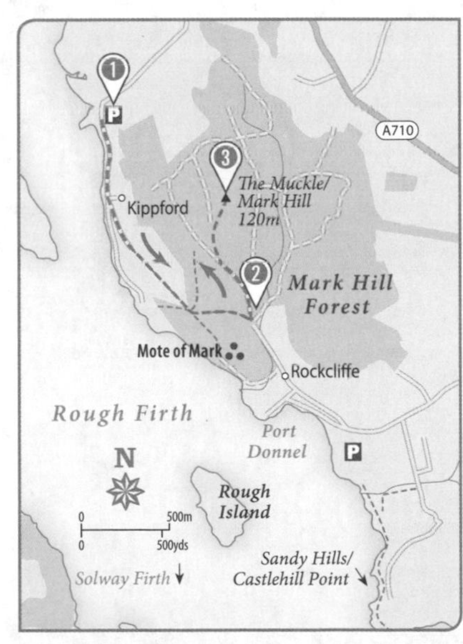

2 Follow the trail uphill, ascending steadily, bearing northwest on a detour marked with a blue arrow. Continue all the way to the top of the feature known as The Muckle (120m).

3 It takes only a little effort to get here, yet the views are spectacular. You can see Rough Firth and the islands out in the Solway, and beyond into Cumbria. To return, providing you don't want to explore further, just retrace your steps to the start (via the Mote of Mark if you want to see the fort; see *Little adventurers*).

ADDED ADVENTURE

At low tide you can walk to Rough Island where – except during the breeding season (May to mid-July) – you can while away the time watching the shorebirds that call this place home. Compare the carrot-like bill of an oystercatcher with the stunted beak of the smaller ringed plover. Tidal access means you'll need to time your visit carefully – though getting stranded for a few hours (with a bivvy bag that just so happened to find its way into your rucksack) would be the perfect adventure.

MAKE IT BIGGER

After you've taken The Muckle continue to Rockcliffe (nts.org.uk/visit/rockcliffe) and pick up the coastal trail that leads round to Castlehill Point and onwards to Sandyhills. Although only about 8km (5 miles), the terrain is a little more challenging.

FOR LITTLE ADVENTURERS

Aside from exploring the site of the old Mote of Mark hillfort, this is one of the best places to make a wildlife checklist for little ones. From oystercatcher to peregrine and ringlet, there's plenty look out for. Then go rockpooling on the shores of Rockcliffe – an activity that brings out the inner child in adults.

FOR CAMPERS

Nearest is Castle Point, which offers pitches right by the sea (castlepointcc.com; Apr–Oct; from £19.50pn).

FOR ADRENALINE LOVERS

With its waterside location you should consider exploring the Solway Firth by canoe or packraft either pre- or post-walk. You just need to pay a nominal fee (currently £5) at Kippford slipway.

FOR HUNGRY HIKERS

Several options in Kippford. For a daytime snack or tea try The Ark (tinyurl.com/kippfordark) which offers a gift shop as well as food and drink. For an evening meal or drink head to The Mariner Hotel (themariner-kippford.co.uk), which has terrace tables overlooking the estuary. The nearest supermarket is in Hillowtown, 14km (9 miles) northwest.

OTHER PRACTICALITIES

From Dumfries (where there is a train station), Bus 372A runs sporadically to Kippford (dumgal.gov.uk/timetables). The nearest public toilets are in the car park at the start.

The Muckle watches over the rockpool-covered beach at Kippford. (Johncox1958/D)

42 SEA TO SUMMIT

STROLL ALONG GIRVAN PROMENADE BEFORE SUMMITING CLYDESIDE'S BASHFUL BUMP

WHERE	Byne Hill, South Ayrshire
STATS	↔ 7km (4¼ miles) ↕ 214m ↗ 210m ↻ 2½ hours
START/FINISH	Girvan car park ⚲ NX182963
TERRAIN	Seafront, farm tracks and grassy slopes
MAPS	OS Explorer (1:25,000) 326, 317; OS Landranger (1:50,000) 84

Let's just say it straight out. The Firth of Clyde doesn't get much attention. Not from outdoor lovers, or in general, but hopefully there's one little hill that may go some way to changing that. Enter Byne Hill, a bashful bump at just 214m high.

This peak, fortunately, is not about the altitude. It's about access and about vistas. Because from this hill not only can you reach an abundance of other lovely lumps and give yourself the opportunity to claim the distinct accolade of walking from the sea (don't forget to dip your walking boot before you start) all the way to a summit, but you are also rewarded with amazing vistas of a shamefully overlooked firth.

From the dramatic summit pillar, placed here to mark the 300th anniversary of the borough of Girvan in 1968, you can peer along the Ayrshire coast towards Turnberry Lighthouse, look out to the volcanic plug that is the seabird-rich Ailsa Craig – floating as it does, almost crouton-like, in a soupy sea – and gaze across to both the west and the northeast at a whole host of other hills that few people will ever take the time to bother with, never mind summit. Chances are when you do so, you will have them entirely to yourself.

↑ The view from Byne Hill looks out all the way to Turnberry Lighthouse. (www.scottishhorizons.co.uk/Keith Fergus)

WALK THIS WAY

❶ Just south of Girvan, from the car park at Shallockpark, head south along the footpath alongside the A77, on the fairly new Ayrshire Coastal Path (ayrshirecoastalpath.org). After you've crossed the burn, take the second turning on your left. ❷ Following the farm track heading uphill (south). You'll go through two gates, through some woodland and past a quarry until you reach a monument to Major A C B Craufurid, who took part in the capture of the Cape of Good Hope in 1795. ❸ Continue, heading northeast now, looking for a gate on your left. Go through this and begin your ascent to the summit of Byne Hill, crossing a stile then traversing rocky ground, until you reach the top (214m). ❹ Here you'll find a toposcope that indicates landmarks in the Firth of Clyde and beyond. Assuming clement weather, you should be able to see the impressive Ailsa Craig, Isle of Arran and – on a really clear day – Northern Ireland. To return, continue along the ridgeline bearing northeast, descending steeply, then swing back on yourself, tracking southwest to pick up the path you left just before stage 3. (It is best not to try cutting through Brochneil as there have been access issues on this route in recent years.) Then simply retrace your steps to the start.

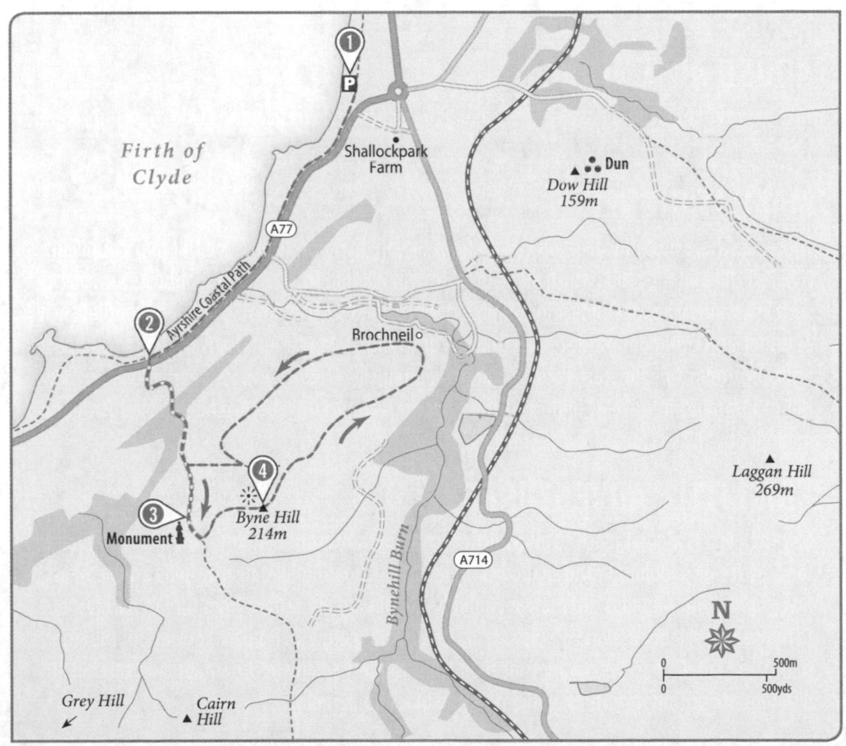

ADDED ADVENTURE

Take your tent for a night out anywhere along the ridge for views over the Clyde coast right from your sleeping bag.

MAKE IT BIGGER

There's a whole host of walks you can do from Girvan. Carry on from Byne Hill to pick up Cairn Hill, Fell Hill and Grey Hill (which all lie in a Scottish Wildlife Trust reserve that hosts rare plants such as common juniper and spring sandwort, butterflies such as small heath, and reptiles such as adder and common lizard; tinyurl.com/greyhillgrassland). Alternatively, head southeast after returning to your start point to tackle Laggan Hill (269m) and its nearby loch, or Dow Hill (159m) and its ancient hillfort. A third option is to pick up the Ayrshire Coastal Path and meander by the sea for as long as you care.

FOR LITTLE ADVENTURERS

Girvan beach is a great place to allow little legs to burn off some energy, whether by building sandcastles or paddling in the shallows. There's also a boating lake nearby, plus amusements. A very different, fabulous alternative would be to join a daily sailing from Girvan harbour out to the seabird-clagged island of Ailsa Craig (ailsacraig.org.uk). Prepare yourself for the sight, sound and smell of 36,000 gannets at their third-biggest colony in Britain, or look carefully to differentiate puffins, razorbills, guillemots and black guillemots.

Turnberry Lighthouse shines a light on the craggy Ailsa Craig. (www.scottishhorizons.co.uk/Keith Fergus)

FOR CAMPERS

The nearest one that takes tents is the Walled Garden Camping & Caravanning Park (tinyurl.com/walledgardencamp; Mar–Nov, from £14pn) in Carrick, 16km (10 miles) northeast.

FOR ADRENALINE LOVERS

Pre- or post-summit head out on the Ayrshire Coastal Path, which sits beneath this summit. A 'practical route rather than a formal laid-out path', this runs for 160km (100 miles) between Glenapp and Kelly Burn. Take your tent and sense of adventure for a rugged multi-day excursion; the Path is targeted at 'well-equipped agile walkers'.

FOR HUNGRY HIKERS

There are a few options in Girvan. For a light bite try Dowhill Country Fayre (dowhillfarm.co.uk; closed Wed), which also has a farm shop where you can get supplies. For sit-down food and drink near the harbour try Flynn's Boatyard (flynnsboatyard.co.uk), which offers typical pub grub. There are a couple of supermarkets (Asda and the Co-op) in Girvan where you can pick up supplies pre-walk.

OTHER PRACTICALITIES

There's a train station in Girvan from where you can start the walk. There are public toilets in the car park at the start.

43 STRIDING ARCHES

MAKE HILLWALKING AN ART FORM BY ADMIRING ANDREW GOLDSWORTHY'S CREATIONS AS YOU ASCEND COLT HILL

WHERE	Colt Hill, Dumfries and Galloway
STATS	↔ 9.5km (6 miles) ↕ 598m ↗ 328m ↻ 3½ hours
START/FINISH	Cairnhead car park NX702971
TERRAIN	Forestry tracks and grassy moorland near summit
MAPS	OS Explorer (1:25,000) 328; OS Landranger (1:50,000) 77, 78

It's rare that you get to combine hillwalking with modern art – especially that emanating from one of Britain's most renowned outdoor sculptors. But along this ascent of Colt Hill, above the funky Dumfries village of Moniaive, you will find just that.

Colt Hill is the tallest of several rounded humps that stretch towards 600m altitude. Their form is echoed by a series of arch sculptures by none other than Andy Goldsworthy, who has lived locally for over 20 years. *Striding Arches* is Goldsworthy's series of large, self-supporting arches yawning like stone rainbows in the landscape (stridingarches.com). Launched in 2002, the project's aim is to focus on a part of Scotland often neglected by tourists and to the hills themselves. Goldsworthy was not the only artist involved: poet Alec Finlay and artist Pip Hall were both inspired to produce work linked to the project.

All four arches in the area stand just under 4m high, span 7m and are made from 31 blocks of local sandstone. Goldsworthy has made similar outdoor installations in Canada, the USA and New Zealand, a nod to the emigration of Scottish people over the last two centuries. Indeed, the stone is said to

↑ Colt Hill's rainbow-like arch. (Lynn Fotheringham/D)

represent the ballast used in the ships on the return journey. The series of arches are found on three hilltops – Benbrack (581m), Bail Hill (517m) and of course the target of this walk – Colt Hill (598m), with the set completed by a half-arch emerging from a building at Cairnhead.

Goldsworthy's idea was that from one arch you should be able to see the others so that all are linked together by sight. Accordingly, when you climb Colt Hill you should – depending on the current height of the woodland plantation – be able to see the other summit sculptures.

It is a great idea to bring people to this heavily forested and, pre-project, very little-visited set of peaks. Even without the stone strides it's an area worthy of attention. With a pronounced U-shaped valley rising steeply to rounded, smooth grassy tops, their flanks coated thickly with conifer trees and the odd pocket of broadleaf and ancient juniper, this is a striking place to wander. One thing's for sure: visiting will show soon-to-be-hillgoers that the journey to the top is often a learning curve…

WALK THIS WAY

❶ You can see Andrew Goldsworthy's first Striding Arch even before getting the walk underway. From Cairnhead car park, the upper of the two paths heading northwest leads uphill to The Byre. Here Goldsworthy's curving arch protrudes from the wall of an old barn. ❷ Retrace your steps to the car park then take the main (lower) path uphill. Crossing a bridge over a burn (keep an eye out for Britain's largest dragonfly, the golden-ringed, scudding past), you enter the forest. Birds associated with pine trees are common here;

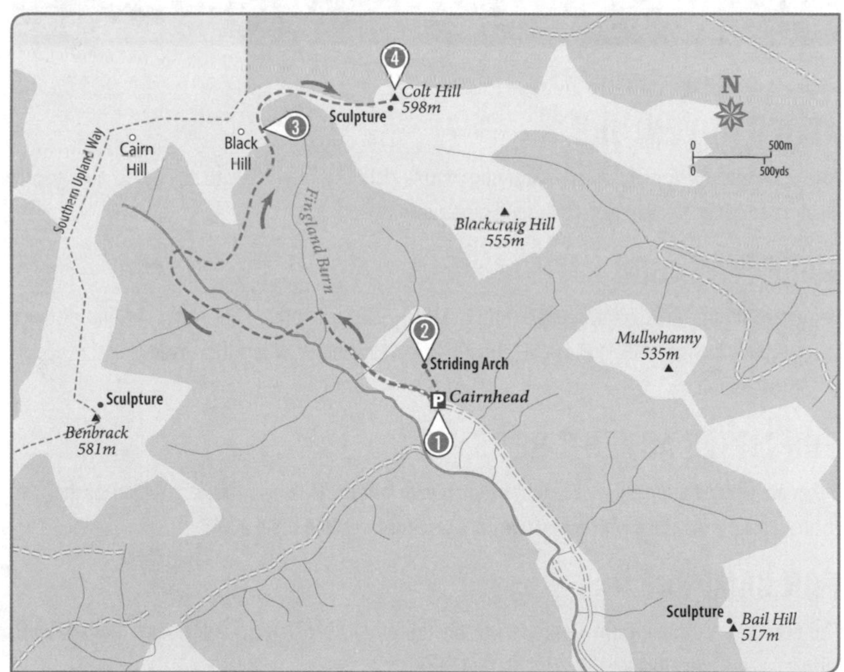

ADDED ADVENTURE

Take your tent for a night spent stargazing in this 'dark sky reserve', with the stone arch gently illuminated by the twinkling of a thousand stars. Cosmic.

MAKE IT BIGGER

Bag a third Striding Arch by cutting west from Colt Hill to join the Southern Upland Way (a long-distance footpath) that loops over Black Hill then Cairn Hill to reach Benbrack, where the curved sculpture adorns the 581m summit.

FOR LITTLE ADVENTURERS

If they are not up for the full walk, it may be enough to visit The Byre near the start. As well as the arch, the barn itself is inscribed with poems: why not take turns reading them out?

FOR CAMPERS

The nearest is Oakbank Farm Campsite (tinyurl.com/oakbankfarm; Mar–Oct; from £12pn), although it is 29km (18 miles) from the start of the walk.

↑ The Byre is a great place to start your walk to the other arches. (AidanStock/A)

NIGHT NAVIGATION

Want to find out which direction you're facing using only the stars? Select a star and stick your walking pole (or a stick) in the ground vertically under it. Check back 30 minutes later and – because of the Earth's rotation – the star will no longer be above the stick. If the star is now to the left – you're looking north, to the right – south, up – east, down – west. Remember it with the phrase 'Lost Nomads Die Wandering', meaning Left North, Down West.

they include siskin, crossbill and coal tit. There are also red squirrels. Ignoring any turn-offs, walk largely parallel to a valley until the path bends sharply right to cross the stream then heads uphill. ❸ On leaving the confines of the forest at the top of Fingland Burn, go through a gate until you see a signpost directing you to Colt Hill Arch. Follow this, staying left of the fenceline. Stonechats and meadow pipits may flit ahead of you, bouncing between fenceposts. The grassy paths lead invitingly on, and the remains of old drystone walls and rocky outcrops litter the slopes. Your ear may catch the gruff honk of a raven or the mewing of a common buzzard. You'll soon reach the – often boggy – hilltop where the burnt-red sandstone arch soon reveals itself above the grassy summit. ❹ From here you will be able to see the third full arch on the hill called Benbrack; this lies to the southwest, on the opposite side of the valley you ascended. To return to the car park, simply retrace your steps.

FOR ADRENALINE LOVERS

For those determined to see all the sculptures there is also one on Bail Hill (517m), 2.5km (1½ miles) southeast of Cairnhead. No paths reach the sculpture, so seeing it involves cutting uphill through thick trees. Reserved for the keenest of walkers and arch-collectors only!

FOR HUNGRY HIKERS

The funky 'festival village' of Moniaive (🖱 moniaive.org.uk) is the place for food, drink and supplies. During the day try Glen Whisk Café & Bistro (🖱 glencairnepm.com/glenwhiskhome), which has cracking cakes and daily specials. In the evening head to Craigdarroch Arms Hotel (🖱 craigdarrocharmshotel.co.uk), which serves hearty, homemade fare. Alternatively, grab some sandwiches from the supermarket in Moniaive and head to the picnic area near the lower flanks of Bail Hill where a stream invites you to skim stones.

OTHER PRACTICALITIES

No public transport to the start of the walk. The best is to take the 81 bus from Dumfries to Moniaive. Nearest toilets are in Moniaive.

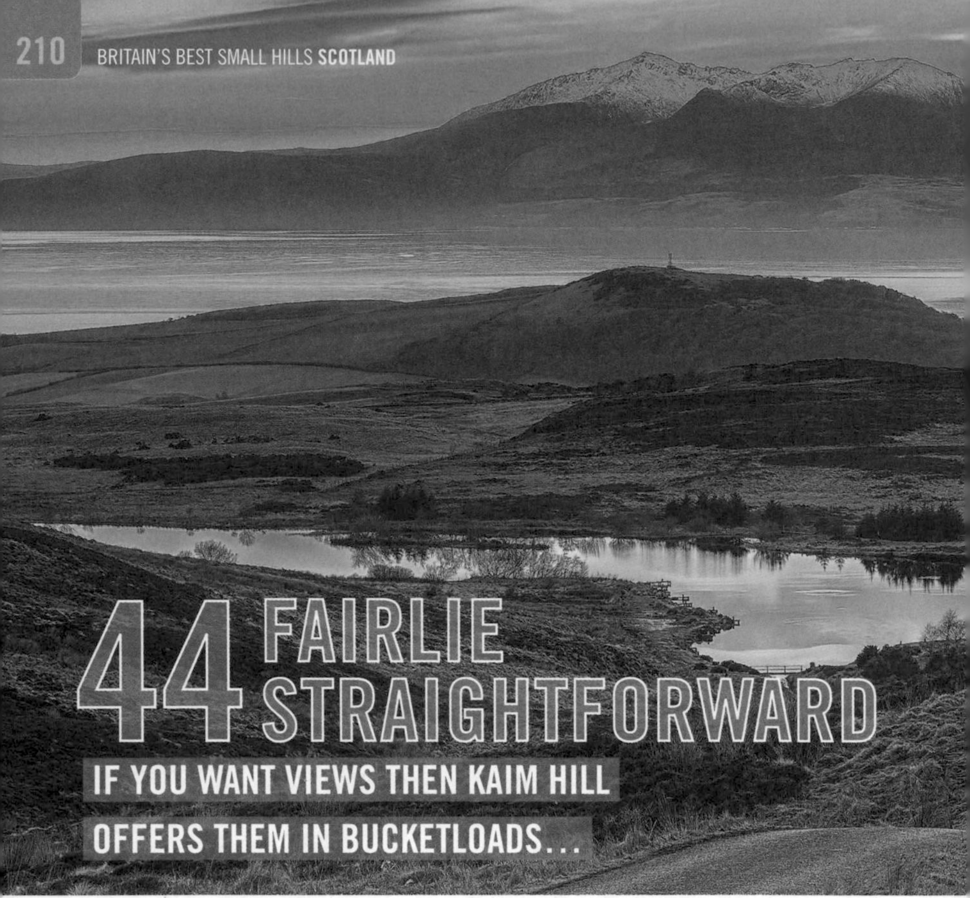

44 FAIRLIE STRAIGHTFORWARD

IF YOU WANT VIEWS THEN KAIM HILL OFFERS THEM IN BUCKETLOADS...

WHERE	Kaim Hill, North Ayrshire
STATS	↔ 5.5km (3½ miles) ↕ 387m ↗ 387m ↻ 2½ hours
START/FINISH	Fairlie train station car park NS210546
TERRAIN	Tarmac then narrow winding paths, open fellside that's a little rough
MAPS	OS Explorer (1:25,000) 341, 333; OS Landranger (1:50,000) 63

Just to hammer home the point that the area that lines the Firth of Clyde is well worthy of your exploration, here's another cool but effortlessly modest mini-mountain to add to your list. North along the coastline from Girvan and its adjacent peak of Byne Hill, and accessed from the sweetly named town of Fairlie, is Kaim Hill.

This tempting prospect is veined on all sides by waterfalls, burns, rivers and reservoirs, creating an almost island-like peak. Kaim Hill offers great views over to Bute, Cumbrae and the Isle of Arran as well as the surrounding hills (those to the east are studded by wind turbines, to the consternation of some) and all the way along the Firth of Clyde.

This peak has another claim to fame. There used to be an active millstone quarry here whose tumbledown remains can still be spotted (including the Quarry Office & Stores, the Smithy and old workings); its raw material was first exported all over the world – from the USA to Australia – in

↑ Take the road less travelled – Fairlie Moor Road provides the access point to Kaim Hill. (James Mcdowall/S)

the 18th century. It's also possible to spot a number of birds on this walk: keep your eyes peeled for golden plover, raven and hen harrier. If walking across boggy areas in summer, look for the fluffy white pompoms of common cotton-grass and the searing yellow spikes of bog asphodel.

WALK THIS WAY

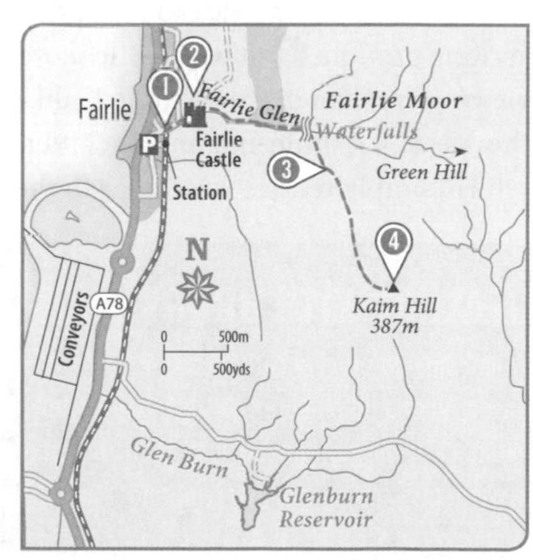

1 From the car park at Fairlie railway station go along the path heading north and follow it to reach Burnfoot Road; turn immediately right on to Castlepark Drive, heading east. Where Castlepark Drive swings north (left), a path veers right. Take this path to enter the area marked on the map as Fairlie Glen. 2 You'll pass Fairlie Castle, an old semi-preserved stronghold that used to house the town's namesake family.

You then ascend gradually into deciduous woodland over a burn and above the enchanted waterfalls (filled with moss-covered boulders, and housed in a sneaky gorge), and on to open moorland. From here onwards, start looking for the birds and plants already mentioned. The path can be a little faint but keep tracking uphill (east) following the gully, before crossing over on to the south bank via a footbridge and then heading out on to the hillside. You'll find the terrain here is tussocky and covered in heather, which can be a little tricky underfoot. **3** Follow the path southeast as it gradually ascends to the summit of Kaim Hill. Despite the short distance involved, it takes a surprisingly long time to reach the top due to the sprawling nature of the incline and the ankle-sucking ground. **4** It was a little more effort than you perhaps thought, but the views more than make up for it. Unlike Byne Hill further south along the coast, this peak has little manmade clutter, making the walk feel even wilder. To return, simply retrace your steps to the start.

DEALING WITH BOGGY GROUND

When walking on very saturated ground it's advisable to carry walking poles as they can help 'test' the depth of a bog before you slip into it up to your waist! If you do plunge in, stay calm and try and backtrack releasing one leg first, then the other. Remember that slow and steady is key as quick movements – no matter how tempting – will only exasperate the problem.

↑ Fairlie Glen Waterfall, just before stage 2. (James Armstrong/Flickr (ItsJamesy))

ADDED ADVENTURE

Keep your eyes peeled for cup and ring markings (resembling water ripples) on the summit rocks. These marks are thought to be a form of prehistoric art whose importance and meaning are still being debated. Given that this place was clearly significant for our ancestors, why not consider spending a night up here?

MAKE IT BIGGER

There's a fair few sprawling peaks in this area, though many are adorned with wind turbines and the wide paths that reach them. From Kaim Hill, try tacking on Green Hill (⚲ NS239547) or Blaeloch (⚲ NS243553) or descend via its south face to check out the waterfall at Glen Burn (⚲ NS216520), then walk down to the Ayrshire Coastal Path (immediately west of the A78) which you can follow north back to your start point.

FOR LITTLE ADVENTURERS

Nearby Kelburn Castle & Estate (🖱 kelburnestate.com; 🕒 daily; from £3) has lots to entertain the kids, from their Secret Forest adventure walk for older kids to the Playbarn for tiny tykes. There's also the chance to try some mountain biking and horseriding.

FOR CAMPERS

The nearest one for tent campers is South Whittlieburn Farm (🖱 largsonline.co.uk/swf/home.html; from £15pn), which is on a working sheep farm.

FOR ADRENALINE LOVERS

Run it: every year around April a fell race takes place on this unassuming summit (🖱 tinyurl.com/kaimhillrace). But you don't have to wait for the official starting pistol to try your hand – or rather feet – at hill-running. Take your trainers, some water and start slowly. Just in case you wondered, the record to beat is 25 minutes 52 seconds – set back in 1995 and as yet unbeaten.

FOR HUNGRY HIKERS

Not loads of choice in Fairlie but there is a decent snack/coffee shop inside the Kelburn Estate (see *For little adventurers*). For a sit-down meal head to Fins Restaurant (🖱 fencebay.co.uk/the-catch-at-fins-restaurant) for great (indeed, award-winning) seafood (bring your own bottle).

OTHER PRACTICALITIES

Fairlie has a train station from which the walk starts. Public toilets are in Fairlie at the south picnic site (⚲ NS207545).

Hen harriers are also frequent visitors to this small hill. (James Lowen) ↑

45 WHANGIE-FUL

TACKLE THE BIZARRE ROCK FORMATIONS OF A MOST CURIOUSLY NAMED PEAK IN THE AUCHINEDEN HILLS

WHERE	The Whangie, East Dunbartonshire
STATS	↔ 4km (2½ miles) ↕ 357m ↗ 165m ↻ 1½ hours
START/FINISH	Queen's View car park NS511808
TERRAIN	Clear (although often boggy) path at start then faint and muddy nearer summit
MAPS	OS Explorer (1:25,000) 348; OS Landranger (1:50,000) 64

For those of you in any doubt the answer is, unequivocally, yes. I did indeed select this small hill primarily because of its wonderful name. But, luckily for me, this wee bump also hides a feature worthy of note – a 100m-long corridor of 10m-high rock that you can walk through as if stepping into a secret chasm.

Known as The Whangie (which, it's theorised, comes from the colloquial term for 'slice'), the corridor is essentially a landsplit. It is believed to have been formed when a glacier tore through the area, splintering it from the main hill via a vulnerable crack in the basaltic rock. However, the folklore version is that the devil caused the fissure when flicking his tail as he flew away from the area, heading for a tryst at Stockie Muir. Whichever version you prefer there's no getting away from the fact that, in a place synonymous with extensive moorland, its very presence is a wonderfully bizarre fluke and one – even putting to one side its glorious name – that means it wholeheartedly deserves a place in this book.

The Whangie is also a cracking place to watch wildlife as you walk. If you arrive at dawn in spring, you may see a group of male black grouse displaying over towards Stockie Muir, the puffed-up velvet males cooing and sneezing at one another. Easier to see are red grouse, curlew and raven. In summer, whinchats perch atop exposed gorse bushes, whilst small pearl-bordered fritillary (an orange butterfly) and golden-ringed dragonfly bring colour and charisma to the moors.

↑ Auchineden Hill – home of the delightfully named Whangie. (Ewan Adamson)

WALK THIS WAY

❶ Starting at the car park, first stand on a hillock to the left, from which Queen Victoria reputedly first admired Loch Lomond. Then climb the stile and follow the boardwalk heading roughly west, keeping the forest to your left, before heading uphill. On your ascent, stop to take in the view of Loch Lomond, Ben Lomond and the Arrochar Hills. After the boardwalk, the ground is often boggy (walking poles will be useful). ❷ Where the path forks, head left to pick up the summit – actually called Auchineden Hill (357m) – taking care if the terrain is boggy. From the top, stop to take in the wonderful views of the Kilpatrick Hills and Campsie Fells nearby. Look too for Burncrooks and Kilmannan reservoir, with Cochno Loch beyond the latter. ❸ From the summit head downhill (north) to the lower path, which turns right near the bottom. You'll soon come to the rocky entrance of The Whangie proper. It's easy to miss, so look carefully. Pass through the cleft in the huge rock face and follow the path for about 100m. Exit The Whangie and continue on the path to rejoin your ascent route, where you forked left at stage 2. From here continue back to the start.

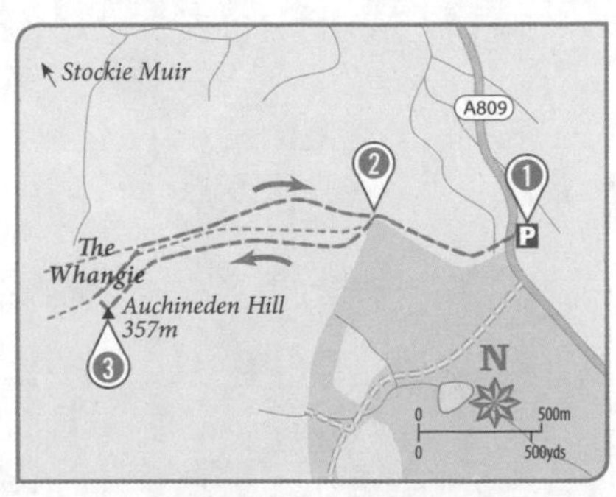

The Whangie rock feature – lovely to say and even better to stroll between. (Kevin McKell)

ADDED ADVENTURE

Linger longer. The Whangie is a place well worth hanging around (pardon the climbing pun) come the evening, checking out its nooks and crannies by the light of the moon. Don't forget your headtorch.

MAKE IT BIGGER

This peak is surrounded by masses of moorland stretching off into the distant Highlands. Admittedly, most of this is boggy and featureless, but there are options (tent in tow) to extend the walk to the Campsie Fells and Kilpatrick Hills to the west... Alternatively, couple it with an ascent of nearby Dumgoyne (page 222) and a celebratory trip to Glengoyne distillery.

FOR LITTLE ADVENTURERS

Nearby Craigend Castle in Mugdock Country Park (mugdock-country-park.org.uk) is a great place for exploring ruins and walking more trails – plus there's an adventure playground too.

FOR CAMPERS

As with Duncolm (page 234), the best place nearby is Bankell Farm (bankellfarm.co.uk; from £8pn).

FOR ADRENALINE LOVERS

The Whangie has served as training ground for many a climber. Several routes are available, with varying degrees of difficulty. Hire a guide or check tinyurl.com/thewhangieclimbing to help you figure them out.

FOR HUNGRY HIKERS

Although there is nowhere right by the walk, Blane Valley Inn in Blanefield (blanevalleyinn.co.uk) is worth a stop for a pint post-walk. It also offers a 'chipshop-style takeaway' for which you phone ahead; the menu includes vegetarian haggis. For supplies pre-walk, the nearest place is Londis or Tesco in Milngavie.

OTHER PRACTICALITIES

Bus 8 from Milngavie will drop you near the car park at the start. Toilets nearest here are in Mugdock Country Park (see above).

46 THE GREAT DIVIDE

LEARN GEOLOGY FROM A PEAK OVERLOOKING THE FAULT LINE WHERE SCOTLAND'S LOWLANDS AND HIGHLANDS COLLIDE

WHERE	Conic Hill, Stirling
STATS	↔ 4.2km (2½ miles) ↕ 361m ↗ 341m ↻ 2 hours
START/FINISH	Balmaha visitor centre car park ⚲ NS421909
TERRAIN	Well-defined woodland paths with steps, grassy slopes and tracks
MAPS	OS Explorer (1:25,000) 46; OS Landranger (1:50,000) 56

Unless you're a geologist, it can be difficult to make out certain land formations and demarcations without the assistance of an enthusiast. Come to Conic Hill, however, and you don't need to be an expert to see one of Britain's most fascinating geological features.

Formed when the ancient continents collided more than 400 million years ago – causing the uplands to rise into the mountains we see today, and the lowlands to sink into valleys and flatter landscapes – the Highland Boundary Fault is a geological line that runs from Arran on Scotland's west coast to Stonehaven in the east. Scything right through the peak of Conic Hill, the Fault marks the actual edge of the Highlands.

From its summit (or, more easily, from its first, false summit), gaze towards Loch Lomond and you will see how the island of Inchcailloch and other smaller islets run in a line – a continuation of the Fault – so straight you swear you could actually connect them with a ruler. So though you may come for the views, it's the ability to actually see how the earth was formed here that will keep you standing on the summit for longer than you ever imagined. Never has a geology lesson been such fun.

WALK THIS WAY

1 Head to the far north end of the car park to pick up the path to Conic Hill. Turn right on to it and follow it northeast through the woodland, passing through a mix of broadleaf, conifer, oak and beech trees, with the odd splash of

↑ Conic Hill rises above Loch Lomond on the line of a geological fault. (Garyellisphotography/D)

a rhododendron (particularly colourful in springtime) and keeping alert for a leaping red squirrel, before entering open country. Where the path forks take the left-hand track, following the West Highland Way. ❷ Continue as the long-distance path heads uphill, the terrain comprising steps, mud and rocky paths. Pass through a gate, climb more steps and cross a stream. Look for hen harriers quartering the grassy tussocks or for common buzzards soaring effortlessly past. ❸ Shortly afterwards (approximately 10m) – though not marked on the map – you will see a faint path tracking uphill, taking on the nose of Conic Hill. Turn right to do the same, using your hands in some places. Don't forget to look back every now and again as the full extent of the Highland Boundary Fault begins to reveal itself. The path reaches a false summit first then descends into quite boggy ground before taking you back up to the true summit of Conic Hill. ❹ Once you've enjoyed the views down to Loch Lomond and the isle of Inchcailloch (see *Added adventure*), and given yourself a geology lesson, leave the summit by a much more distinct path that tracks steeply downhill, roughly west, then joins the West Highland Way. Follow this southwest until it turns southeast to reach the point where you left the uphill path at stage 3. Now simply retrace your steps downhill through the woodland back to the start.

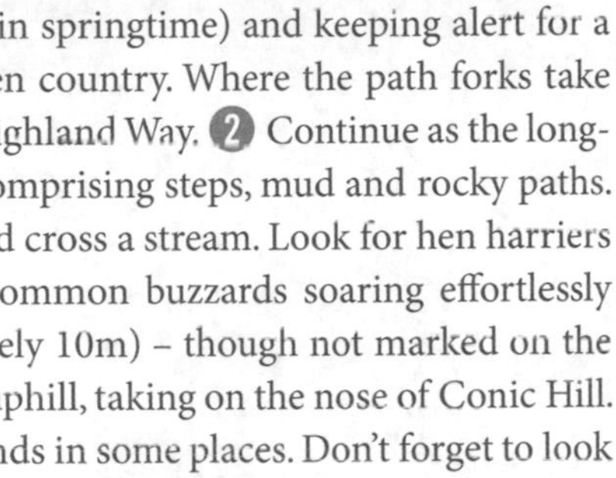

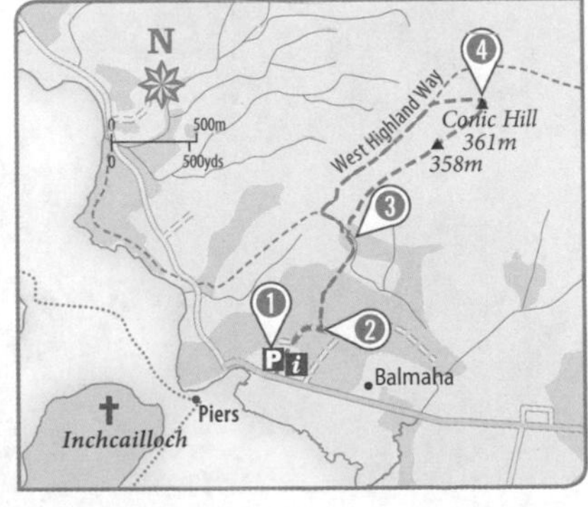

ADDED ADVENTURE

After you've summited the peak (the col adjacent to which, incidentally, makes for a good bivvy spot should it not be too windy), consider taking the regular summer ferry (balmahaboatyard.co.uk) over to Inchcailloch to explore the island. There are two walking trails – one through the woodland, another up to the highest point. It's a great place to wander through the oak trees that would once have encircled the loch, as well as through alder woodland and Scots pines. Also keep your eyes peeled for wildlife in the form of fallow deer, ospreys in the summer, Greenland white-fronted geese in the winter – which have flown here from above the Arctic Circle – and woodland birds such as siskin, goldcrest and crossbill. Then there's the burial ground at the former site of a church called St Kentigerna, which was used up until 1770.

MAKE IT BIGGER

Passing by Conic Hill's lower flanks is the West Highland Way (west-highland-way.co.uk), a long-distance footpath that runs from Milngavie, near Glasgow, to Fort William. You could walk a portion of the 151km (97-mile) route or use this hill as a starting point to walk the southern section back to Glasgow.

FOR LITTLE ADVENTURERS

The National Park's Balmaha visitor centre (lochlomond-trossachs.org), at the start of the walk, offers excellent resources to inspire kids to look for wildlife on their walk, and to learn about and draw the people who used to call this part of Loch Lomond home. There's a children's play area too.

FOR CAMPERS

Aside from the Camping and Caravanning Club site at Milarrochy, which is a bit more motorhome than tent, the nearest campsite is Drymen Camping (formerly known as Easter Drumquhassle Farm; drymencamping.co.uk; from £5pn).

FOR ADRENALINE LOVERS

Pack your swimsuit (or wetsuit) and take the plunge into Loch Lomond after your hike. In August, the famous loch is home to the annual Great Scottish Swim (greatrun.org/great-swim/great-scottish-swim), a sure sign that it's a good spot to dip your toe (or more, if you're feeling brave).

FOR HUNGRY HIKERS

The Oak Tree Inn opposite the car park (theoaktreeinn.co.uk) is a fine (indeed, award-winning) place to have a bite to eat or coffee before or after your hike. The nearest place to pick up supplies is the Co-op in Balloch.

OTHER PRACTICALITIES

Buses 309 and 308 from Glasgow and Milngavie drop off near the visitor centre (travelinescotland.com). There are public toilets inside the centre, which can be used for a nominal charge: income is ploughed back into running and maintaining the centre.

← Taking the more direct approach with a scramble up the nose of Conic Hill. (Neil S Price)

47 HILL SHOT

ASCENDING DUMGOYNE MAKES FOR THIRSTY WORK, SO GRANT YOURSELF A WEE DRAM FROM ITS DISTILLERY

WHERE	Dumgoyne, Stirling
STATS	↔ 3km (2 miles) ↕ 427m ↗ 400m ↻ 1½ hours
START/FINISH	Distillery car park NS526827. If not visiting the distillery, use limited spaces opposite or the layby at NY525833.
TERRAIN	Track, and steep, eroded hill paths
MAPS	OS Explorer (1:25,000) 348; OS Landranger (1:50,000) 57

Visible even from the city of Glasgow, 22.5km (14 miles) south is the small, stud-like peak of Dumgoyne. Part of the rarely mentioned Campsie Fells, Dumgoyne has long intrigued urbanites from afar. The hill's wonderfully protruding summit announces its heritage as a volcanic plug (formed when magma hardens in a vent of an active volcano). For a sublime example of the peak's explosive past, you need only gaze upon the wonderful line-up of perpendicular basalt columns (formed when magma cools very quickly close to the surface) that girdles its western face. On the summit is yet more evidence of this red-hot formation, with small air holes visible within the rocks.

Enjoy all these geophysical relics before heading back down to enjoy something equally as intoxicating at Glengoyne Distillery (www.glengoyne.com) – single malt whisky. In operation since 1833, the distillery sits on the physical fault line that separates Scotland's Highlands from its lowlands (the Highland Boundary Fault). This means that the amber spirit that you may taste here has the unique distinction of being distilled in the Highlands, but then matured in the lowlands (even if it is literally only across the road). It's also made with water that flows down from the very hill you've just climbed.

When walking here it's worth remembering that during the 1800s (when the government imposed ridiculously high taxes on alcohol sales) whisky was distilled covertly – and illegally – out on these tops.

↑ Dumgoyne rises above the local whisky distillery. (David Robertson/A)

The whisky makers were forced to conceal their equipment in the hidden folds of the hills and woodlands, remains of which can sometimes be made out by the eagle-eyed today. Nowadays, at least, we can celebrate this Scottish staple without secrecy – we'll certainly drink to that! *Slàinte*!

WALK THIS WAY

1 From the parking area, go up the track on your right, heading east. You'll pass some houses, soon after which the track forks. Keep right here, crossing the stream, and cut through the trees to emerge below another house (marked Blairgar on maps). Go through the farm gate and, at the edge of the trees, you'll pick out a faint path. Turn left on to it, cutting through fields and over a stile, until you are deposited on to the path that leads up the open hillside of Dumgoyne. **2** Follow the path as it heads uphill, straight up, then swings to the right to tackle the top from its less knee-busting side via a dirt track on the grassy hillside. Continue to enjoy the peak, keeping your eyes peeled for air holes in the rocks that nod to Dumgoyne's volcanic past. The highest point is marked by a large stone. **3** After enjoying your summit success, with views over to the city of Glasgow and beyond, simply retrace your steps to the start.

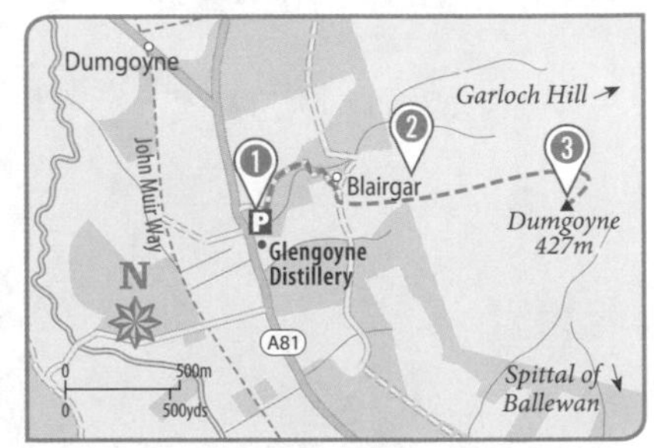

Glengoyne distillery – the perfect reward post-peak. (Mari Hobkirk)

ADDED ADVENTURE

Keep a lookout for a small area called the Spittal of Ballewan (NS545811), which was once owned by the medieval Knights Templar. After this detour, raise a glass to the troops at the hillside distillery where you can also learn all about the distilling process.

MAKE IT BIGGER

For views of the volcanic plug you've just claimed continue on to bag Garloch Hill (NS555835) and then on to Earl's Seat (NS569838) before looping back round to your start. To lengthen it further, start the whole walk at Strathblane (NS564793), around 5km (3 miles) to the east, and consider coupling it with The Whangie (page 214). For a real challenge you could add this hill to walking the nearby John Muir Way (johnmuirway.org), which stretches 215km (134 miles) from Helensburgh on Scotland's west coast to Dunbar on its east.

FOR LITTLE ADVENTURERS

With the promise (for adults) of a distillery at the end, this walk's pleasures lie for little ones in taking the bus from Glasgow city centre and simply claiming the summit itself. Afterwards head to the Beech Tree Inn (see *For hungry h*ikers) where there are farm animals on hand to entertain little ones.

FOR CAMPERS

There are not many options near here. The best is Drymen Camping (drymencamping.co.uk; from £5pn).

FOR ADRENALINE LOVERS

Take your mountain bike. Starting from the town of Milngavie head north to the hill to do a 17-mile loop with Dumgoyne as the highlight before looping back via Carbeth to the start. (See tinyurl.com/dumgoyneMTB for route information.)

FOR HUNGRY HIKERS

The Beech Tree Inn in Dumgoyne (thebeechtreeinn.co.uk) is a restaurant and bar with a large garden and farm animals to keep the kids amused. Best to grab supplies in Glasgow or Milngavie on your way here.

OTHER PRACTICALITIES

Take bus number 10 from Glasgow: you'll need to request a stop at the distillery. There are no toilets at the start: go in Glasgow before you leave or (if you are a customer) use those at the Beech Tree Inn.

48 CITY CENTRE SUMMIT

ADD A SUMMIT TO YOUR SHOPPING WITH AN ASCENT OF CITYSIDE ARTHUR'S SEAT

WHERE	Arthur's Seat, Edinburgh
STATS	↔ 3.5km (2¼ miles) ↕ 251m ↗ 216m ↻ 2½ hours
START/FINISH	Holyrood Palace car park ⚲ NT270737
TERRAIN	Clear tracks over some rough and rocky ground, particularly near summits and crags
MAPS	OS Explorer (1:25,000) 350; OS Landranger (1:50,000) 66

Very rarely do you get the chance to build a stellar hill into a day on the high street, but when it comes to the city of Edinburgh, it would be a travesty not to do so. Sitting in Holyrood Park, at the end of the Royal Mile, is the distinctly shapely summit of Arthur's Seat. Formed by a volcano that erupted 350 million years ago, then sliced by glaciers into the wedge we see today, it has seen more than 10,000 years of human usage. Nowadays it is a place just for walking outdoors, but previously it has served (as is the case for many of this book's little hills) as the site of an Iron Age hillfort, as well as a quarry, farmland and hunting-gathering territory.

The name of this 251m-high peak is the subject of dispute, but probably derives from links with the legendary King Arthur. Some believe it is the actual location for Arthur's castle, Camelot. A rather different legend linked to the site, enshrined in Robert Fergusson's 1773 poem *Auld Reekie*, tells that if young girls wash their face in fresh morning dew on May Day they will become even more beautiful.

Whether or not you are a young girl, there's no need to wash your face in dew to experience the rejuvenating powers of this peak. A simple walk up to its summit will clear away any cobwebs and materialistic cynicism brought on while gazing into the city's shop windows!

WALK THIS WAY

❶ Leave the car park, cross Queen's Drive and head south towards Holyrood Park (tinyurl.com/holyroodpark). Once inside turn right and take the main track that bears left towards the back (east) of Salisbury Crags. You'll be heading up towards a gap between the two craggy lines. ❷ Stay on the main track, ignoring the turning to your left, then take the grassy track that cuts

↑ From shops to sheer edges – the joy of a city-side peak. (Aleksandr Vrublevskiy/S)

uphill steeply, aiming for the top of Salisbury Crags. Follow the path along the top of this ridge, going as close to the edge as you safely dare, and you'll begin to see people on the summit of Arthur's Seat to the east. ❸ Just before the crag ends, take the path on your left and descend to a lower path, then cut right to join the central path. This comprises steps that zigzag upwards all the way to the summit trig of Arthur's Seat. ❹ Take in the views of the city, looking for landmarks such as Holyrood Palace, Edinburgh Castle, and the Princes Street shops, but also taking in the southern vista to discern Duddingston Loch and the sneaking pathway of the John Muir Way. To start your descent head northeast on a track with a safety railing, at the bottom of which there are myriad paths from which to choose. Go straight ahead, initially climbing, then contouring around the flanks of Whinny Hill (an optional add-on). As St Margaret's Loch nears, follow the path round to the west, heading steadily downhill and back towards your entry point from Queen's Drive.

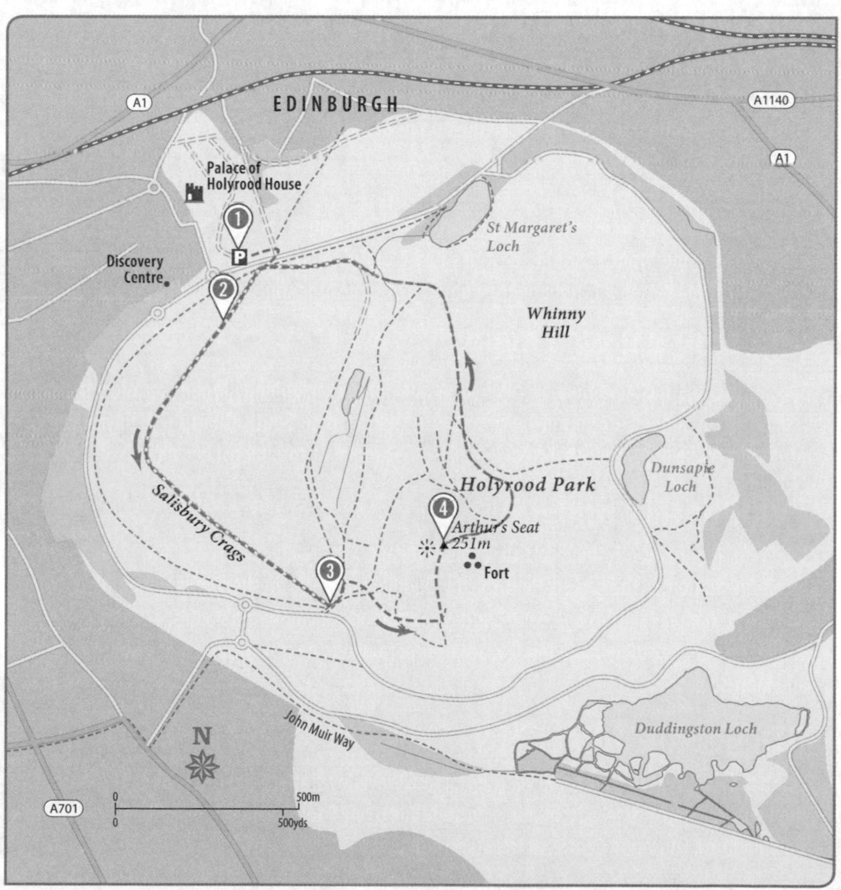

ADDED ADVENTURE

Be sure to spend time checking out all the nooks and crannies on the crags around this hillock. It was here in the 1830s that some boys discovered a set of small coffins that are often linked to the Burke and Hare murders. (These comprised 16 killings over ten months in 1828, all to supply an Edinburgh doctor with bodies to dissect for medical research.) See those same coffins now in Edinburgh's National Museum of Scotland (nms.ac.uk/national-museum-of-scotland).

MAKE IT BIGGER

The John Muir Way runs below the lower flanks of Arthur's Seat. It's a 215km (134-mile) trail that crosses Scotland from west coast to east. Tick off Arthur's Seat as part of a longer trek, or use the summit it to kickstart a section of the Way.

FOR LITTLE ADVENTURERS

Kids will enjoy the hill for sure, but after explaining to them about the origins of this little volcano, be sure to pop into Dynamic Earth (dynamicearth.co.uk) at the foot of Arthur's Seat. This offers a journey back in time to see the origins of the planet, polar extremes and more.

FOR CAMPERS

The award-winning Morton Hall Caravan and Camping Park (meadowhead.co.uk/mortonhall-home; from £18pn) is best; it's just 15 minutes' drive or an hour's walk from the city centre. Even better, it is right on the doorstep of some other fine hillocks in the Pentlands.

FOR ADRENALINE LOVERS

Salisbury Crags has traditionally been a venue for rock climbing, though erosion means that access is limited to permit-holders and is restricted to South Quarry (tinyurl.com/southquarry). To apply (which is free), email hs.rangers@scotland.gsi.gov.uk.

FOR HUNGRY HIKERS

Being in the heart of the Scottish capital means you really are spoilt for choice. One recommendation is The Sheep Heid Inn in Duddingston (thesheepheidedinburgh.co.uk) where you can play skittles and eat a Sunday roast at one of Edinburgh's oldest watering holes. To pick up supplies there are a fair few small supermarkets nearby including Sainsbury's Local and Morrisons.

OTHER PRACTICALITIES

Edinburgh is very well connected via trains. From Waverley station, you can walk to the start of the walk in approximately 20 minutes or grab Bus 6 or 35 to Holyrood House. Toilets are near Holyrood Park Education Centre, at the start of the walk.

A heavenly view of Arthur's Seat as seen from above the graveyard at Canongate Church. (evenfh/Shutterstock)

49 DUMPLING ON THE SIDE

MAX OUT ON VIEWS WITH MINIMUM EFFORT ON A DUNBARTONSHIRE PEAK WITH AN ENDEARING NICKNAME

WHERE	Duncryne, West Dunbartonshire
STATS	↔ 1.25km (¾ mile) ↕ 142m ↗ 72m ↻ 1 hour
START/FINISH	Car park in Gartocharn ♀ NS428863
TERRAIN	Grassy paths (can get muddy)
MAPS	OS Explorer (1:25,000) 38; OS Landranger (1:50,000) 56

Names can say an awful lot about a hill. Typically they hint at the difficulty involved in climbing the peak (such as Scotland's Devil's Peak) or are simply slightly rude (The Paps of Jura, anyone?). So it's nice to come across a peak with a nickname so heart-warmingly endearing and so tongue-tantalisingly tasty that it instantly holds a special place in walkers' hearts. Enter Duncryne, aka The Dumpling – in recognition of its lump-like shape – which rises above the hamlet of Gartocharn. Have you ever heard such a wonderfully succulent sobriquet? Too delicious an hors d'oeuvre for any visitor to the Loch Lomond area to resist taking a gargantuan bite out of. It also nods to the perfect Sunday lunch, which this little hill pairs up with beautifully being either a fantastic pre- or post-meal stroll.

Better still, Duncryne's nickname is far from the sole appetising thing about it. The views you get from the succulent summit (142m) are equally as mouth-watering. Don't just take my word for it. The legendary hillwalker, author and broadcaster Tom Weir reckoned that The Dumpling offered the very best views of Loch Lomond and its islands, as well as a sweeping vista of the southern Highlands including The Cobbler (worth a walk too, incidentally), Ben Lomond and Ben Vorlich to name but a few of the landmarks visible. So whet your appetite with this scrumptious summit and find your legs aching for a second helping.

↑ Looking over Loch Lomond from the perfect perch of Duncryne Hill. (Joop Snijder Photography/S)

WALK THIS WAY

❶ The walk starts from Gartocharn car park. From here head along Church Street back to the main road on which you entered the hamlet (Old Military Road). Cross this and turn left, then take the first road on your right (auspiciously called Duncryne Road). Follow this up to a pull-in by some houses at ⚲ NS428863. ❷ From here take the signposted path through a gate on the left into the trees. Follow the path northeast until another gate leads you out of the woods. ❸ Bearing northeast, the path funnels you along between two fences with fields either side. You'll come to a final gate; pass through this to access open woodland on the hill flanks, with scattered gorse bushes adding vibrant colour. At the fork, follow the path veering right, climbing uphill over bracken-covered slopes and out on to the clear summit, where bluebells shimmer in spring. ❹ Eat up the far-reaching views that this tiny, unassuming dumpling offers, especially the famous vista to the north and west – of Loch Lomond itself – before returning along the same route to the start point.

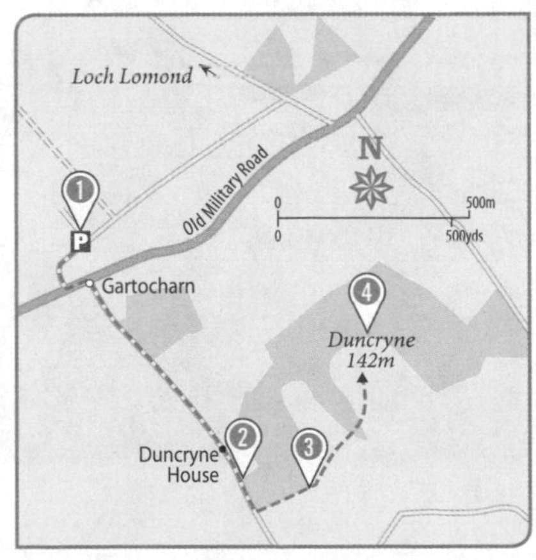

Don't be fooled by its stature, Duncryne packs a view-filled punch. (Phil Seale/A)

ADDED ADVENTURE

Before the walk, cross Loch Lomond by taking a ride on the steamship *Maid of the Loch*, the last major paddle steamer to be built in Britain (maidoftheloch.org).

MAKE IT BIGGER

This really is the hill to inspire you to climb more (and higher). From its summit you'll be rewarded with views of The Cobbler, Ben Vorlich and Ben Lomond. You may want a slightly nearer starting point, but the choice is yours.

FOR LITTLE ADVENTURERS

Loch Lomond (lovelochlomond.com/activities/kid) offers a host of things to do with kids – from an aquarium to a bird-of-prey centre and more besides.

FOR CAMPERS

The nearest is Cashel Campsite (tinyurl.com/cashelcamp; from £14.55pn) which, though geared up more for caravans, offers great views over the water.

FOR ADRENALINE LOVERS

Nothing at the hill itself, but there are options at a certain famous waterbody nearby. Check out Loch Lomond Leisure (lochlomond-scotland.com; from £10) for a range of water-based thrills – from wakeboarding to 'ringo rides' and banana boats.

FOR HUNGRY HIKERS

For something to eat you need to head south to Alexandria, 8.8km (5½ miles) away. Try Corries on Balloch Road (01389 753552) for great breakfast, teas and coffees. For pre-hike supplies head to the Co-op in Balloch.

OTHER PRACTICALITIES

Bus 309 calls in at Gartocharn as it travels between Balloch and Alexandria (which, in turn, are each served by buses from Glasgow; tinyurl.com/gartocharn-bus). Nearest toilets are in Balloch, 6.5km (4 miles) southwest.

50 ACCESSIBLE WILDERNESS

ON GLASGOW'S FRINGES LIES A TOUGH LITTLE PEAK THAT REWARDS WALKERS' STRENUOUS EFFORTS WITH TRANQUILLITY

WHERE	Duncolm, West Dunbartonshire
STATS	↔ 13km (8 miles) ↕ 401m ↗ 370m ↻ 4–5 hours
START/FINISH	Old Kilpatrick Braes car park ⚲ NS469728
TERRAIN	Well-defined track to start, then grassy, rough and boggy from Loch Humphrey
MAPS	OS Explorer (1:25,000) 342, 348; OS Landranger (1:50,000) 64

'Nothing in this world worth having comes easy.' I can't help but think that whichever wise soul first said these words had previously paid a visit to the highest point in West Dunbartonshire's Kilpatrick Hills, the steep grassy dome of Duncolm. Its stature may be unremarkable compared with other Scottish peaks – barely making it to the 400m mark – yet the distance required to reach it certainly takes some effort. Given the length of the walk, you may as well tack on other 'Duncolms' in the process – with Lower and Middle Duncolms being easy to bag on the way.

The beauty of this peak, set amidst rolling bronze, green and gold moorland, is the contrast between the toil required to gain it, and its proximity to Scotland's second city. After only a 20-minute train ride from Glasgow's bustling centre, you will find yourself amidst profound tranquillity. Striding outwards and upwards, you will feel a million miles away from the urban sprawl you so rapidly left behind. Bliss.

WALK THIS WAY

❶ From the car park take the road that goes through an underpass beneath the A82. Turn left on to the minor road, passing the gasworks, then turn right on to the lane that is marked as a path to the Kilpatrick Hills. Stay on this until the road becomes a track – passing dark, dense pine forest on your right – and starts to curve right and steeply uphill. Look back for views of

↑ The wild peak of Duncolm – handily accessible from the centre of Glasgow via a bus ride. (Anne Neilson)

the River Clyde as the grassy track stays northeast. Soon the grass-edged waters of Loch Humphrey appear ahead; the track descends to it. ❷ As you reach Loch Humphrey's shores, ignoring any turn-offs, cross the outflow and keep heading straight on (northeast). The track becomes grassier and narrower before contouring around the flanks of Little Duncolm (380m; feel free to climb and tick off). ❸ Ahead is the second Duncolm – this time the Middle one (393m). You can go up and over the hill, or, to bypass it, veer left at the fork to skirt its base before rejoining the summit path. You will now see (the final and true) Duncolm in front of you. ❹ Follow the path to climb directly to the summit you've been targeting. Enjoy views over to Loch Lomond and the Campsie Fells (see if you can spot Conic Hill, page 218; and Dumgoyne, page 222). Or look south to see Erskine Bridge that marks the start of Glasgow: so near, yet feeling so far. ❺ Simply retrace your steps to the start.

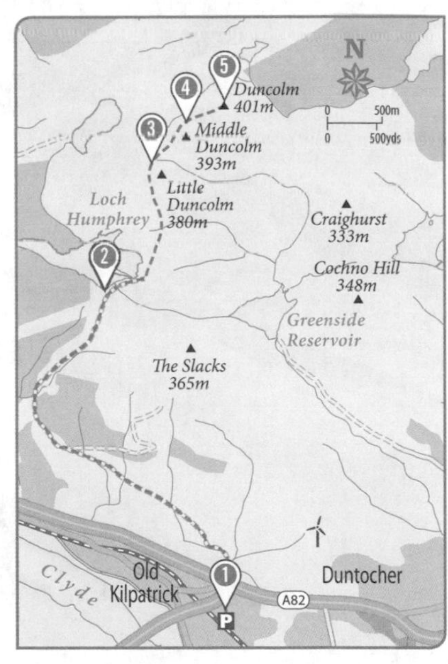

Middle and Little Duncolms looking epic under a thick coating of snow. (Ross Vernal)

ADDED ADVENTURE

The area may be easily accessible, but once up in its hills, it feels properly removed from the town: true adventure stuff. For an overnight stay, you could pitch a tent by one of the lochs or sling up a hammock in the Kilpatrick Braes woodland.

MAKE IT BIGGER

There's a smattering of little lumps and bumps to tick off while you're here. To the west you can try Doughnot Hill (375m). To the east there's Craighurst (333m) and Cochno (348m), then, on your return to Kilpatrick, you can opt to include an ascent of the deliciously named The Slacks (365m), southwest of Greenside Reservoir.

FOR LITTLE ADVENTURERS

Not much more to recommend on the hill itself, though nearby Glasgow obviously has a lot of child-friendly activities to try (peoplemakeglasgow.com).

FOR CAMPERS

The nearest is Bankell Farm (bankellfarm.co.uk; from £8pppn), which offers sheltered pitches and is popular with walkers doing the West Highland Way (west-highland-way.co.uk).

FOR ADRENALINE LOVERS

On the River Clyde nearby you can try your hand at urban bungee jumping. Highland Fling Bungee Jumping (bungeejumpscotland.co.uk) offer jumps from £79.

FOR HUNGRY HIKERS

Lots of options in Clydebank, 5km (3 miles) away. Go for chips or cocktails (plus much else besides) in a converted ship at McMonagles in Clydebank (mcmonagles.co.uk). For supplies there's Nisa in Old Kirkpatrick, near the start of the walk, or supermarkets in Clydebank.

OTHER PRACTICALITIES

Kilpatrick is reached by train and bus from Glasgow city centre (traveline-Scotland.org.uk). No toilets at the start. Try Clydebank (in the supermarket) before your walk.

51 ARROCHAR ALPS ADJACENT

JUDGE WHETHER THE POINTY PEAK OF BEN A'AN IS ALSO WORTHY OF AN ALPINE MONIKER

WHERE	Ben A'an, Stirling
STATS	↔ 4km (2½ miles) ↕ 461m ↗ 362m ↻ 2½ hours
START/FINISH	Ben A'an car park ⚲ NN509070
TERRAIN	Clear path through woodland, then steep ascent over rocks and heather to summit
MAPS	OS Explorer (1:25,000) 39; OS Landranger (1:50,000) 56

When it comes to giving out names, Ben A'an (Gaelic for 'small pointed peak') certainly received the right one. With its pyramidal profile and modest height of 461m, its moniker effectively takes the Ronseal approach to appellations. Yet perhaps the funniest thing about this Stirling peak is that it's not even a complete hill in its own right. Although it stands boldly sandwiched between the inviting lochs of Achray and Katrine, and has the appearance of a perfect mini-mountain, it is in fact just an outlier of the much more rounded and boring Meall Gainmheich, which lies to the north.

But who cares about such a mere technicality when Ben A'an offers such an exciting ascent, such a dramatic profile and some of the best views of the Trossachs you could ever hope to get. Rising above the Trossachs Forest Ben A'an sits in an area rich in wildlife. Red and roe deer browse along its flanks, golden eagles soar overhead and red squirrels clamber in the trees above you as you walk. After all, this is the peak that offers a panorama over the Arrochar Alps, a slightly tongue-in-cheek name. So throw detail to the wind and go climb the hill that's not really a hill – but looks like a mountain.

↑ The Alps? Or Arrochar? A trip to Ben A'an is the only way to decide. (mountaintreks/S)

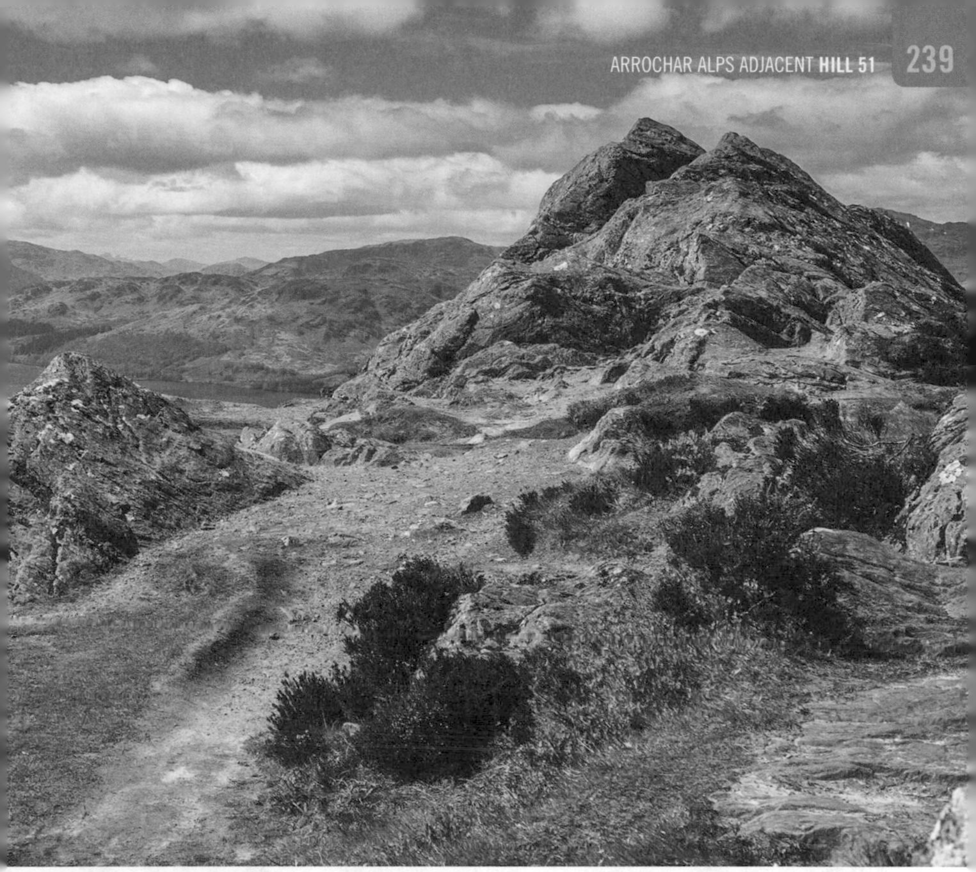

WALK THIS WAY

❶ Cross the road (north) from the car park in order to take the track opposite. The climb begins straight away, initially on tarmac then on a rough and rocky path, through some trees and over the stream via a bridge. ❷ Continue to climb on the well-marked path. The OS map suggests the area to be forested, but this is not presently the case. Forestry Commission Scotland has felled non-native trees, and is replacing them with indigenous species. At the time of writing, this part of the walk is thus quite bare, but that should change within a few years. Soon you'll see the conical Ben A'an summit rising straight ahead – its profile belying its small size. As you return to the cover of trees, it's worth stopping for a breather before the steep climb begins. ❸ Continue upwards to the right, bearing northeast of the summit and gradually leaving the trees behind. The climb increases in

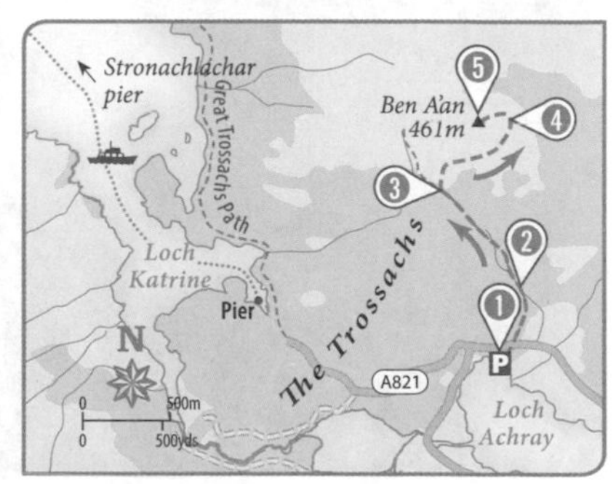

steepness throughout, and you may need to use your hands occasionally; the path is rough and can wash away a little after a lot of rain. Eventually the gradient relents just before the path swings back on itself to crest the summit from behind and head southeast. You are now on an open grass- and heather-covered hillside that is punctuated by the odd well-positioned boulder (perfect for taking a seat or standing atop). Before taking the final steps, take a minute to walk a few metres north to check out the beautiful view down tree-lined Loch Katrine to the west. Rimmed by rising peaks, the loch's water sparkles as it stretches further than the eye can see. ❹ Facing south, now head up to the summit on one of the many boot-beaten paths through the heather. ❺ From the top the views really open out. Looking south, you can see the woodland-coated Trossachs and craggy Ben Venue. To the west lie the perfectly pointed Arrochar Alps (from which this little summit definitely feels as though it was separated at birth). Enjoy the vista for as long as you like then retrace your steps to the start.

↑ The newly pitched path makes the first part of the ascent to Ben A'an a breeze. (Neil S Price)

ADDED ADVENTURE

Make getting there part of the adventure. In summer a steamship (lochkatrine.com) runs from Stronachlachar pier (NN404102) to Trossachs pier at the visitor centre on Loch Katrine (NN495072), from where it is approximately 2km (1¼ miles) along the A821 to the start.

MAKE IT BIGGER

Ben A'an can be the start of your exploration of the peaks that make up a diminutive ridge running northwest that includes Meall Gainmheich, Bealach na h-Imriche, Cnoc Odhar – and beyond. Or simply make the getting there bigger. Take the ferry from Stronachlachar pier, climb Ben A'an then hire a bike at Loch Katrine (tinyurl.com/lochkatrinebikes) and take the cycle route back to the pier. Perfect.

FOR LITTLE ADVENTURERS

The climb itself and the rocky summit are really quite an adventure for kids, as would be the boat ride and cycle route. For those not up to the challenge you could simply have a short walk along the bridleway (Great Trossachs Path) that runs along Loch Katrine's northern shore or do one of the other strolls waymarked from Loch Katrine visitor centre (lochkatrine.com). Children older than ten may fancy 'going ape' (see *For adrenaline lovers*).

FOR CAMPERS

The nearest is Cobleland Campsite (tinyurl.com/cobleland; Apr–Oct; from £14.55pn) just south of Aberfoyle, 26km (16 miles) away. Pitches are set beneath towering oaks, and the River Forth flows through the site.

FOR ADRENALINE LOVERS

Go Ape: literally. At The Lodge forest visitor centre in Aberfoyle (tinyurl.com/thelodgetrossachs) nearby is a Go Ape treetop assault course (goape.co.uk; from £25). Clip in to experience two of the longest zip lines in Britain.

FOR HUNGRY HIKERS

There's a café at Trossachs pier, Loch Katrine, where you can grab snacks and hot and cold drinks. Further east along the A821 The Byre Inn (byreinn.co.uk) is a refurbished cowshed where you can try locally sourced, seasonal food and drink including wine and beer. For supplies pre-trip try the Co-op in either Aberfoyle or Callander.

OTHER PRACTICALITIES

No bus to start. The nearest you can get to is Aberfoyle but then you'd need a taxi from there. The nearest toilets are at the car park at Loch Katrine visitor centre.

Keep your eyes peeled for resident golden eagles. (Vladimir Kogan Michael/S) ↑

52 TROUBLE AND FIFE

ASCEND A TOWNSIDE HILL COMPLETE WITH IRON AGE FORT THEN WANDER THROUGH SOME GORGEOUS GORGES

WHERE	Falkland Hill, Fife
STATS	↔ 2.1km (1¼ miles) ↕ 434m ↗ 90m ↻ 1 hour
START/FINISH	Relay station car park NO251058
TERRAIN	Typical hill paths on grassy and rough ground
MAPS	OS Explorer (1:25,000) 370; OS Landranger (1:50,000) 58

The dome-shaped summit of East Lomond, aka Falkland Hill, lures many a visitor from the nearby historical town of Falkland. Looming majestically from the southwest over Falkland's old buildings, many of which have stood for three centuries or more, East Lomond seems to call out for people to head to its top.

And many do. From mountain bikers to paragliders, runners to walkers, anyone who takes the time to make it to the summit (434m) will be rewarded with views of the Borders and the Fife coast. Once you've climbed up, you can also explore the depressions that mark an Iron Age hillfort and imagine being an ancient inhabitant standing on this prime point. Plus there's ample opportunity to extend the hike by adding on more adventurous routes both on and off the summit – and there are moorland birds such as red grouse to admire as well. Nae bad for a wee hill…

↑ The sprawling summit of Iron Age hillfort studded Falkland Hill. (Sasalan999/D)

WALK THIS WAY

1 From the car park and picnic site, follow the road back to the masts of the relay station then turn left on to the track that heads uphill to the west. **2** Where it forks, keep to the left for easy access to the trig point and the high point of East Lomond/Falkland Hill. **3** At the summit take time to enjoy the view northeast to the town of Falkland, east to the Fife coast and south to the Borders. Be sure to check out the remains of the fort. Remains of a cairn – a circular, grass-covered cluster of stones – can be made out on the summit over an impressive diameter of approximately 13m. Afterwards simply retrace your steps to the start, trying not to start should a grouse whirr up from your feet.

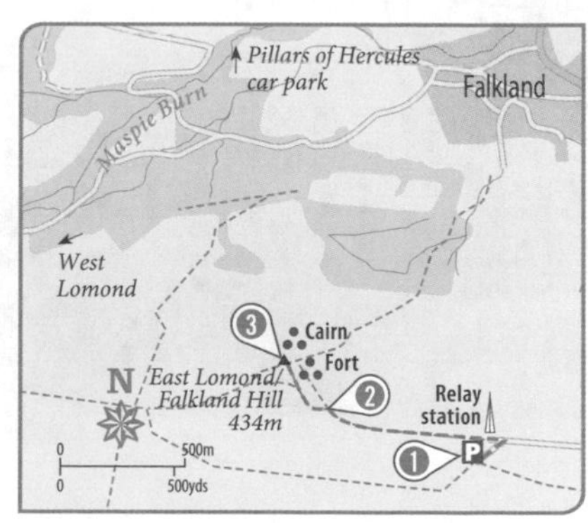

Maspie Glen waterfall – a perfect place to linger. (Sasalan999/D)

ADDED ADVENTURE

Start your walk from the Pillars of Hercules car park west of Falkland. Follow the path south out of the car park heading for Falkland House School. Take the path that runs southwest alongside the gorge of Maspie Burn to an undercut waterfall at the top. This route offers dramatic landscapes before you even reach the heights of the hill. From the summit, return to town via the steep north side to descend into Douk Plantation and its ravine-encased burn.

MAKE IT BIGGER

Continue west from the summit to tick off the sister peak and tip of the sprawling escarpment: West Lomond (522m) lies around 6km (3.7 miles) away. Collectively, this pair of volcanic hills is known as the 'Paps of Fife'. Keep your eyes peeled on West Lomond's lower (southern) end for eroded scarring and a cleft in the rocks. This was once known as John Knox's Pulpit, site of religious ceremonies in the 17th century.

FOR LITTLE ADVENTURERS

Want more outdoor space for the kids to run around in? The National Trust of Scotland's Falkland Palace and Garden is a stone's throw away (tinyurl.com/falklandpalace). Experience the splendour of Mary Queen of Scots' favourite abode and the ruins of this 12th-century castle.

FOR CAMPERS

Pillars of Hercules (pillars.co.uk; from £6pn) is a gem of a site close to the start of the walk. It offers a basic place to pitch with campfires encouraged – so remember to bring your marshmallows. . . It also houses an organic café (see *For hungry hikers*).

FOR ADRENALINE LOVERS

Skydive St Andrews offers tandem jumps at £270 that guarantee a huge adrenaline rush (skydivestandrews.co.uk). Alternatively, join the annual fell race to East Lomond's summit every August (tinyurl.com/lomondfellrun), enjoy a series of downhill mountain-bike tracks or become one of the paragliders often seen running off its grassy slopes.

FOR HUNGRY HIKERS

Best place is at Pillars of Hercules campsite (see above), where a café offers organic vegetarian and vegan food with veggies fresh from the garden. All cakes are homebaked, and the farm shop sells bread and other produce – perfect for making sandwiches. After hours, try a pint at The Bruce Inn (thebrucefalkland.co.uk), where the cosy bar has a woodburning stove.

OTHER PRACTICALITIES

There are toilets in the car park at the start. An alternative start point can be the car park (also with toilets) to the west near Craigmead (NO227061), from where a path leads east to the summit. Buses (stagecoachbus.com) run to Falkland from Perth, Kinross, Cupar, and Ladybank railway station.

53 SUMMITS AND SPECTRES

ASCEND BEN HIANT TO ADMIRE A REMOTE SCOTTISH PENINSULA AND EXPLORE A GHOST VILLAGE

WHERE	Ben Hiant, Highlands
STATS	↔ 4.5km (2¾ miles) ↕ 528m ↗ 357m ↻ 2–3 hours
START/FINISH	Roadside parking at NM551641
TERRAIN	Gravel track to start then rough grassy paths that can be boggy
MAPS	OS Explorer (1:25,000) 390; OS Landranger (1:50,000) 40

Being the westernmost finger of land in mainland Britain, you might imagine the Ardnamurchan Peninsula to be pretty well known – but it's not. The explanation, perhaps, is to do with access. To reach somewhere this remote requires either a long drive along some fairly dicey single-track roads or all the faff of a ferry over Loch Linnhe (which, even then, is followed by driving along some fairly dicey single-track roads).

But then it's the tricky access that has helped Ardnamurchan remain blissfully free of people, whether tourist crowds or residents. Consequently, it's a sprawling slither of wilderness-walking potential, with coastal trails, wild woodland and curvaceous peaks all ripe for adventure.

The little mass of Ben Hiant is arguably the best of the lot. Not only does it have a very fetching rump on which to climb, but the reward for doing so is some incredible views (including over to the Inner Hebridean islands of Muck, Eigg and Rum, to name but a few). Moreover, on the hill's lower flanks sit the remains of an old village, reluctantly abandoned in 1828 during the infamous Highland Clearances of the 18th–19th centuries.

And then there's the not insignificant matter of the Scottish wildcat. This precise stretch of Ardnamurchan offers the country's highest chance of spotting this increasingly rare creature;

↑ Impressive volcanic bumps can be spotted on Ben Hiant. (App555/D)

particularly in the hours after dusk. Take your binoculars with you and – it goes without saying, but I'll say it anyway – keep your camera to hand, too. You can get your small summit, with a side of historical ruins, and the possibility of a celebrity animal, all wrapped up on a far-flung peninsula. Perfect.

WALK THIS WAY

1 From the layby parking area head north for a few metres to pick up the gated gravel track on your left. Keep your eyes peeled to spot the cairn from where the hill path starts and head steeply up it. You soon reach an escarpment where the path cuts to your left on to a grassy slope that takes you up on to the ridge. **2** The summit will lie ahead of you as you follow the ridgeline to a shoulder, from where the path cuts left under the hill's southern flanks before taking you to the summit. **3** Enjoy the views and then simply retrace your steps back to the start. Only the sharpest (or luckiest) eyes will spot a wildcat, but you have a fair chance of red, roe or fallow deer brooding across the fells.

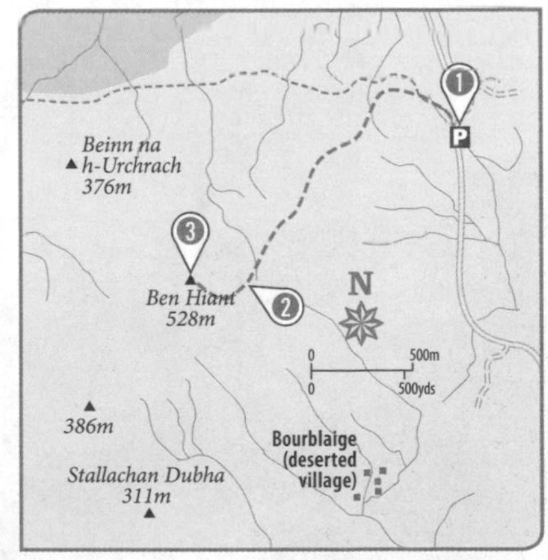

The jaw-droppingly gorgeous view from Ben Hiant out to Camas nan Geall. (Derek Beattle Images/S)

ADDED ADVENTURE

Take time to check out the deserted village of Bourblaige, a once-thriving community whose inhabitants were turfed out to make way for sheep grazing during the infamous Highland Clearances. Now all that remains is a few ruined buildings and the sad shadows of parallel lines in the ground where the villagers once grew vegetables. This is a truly haunting place to contemplate a dark moment in Britain's history.

MAKE IT BIGGER

Why stop when you're so close to being the westernmost thing on mainland Britain? Continue west, across the peninsula to Ardnamurchan Point. Don't be fooled by the lighthouse – as it's the tiny bump of Corrachadh Mor to the south that marks the geographical extremity. By pure coincidence, it's also the perfect peak on which to pitch your tent for a spot of wild camping.

FOR LITTLE ADVENTURERS

Situated nearby, the Ardnamurchan Natural History Visitor Centre in Acharacle (ardnamurchannaturalhistorycentre.co.uk) offers the chance to learn about the wildlife located on this isolated peninsula. There are also several little beaches along the way to Acharacle where the nippers can burn off some energy.

FOR CAMPERS

Lochan Nan Al (ardnamurchancamping.co.uk) offers pitches for tents (as well as a field and hook-up for campervans/caravans) right on the tip of the Ardnamurchan Peninsula. There are views over to the Isle of Mull, and the site lies within 10 minutes' walk of the local pub.

FOR ADRENALINE LOVERS

The coast around the Ardnamurchan Peninsula is a great place for spotting minke whales and bottlenose dolphins come summer. So consider hiring a sea kayak to look for them from the water.

FOR HUNGRY HIKERS

There are not masses of options here especially since the nearest hotel offering food has now closed. Nearest option is Ardshealach Lodge in Acharacle (ardshealach-lodge.co.uk), 23km (14½ miles) away from the start, which serves seasonal and home-grown food. The best place for supplies is Fort William before you come out this way.

OTHER PRACTICALITIES

If coming from the south, save time on long winding roads by taking the Corran Ferry over to Ardnamurchan (argyll-bute.gov.uk/corran-ferry-timetable; from £8.20/vehicle). Shiel Bus 506 (shielbuses.co.uk) runs between Fort William (where there's a train station, accessed by a number of routes including the Caledonian Sleeper from London) and Kilchoan, so can drop you near to the start of the walk. No toilets at the start: the nearest are in Acharacle village centre or in Kilchoan Community Centre (which also has a shower).

54 WALKING WARM-UP

WARM UP FOR THE BEN ON FORT WILLIAM'S UNASSUMING WEE HILL OF DRUIMARBIN

WHERE	Druimarbin, Highlands
STATS	↔ 1.2km (¾ mile) ↕ 287m ↗ 150m ↻ 1 hour
START/FINISH	Parking area above Upper Auchintore ⚲ NN096720
TERRAIN	Grassy path – often boggy and slippery
MAPS	OS Explorer (1:25,000) 392; OS Landranger (1:50,000) 41

Let's be honest – if the town of Fort William (affectionately known as 'Fort Bill') is famous for anything it's certainly not *small* hills. Located adjacent to the highest mountain in Britain, Ben Nevis, means that most hikers who descend on the town come with one purpose and one purpose alone – to stand atop this great peak. And, chances are, if you've come here with hills on your mind, that's what you intend to do too.

However, such lofty intentions do not prevent you from using one of the peaks that stands less tall and proud as a warm-up for travel-weary muscles, whether before breakfast or the night before your big hike. With a short track leading from a roadside parking area, plus, weather permitting, the views offered of the mighty Ben (as well as over forest to Loch Linnhe, to the west), Druimarbin fits the bill for such a leg-stretch.

It's not a bad place for wildlife either. In spring, male black grouse congregate near the roadside to hiss and pop in display; please stay in your car if you wish to watch these gamebirds, which are very

↑ Fort William, complete with the diddy Druimarbin in the Ben Nevis foothills. (John A Cameron/S)

sensitive to disturbance. And, also in spring, grasshopper warblers utter their distinctive song (like a clunky freewheeling bicycle) from streamside vegetation downslope.

WALK THIS WAY

❶ From the parking area, viewpoint and picnic spot, cross the road and head southwest through the metal gate. Keeping the fence on your right, you'll soon come to a second gate. Go through this on to open hillside and follow the peat path (often wet) all the way to the rounded rump of the summit of Druimarbin, which is adorned by a trig point. ❷ Enjoy the views of Loch Linnhe and, if you're lucky, Ben Nevis ('The Ben' is seemingly clagged with cloud 99.9% of the time). Then retrace your steps to the start.

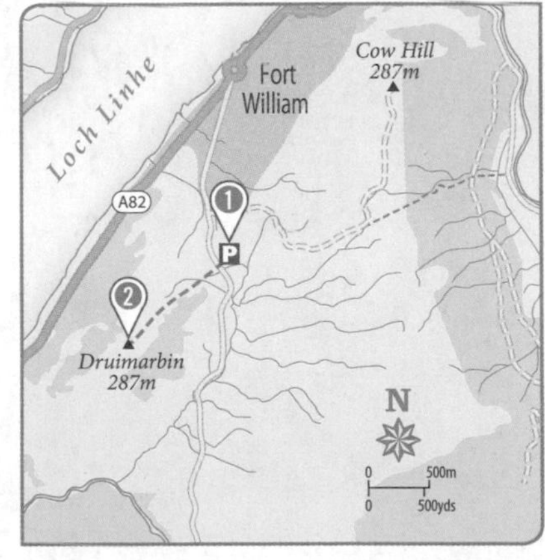

Descending The Ben's Pony Track – the perfect add-on after a training trek on Druimarbin. (Phoebe Smith)

ADDED ADVENTURE

Consider this a warm-up hill perfect for a dawn raid or an evening amble from where you can watch the sun rise or set. Take a bivvy and you can enjoy both with views of Loch Linnhe and the Great Glen at your feet.

MAKE IT BIGGER

Start from Fort William itself and go via the summit of nearby Cow Hill (NN113735) for a longer walk post-breakfast.

FOR LITTLE ADVENTURERS

After they've climbed their mini-mountain why not treat the kids to a cable-car ride over the Nevis range (nevisrange.co.uk; adults from £13 single/£16 return) on the slopes of Aonach Mor. Or look for otters and seals from Fort William pier.

FOR CAMPERS

The award-winning Glen Nevis Caravan and Camping Park (glen-nevis.co.uk; Mar–Nov; from £23pn) is the nearest. There are also camping pods, holiday chalets and a restaurant/bar.

FOR ADRENALINE LOVERS

For the hardy it has to be an ascent of Ben Nevis even if, as Britain's highest peak, it is the antithesis of this entire book! No matter which route you take to the top it's a proper mountain, but the really adventurous might choose to approach from the north, via the knife-edge *arête* of Carn Mor Dearg. You will need a head for heights and winter skills, plus ice axe and crampons if any snow remains.

FOR HUNGRY HIKERS

Supplies can be picked up easily from the large Morrisons supermarket by Fort William train station. There's also the excellent Ellis Brigham camping store for gas and lightweight camping. For proper lunch and dinner, try Ben Nevis Inn (ben-nevis-inn.co.uk), a 200-year-old converted barn specialising in local produce, which is proudly located 'at the foot of the Ben'.

OTHER PRACTICALITIES

Fort William train station gives access to the rest of the country's network. Although there is no bus to the start, you can easily walk to Druimarbin straight from town. Toilets are in Fort William station and on the corner of Bank Street.

55 MONSTER MOUNTAIN

SCAN FOR THE LOCH NESS MONSTER FROM THE MUSCULAR HIGHLAND TOP OF MEALL FUAR-MHONAIDH

WHERE	Meall Fuar-mhonaidh, Highlands
STATS	↔ 8km (5 miles) ↕ 699m ↗ 479m ↻ 2½ hours
START/FINISH	Grotaig car park ⚲ NH490236
TERRAIN	Clear track to start then rough hill path over rocks and heather
MAPS	OS Explorer (1:25,000) 416; OS Landranger (1:50,000) 26

The name Loch Ness immediately conjures up one thing and one thing only – 'Nessie'. Ah, the Loch Ness monster – or prehistoric plesiosaur – which is fabled to lurk in the depths of this large waterbody, waiting for believers and sceptics alike to see it emerge from the ripples and take a photograph. Which would, of course, send the whole country into yet another frenzy of excitement – just as we have done regularly ever since the inaugural 6th-century 'sighting' by St Columba, or, in modern times, since 1933 (when the first-known photograph was 'taken').

The 'elusive' Nessie has perhaps more in common with the small peak of Meall Fuar-mhonaidh than you might first think. For a start those disinterested in hillwalking will likely be suspicious should you try to persuade them of the joy produced by the simple act of walking up a slope. Is this not rather similar to those sceptics who would never dream of devoting hours of their life to

↑ Reaching the summit cairn atop Meall Fuar-mhonaidh. (Neil S Price)

spotting mysterious monsters? Then there's the shape. Both – depending on cloud cover for the peak – exhibit a muscular, ridged back that hints of something far more momentous lying beneath.

So proceed with an open mind to discover the joys of small hills and make-believe monsters by committing to a real physical challenge on this rising hilly giant. One thing's for sure – one of the pair is definitely real and unambiguously worthy of your time.

WALK THIS WAY

❶ From the car park at the hamlet of Grotaig, take the pathway south, twice crossing Grotaig Burn. Then head west through the woodland, wandering under the canopy of birch, rowan, willow and oak, where blaeberries (bilberries) ripen in the autumn and sika deer stroll, keeping north of Inchtellach House, and out on to the open slopes of Meall Fuar-mhonaidh.

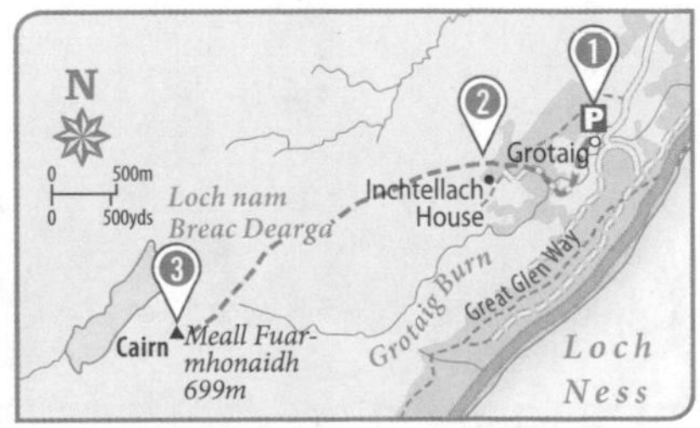

Nessie spotting from the slopes of Meall Fuar-mhonaidh. (Neil S Price)

ADDED ADVENTURE

To the west of Meall Fuar-mhonaidh is a lovely waterbody called Loch nam Breac Dearga – the perfect place to retire to your tent or bivvy bag after a day spent Nessie-spotting. The other (mainly pathless) fells make for additional ample exploration.

MAKE IT BIGGER

This hill stands proudly above the Great Glen Way (greatglenway.org), a long-distance footpath that runs 117km (73 miles) from Inverness to Fort William, including along much of Loch Ness. Tack Meall Fuar-mhonaidh on to a five to seven-day amble along the Way (or part of it).

FOR LITTLE ADVENTURERS

Fuel their imagination before you climb the hill by visiting the Loch Ness Monster Exhibition in nearby Drumnadrochit (lochness.com). This transports visitors through half-a-billion years of 'history, natural mystery and legend'. Or take them to lochside Urquhart Castle (tinyurl.com/castleurquhart), the scene of numerous power struggles, so they may spar amongst the ruins.

FOR CAMPERS

Nearby is Borlum campsite (borlum.co.uk; from £9pn), where you can also rent a cottage and go horseriding.

↑ Tackling the gently rising heather-clad slopes at stage 2. (Neil S Price)

WILD CAMP LUXURIES

Just because you're heading out to sleep in the wilds doesn't mean you have to leave comfort back at home. Make sure that in addition to the essentials you save space for some little luxuries such as an inflatable pillow, a half bottle of wine or hip flask, some hot chocolate sachets and real chocolate or even a portable power pack so you can re-charge your phone on the move.

❷ The path runs west then southwest, with a ridge to your right. On the OS map the path disappears before the 400m contour; in reality, it runs all the way to the summit, weaving through heather and over alternately rocky and muddy ground. Follow the path as it makes its way up and over the northwest ridge up to the summit cairn at 699m. ❸ As the highest hill featured in this book, you'd expect the views to be great. And you would be right. Your vista encompasses little-explored hills (to the north), via the lovely wee Loch nam Breac Dearga (immediately west of the summit) to the giant expanse of Loch Ness (to the south and east). From up here you can appreciate just how big this body of water actually is, so you'll need binoculars to do some Nessie 'spotting'. Once you've had enough, turn around and retrace your steps to the start.

FOR ADRENALINE LOVERS

You could join a Nessie-spotting cruise but where's the fun in that? Instead hire a kayak, canoe or stand-up paddleboard from Explore Highland (explorehighland.com) and walk this hillock as an aside to completing the Great Glen Canoe Trail (greatglencanoetrail.info).

FOR HUNGRY HIKERS

Lots of choices – both the Loch Ness Monster Exhibition and Borlum campsite offer food (see opposite). Otherwise try the award-winning Fiddlers (fiddledrum.co.uk) for pub grub and the airy Ness Deli (nessdeli.co.uk) for sandwiches and snacks. Both are in Drumnadrochit. The nearest supermarket is in Inverness where you'll also find outdoor shops to stock up on any supplies you may need if you're opting to wild camp (such as gas, dehydrated meals, etc).

OTHER PRACTICALITIES

Stagecoach runs hourly buses (17, 19, 19A) from Inverness to Drumnadrochit. The nearest toilets are at the tourist information centre on the A82 at Drumnadrochit.

Sika deer can often be heard 'barking' in the woodland below the hill. (chris2766/S) ↑

56 REMOTE WANDERINGS

FOR RUGGED WILDERNESS, JOIN THE DETERMINED FEW MAKING IT TO THE ISOLATED GLENS OF STRATHFARRAR

WHERE Meall Innis an Loichel, Highlands

STATS ↔ 3.5km (2 miles) ↕ 391m ↗ 181m ↻ 1 hour

START/FINISH Park at the power station NH183381. Gate open between certain hours only: check before arrival at tinyurl.com/strathfarrar.

TERRAIN Grassy slopes

MAPS OS Explorer (1:25,000) 430; OS Landranger (1:50,000) 25

I don't know about you, but I find that when it's tricky to even reach the start of a walk, the target summit assumes an even more alluring stature, presenting itself as an enticing challenge and one that I find impossible to refuse. So it is with Meall Innis an Loichel, which lies in a remote Highland glen between Inverness and Kyle of Lochalsh (but it is not particularly near either).

The hill's location at the very end of a private road in the little-visited Glen Strathfarrar – which even the bods at Visit Scotland admit rivals more well-known Glen Affric in terms of a true sense of wilderness, Alpine-esque peaks, and swathes of grassy foothills linking the lochs – means that you can't simply rock up on a whim and get strolling. Instead you first need to request permission from the gatehouse (tinyurl.com/strathfarrar). Moreover, there's a rigid daily quota for the number of cars allowed in and fixed opening hours (usually 09.00–20.00), so an early arrival and prompt departure are advisable. The only way round these restrictions – and it's a welcome health-boosting solution – is to walk or bike in. In winter (November–late March) visiting requires advance planning, as the gate is always locked; you will need to contact the Mountaineering Council of Scotland (01738 493942) to get the access code.

With such restrictions and stipulations, it is little wonder that you'll find the area – at whatever time of the year – devoid of other walkers, making it the perfect place to enjoy some solitude. Reward indeed for the trials of getting here. The peak itself is a curious little steep-sided bump with a truly wild feel. There are no buildings or proper roads for miles, a surrounding cirque of higher mountains and a

↑ Meall Innis an Loichel from neighbouring Meall an Tairbh, with the Loch Monar dam in the foreground. (Iain MacDiarmid)

covering of rocky outcrops with a backdrop of serrated peaks. Moreover, there are views down Loch Monar from a hill on which few others will have ever even set foot.

Convoluted though this day out may seem – mark my words – this secret stash of hills is moreish. You may come for diminutive Meall Innis an Loichel but I guarantee you'll be hooked by what you see from its summit and want to stay for more.

WALK THIS WAY

❶ From the car park at the power station, follow the track east above River Uisge Misgeach. After nearly 2km the track forks. Take the left branch headed for the shores of Loch Monar. Once you reach the water take the track on the right and follow it round to stand facing the western nose of the peak. Take a minute (or several) to gaze along the loch, which is lined with mountains on either side. There will likely be nobody else within miles of you. ❷ Continue straight up and simply pick your way along a faint path to the summit of Meall Innis an Loichel. ❸ From the top there is much to see in terms of mountaintops. To the north is East Monar Forest, home to the 1,001m-high, rump-like Maoile Lunndaidh. To the west you'll spy the rocky ridge of An Socach. Look south and you'll be treated to views of Braigh a' Choire Bhig (1,011m). To return, retrace your steps to the start.

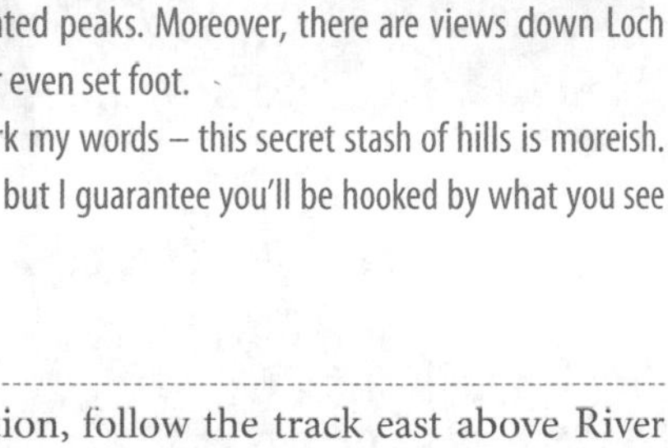

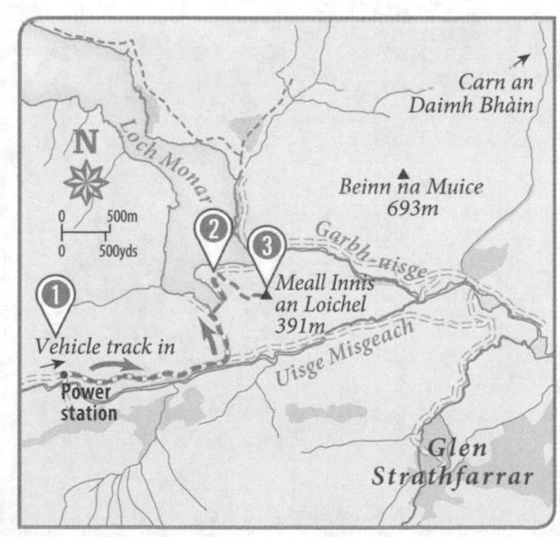

The River Uisge Misgeach at Innis an Loichel adds drama to the wild landscape. (Gordie Broon)

ADDED ADVENTURE

With its isolated hillocks and few other walkers, this whole area screams out for a multi-day adventure of wild walking and wild camping. Remember to bring your tent or bivvy as there are ample spots in which to pitch in Strathfarrar.

MAKE IT BIGGER

You could easily couple this hillock with two higher peaks on the opposite (north) side of Garbh-uisge – Beinn na Muice (693m) and Carn an Daimh Bhain (625m) – and even venture further. Grab your map and decide how many tops you can squeeze in before the gate closes. Then there's the remote Affric Kintail Way. Only open since 2015, this walking and mountain-bike trail runs through neighbouring Glen Affric, from Drumnadrochit on Loch Ness to the remote Morvich, over 70km (44 miles) of well-maintained but wild-feeling paths

FOR LITTLE ADVENTURERS

Not much in the surrounding area as the appeal is its remoteness and lack of services. The nearest town is Beauly, and even that is 45km (28 miles) away. Here you'll find a childrens' farm (⏲ Jun–Aug) plus a farm shop at Robertson's (🖱 robertsonsfarmshop.co.uk).

FOR CAMPERS

The nearest is Cannich Woodland Camping (🖱 highlandcamping.co.uk; from £8.50pn), which offers camping pods as well as sites for tents and caravans. This quiet woodland site lies on the Affric Kintail Way, a new long-distance footpath (🖱 affrickintailway.com).

FOR ADRENALINE LOVERS

Look at the map and you'll rapidly notice that, apart from the one along Glen Strathfarrar, there are no roads for miles around that cut through this great wilderness. If you really want to push yourself take plenty of supplies and aim for a full circuit of the hills surrounding Loch Monar. It's hard, wild and not for the faint-hearted.

FOR HUNGRY HIKERS

The Bog Café at Cannich campsite (see above; ⏲ Mar–Oct daily, Nov–Mar Sat–Sun only) is great for snacks and hot and cold drinks. For a post-walk celebration, best head to the 19th-century, stone-walled Struy Inn in Struy at the head of the road to Glen Strathfarrar (🖱 thestruy.co.uk). It also does take-away fish and chips. For supplies, the nearest place is the Co-op in Beauly.

OTHER PRACTICALITIES

There is no public transport to this hill. The nearest toilets are back in Beauly on the main road.

57 CAIRNGORMS SAMPLER

TRY A WILD SLICE OF CRAIGELLACHIE, STRAIGHT FROM THE TOWN OF AVIEMORE

WHERE	Craigellachie, Highlands
STATS	↔ 5km (3 miles) ↕ 493m ↗ 273m ↻ 2½ hours
START/FINISH	Aviemore Youth Hostel NH893119; parking also available at visitor centre NH902109
TERRAIN	Clear woodland path then rough and steep near summit
MAPS	OS Explorer (1:25,000) 57; OS Landranger (1:50,000) 36, 35

It's not until you see the Cairngorms massif that I feel you can say you've witnessed the true might of British mountains. It's not only size that makes these easternmost Highlands impressive – many top the 4,000ft (1,219m) mark. Nor the fact that the plateau landscape is as near as you can get to that of the Arctic tundra without setting foot on foreign lands. It's also their unpredictability.

Attracting cloud, hail and snow as though a giant magnet for inclement weather, and being fairly featureless once you reach their dizzying heights, the Cairngorm tops can catch out even the most experienced mountaineer. So what better reason to check out a smaller slice of Cairngorm magic on Craigellachie – whether as a warm-up to something more committing or just because it's a perfect pocket-size peak in its own right.

With easy access from the well-connected ski-resort town of Aviemore (meaning you won't need a car at all), this is one summit that can be attempted on a whim. Not only that, but it also offers an amazing opportunity to spy the local nesting peregrine falcons – whether out on the hill itself, above the beautiful silver birch trees during your ascent, or (when the birds are breeding) watching the camera feed from inside the youth hostel at the start.

↑ Looking over to the sprawling Cairngorm massif from the modest Craigellachie. (Chiz Dakin/www.peakimages.co.uk)

This walk also offers glorious variation. You'll experience a bit of a scramble on Craigellachie's lower crags. You'll chill during a peaceful walk on the hill's higher reaches, well above the buzzy town. And you'll savour one of the most beautiful panoramas in the area, with the summit offering views towards all points of the compass – including over the Rothiemurchus Forest, the lower Spey Valley and the distant lonely Monadhliath Hills.

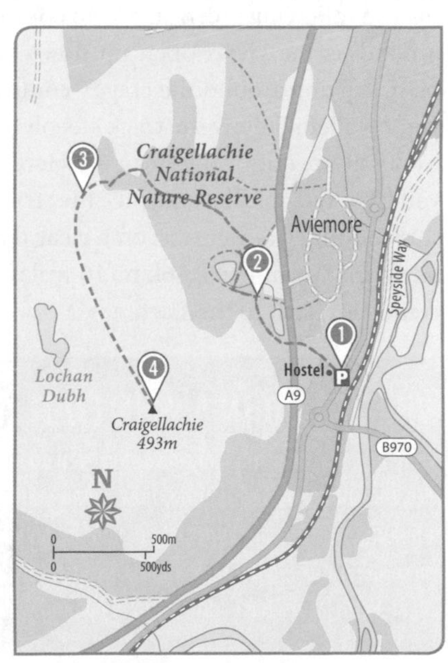

WALK THIS WAY

❶ From Aviemore Youth Hostel car park (where you may park to do this walk) take the path heading uphill then through the tunnel under the A9 road, before climbing uphill once more through silver birch trees, where willow warblers utter their liquid, descending song in spring, and where black darter dragonflies and Scotch argus butterflies bask in late summer. Ignore the turn-off down to the right

to the lochan (although it is worth a detour if you want to see dragonflies), instead following green arrows to continue uphill, bearing left over ever-steeper ground as the views open up down towards Aviemore. ❷ Continue on the path, skirting around the craggy contours until you reach a wider track where you turn left. Follow the track steeply uphill as it changes to become steps that lead you up, out of the trees. ❸ Here a rough path over grass and rock takes you the rest of the way to the true summit. ❹ Enjoy the views of the surrounding Cairngorms: on a clear day you can even see over to the ski slope on Cairn Gorm itself, 16km (10 miles) southeast. Then it's a case of retracing your steps back to the start.

WHAT TO DO IN A WHITEOUT

Whiteouts can occur suddenly in winter, even on lower hills. The cloud may descend and, when coupled with the snow-covered ground, may mean you are unable to orientate. If conditions look likely to deteriorate, ensure you know where you are on your map first. Once it descends stop and think. Plan your route out using defined landmarks such as walls even if they mean a longer descent. If in doubt add on extra layers, have something to eat and wait until it clears.

↑ The only herd of wild reindeer in Britain are found in the Cairngorms. (Fiona Smith)

ADDED ADVENTURE

Take your tent or bivvy and go for a wild camp around Lochan Dubh to get a full Cairngorms experience – all just above the town of Aviemore.

MAKE IT BIGGER

The Speyside Way (speysideway.org) is a long-distance route that starts near to this mini-mountain and runs all the way to Bucklie, 105km (65 miles) away. Consider making this peak your spectacular start or finish.

FOR LITTLE ADVENTURERERS

Think you need to head to the Arctic to see reindeer? The Cairngorms has its own herd, introduced here in 1952. Check out the Cairngorm Reindeer Centre (cairngormreindeer.co.uk; from £3.50) to join a guided walk to find these hefty herbivores grazing in the hills. In spring and summer, visit the osprey centre at RSPB Loch Garten (tinyurl.com/rspbgarten), between Aviemore and Nethybridge. You can watch the nest through a telescope or via a remote camera, as well as enjoy red squirrels and small birds such as siskins at point blank range.

FOR CAMPERS

The nearest is Glenmore Campsite (tinyurl.com/campglenmore; from £16pn), which is surrounded by the Scots pines of ancient Caledonian forest and direct access to the beaches of Loch Morlich.

FOR ADRENALINE LOVERS

Come in winter to practise newly acquired skills when this hillock feels just ever so slightly more arctic. Courses at Glenmore Lodge (glenmorelodge.org.uk) are highly recommended. You'll learn all kinds of key winter skills, from navigating in snow to kicking steps, making platforms, moving safely on ice, avalanche awareness, ice-axe arrest, using crampons, staying warm and even – for the truly adventurous – how to dig and sleep safely in a snow hole.

FOR HUNGRY HIKERS

The Mountain Café in the Cairngorm Mountain Sports gear shop in Aviemore (mountaincafe-aviemore.co.uk) does the best breakfast by far. It's also a great place to pick up supplies. There's also a Tesco in town.

OTHER PRACTICALITIES

Aviemore train station connects this famous winter resort with London, Crewe and Preston via the Caledonian Sleeper train (sleeper.scot) – a must-do if heading this way from England. Toilets can be found on the main street (Grampian Road) and in the railway station.

Come in spring/early summer for the chance to see peregrine falcons nesting. (James Lowen) ↑

58 BRAEMAR BEAUTY

HONOUR 18TH-CENTURY JACOBITE REBELS BY BRAVING THE STEEP SLOPES OF CREAG CHOINNICH

WHERE	Creag Choinnich, Aberdeenshire
STATS	↔ 2.5km (1½ miles) ↕ 538m ↗ 210m ↻ 1½ hours
START/FINISH	Car park at the north edge of Braemar ⚲ NO151916
TERRAIN	Good path, steep towards summit
MAPS	OS Explorer (1:25,000) 58; OS Landranger (1:50,000) 43

Rising up above the surrounding border of pine trees, Creag Choinnich is a peak that seems almost designed to be a viewpoint. From its exposed, cairn-adorned top, the summit offers sweeping peeks down the River Dee. Trace the river's route all the way to the dramatic knolls and flattened, yawning tops of the Cairngorms mountain range beyond, which seemingly beckon you from miles away. Grab your map and on a clear day you'll be able to check off and name a whole host of the eastern highland giants from your viewpoint.

The walk starts straight from the village of Braemar and makes for a short – but steep – stroll among pine forests, heather-coated slopes and rocky outcrops. There's also an abundance of wildlife to spy as you go. Keep your eyes peeled for the native red squirrel often seen among the branches in the woodland, otter poking up along the River Dee, and don't forget to look up – you may be lucky enough to spot golden eagle. Several landmarks of particular interest are visible from the top. One is Lion's Face, a bold lump of craggy rock seemingly protruding from the tree canopy like a stony feline. A second is Braemar Castle, built as a hunting lodge in 1628, but then a key point of control during the 17th-century Jacobite Rebellion: indeed, look on the OS map and you'll see the flanks of this peak were also a key site for the raising of the Rebellion's standard in 1715.

Thankfully it's all peace and tranquillity now amid the pine trees and rocky outcrops, making this the perfect townside escape.

↑ Creag Choinnich overlooks the town of Braemar. (William White)

WALK THIS WAY

❶ You'll see this small hill as soon as you arrive in Braemar village, rising to the northeast from a forested petticoat. From the car park cross the main road (A93) east, and head along the opposite street, which leads left, past a hotel, into Castleton Place. Continue along this street, following the sign for Creag Choinnich and passing a school on your right. As the street bears right, continue straight on through a gate and on to a path entering the woods. Bear left to head uphill. ❷ Ignore turn-offs and instead head on steadily uphill through the trees – a mixture of silver birch and Scots pine, interspersed with heather and dotted with rocks – until you emerge on to the open grass- and heather-coated hillside and the views begin to open out behind you. ❸ The path becomes steep and rocky, but keep on it to reach the summit cairn. ❹ Enjoy the views of the Dee Valley, the royal estate of Balmoral, the throne-like peak of Lochnagar and back down to the village. Beinn a' Bhuird and Ben Avon are over to the northwest, while Lion's Rock is out to the east and directly north are the looming turrets of Braemar Castle. Once finished, unless exploring further (see *Added adventure*), it's a case of following the path back down to where you started.

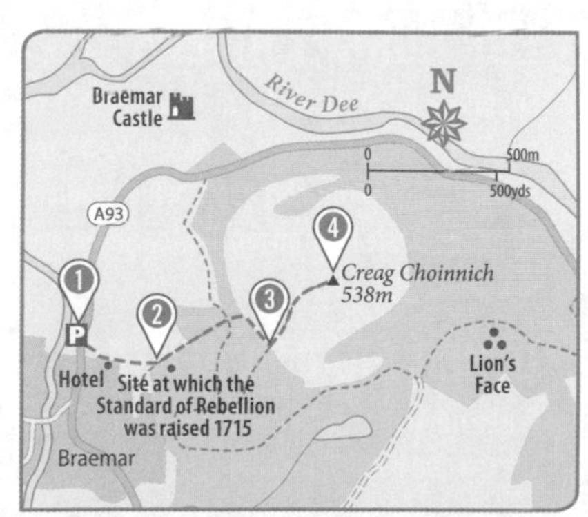

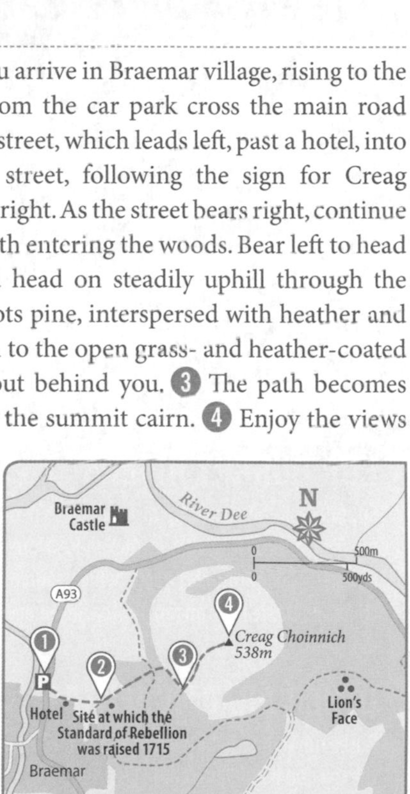

ADDED ADVENTURE

Check out the Lion's Face rock – a gargantuan lump of limestone said to resemble the face of the big cat when viewed from the other side of the River Dee. There's only one way to check… get walking 1km (¾ mile) southeast to NO166915.

MAKE IT BIGGER

There are other hills around Braemar to hike if you have the strength in your legs after this steep ascent. Continue south to hit Carn nan Sgliat (690m) and Creag nan Leachda (784m) for a double-summit hike. Alternatively, go west to tackle Morrone (859m), head east for smaller Craig Leek (635m) or walk north to Little Elrick (576m) or Carn na Drochaide (818m).

FOR LITTLE ADVENTURERS

A visit to Braemar Castle (braemarcastle.co.uk), run by the local community, is worthwhile. You can explore the grounds and listen to a guided tour that includes hidden teddy bears to hunt for in each room, each of which reveals something about the history of the place – so great for kids. There are also other walks from the town along the River Dee: get an OS map, pick a trail and start exploring – minus the ascent.

FOR CAMPERS

The nearest campsite is Braemar Caravan Park (braemarcaravanpark.co.uk), part of the Invercauld estate and less than 10 minutes' walk from the village, which takes tents and offers camping pods.

FOR ADRENALINE LOVERS

In winter, assuming there is snow, go skiing or ski-touring, with special skis to allow you to go uphill. The nearest slope is at Glenshee (ski-glenshee.co.uk), 14.5km (9 miles) away. You can hire equipment from Cycle Highlands (cyclehighlands.com/ski-hire) in Victoria Hall on Glenshee Road in Braemar.

FOR HUNGRY HIKERS

Supplies can be picked up at Braemar's Co-op on Mar Road, close to the car park. For a tasty meal post-stroll there's the Alexandra Hotel (alexandrahotelballater.co.uk) restaurant in Ballater (25km/16 miles east), which sources local produce to make classics such as fish and chips and has real ale on tap. For tea and snacks during the day try The Bothy (01339 741242) in Braemar itself.

OTHER PRACTICALITIES

Buses run regularly between the town of Braemar and Aberdeen. Toilets can be found next to the river on Balnellan Road.

Taking in the views from the summit – a great feeling, no matter how old you are. (Dan Nuttell)

59 BRILLIANT BENNACHIE

ASCEND OXEN CRAIG TO SPEND TIME AMONG MATERNAL HILLS BELOVED BY OUR BRONZE AGE ANCESTORS

WHERE	Oxen Craig, Aberdeenshire
STATS	↔ 4km (2½ miles) ↕ 529m ↗ 354m ↻ 1½ hours
START/FINISH	Back o' Bennachie car park NJ661244
TERRAIN	Hill paths on moorland with some steps
MAPS	OS Explorer (1:25,000) 421; OS Landranger (1:50,000) 37

You can always rely on the Scots to tell it like it is when it comes to hills. Take Bennachie as a perfect example. Rising up like a rack of little lumps from the surrounding forest, its name, translated literally, means 'hill of the breast'. This nod to the 'mammaries' on this hillock near Aberdeen finds its echo in the adjacent peak of Mither Tap, which means 'Mother Top'. Looking at these supple summits from below, you can kind of see what our ancestors might have been getting at, rising and falling as they do like a buxom maiden's chest.

This is particularly true of our Bronze Age relations who – judging from the abundance of standing stones around the area – seemed to regard this hill with spiritual reverie. This may be because of the physical association with the female form, but might equally be down to Mither Tap casting a shadow over the landscape each equinox. Bennachie has another, more recent, significance that earns it a spot

↑ Bronze Age, bronze light, the perfect time to be on the summit of Bennachie is at dusk. (Matt Youngs)

on the 'Best Small Hills' list. From 1801 to 1859, the flanks of the hill were inhabited by a community of – for want of a better word – squatters. Residents of 'The Colony' were crofters who also provided skilled labour for local landowners. However, when the common land entered private ownership, the community ebbed away. The last of the Colonists, a man called George Esson, died in the 1930s.

Nowadays archaeologists and the University of Aberdeen are studying the history of The Colony. Findings should be shared via interpretation boards on site as well as on the website of a charity – Bailies of Bennachie – that cares for and promotes the site (bailiesofbennachie.co.uk).

There is often plenty of flora and fauna on this walk, including three noteworthy orchids during summer. Heath spotted orchid blooms in damper parts of the moorland, and the titchy lesser twayblade hides beneath clumps of heather. In July and August, creeping lady's-tresses, a delicate whirl of a plant, flowers in the pine forests. Easier to spot are common lizard and red grouse, both typically found on the open moorland.

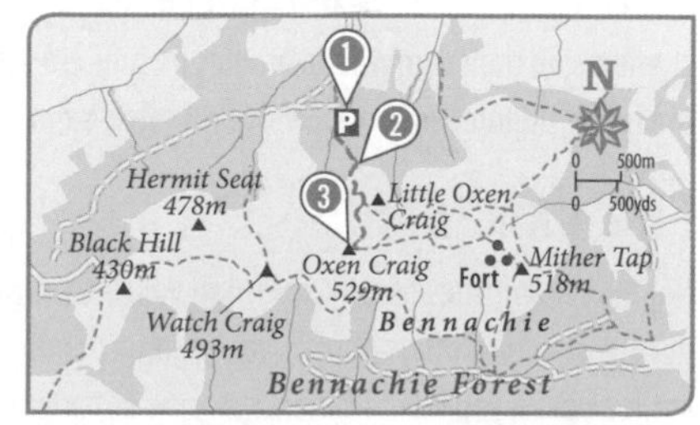

ADDED ADVENTURE

Take your hammock and tarp to enjoy a wild woodland sleep – Colony-style – amidst the trees that surround the peak.

MAKE IT BIGGER

It would be worthwhile to tack on the four other peaks that make up the Bennachie ridge: Black Hill, Hermit Seat, Watch Crag and the splendidly named Mither Tap, which comes with a hillfort that may date from 1000BC.

FOR LITTLE ADVENTURERS

There's a lot to see in nearby Insch (16km/10 miles) in terms of more small hills with interesting elements on their summits. Examples include the Hill of Christ's Kirk (with its unfinished fort on top) to the Hill of Dunnideer (with its fort and settlement).

FOR CAMPERS

Not many campsites nearby. Try Ythan Valley Campsite (✆ 01358 761400; from £8pn) 30km (19 miles) northeast, which offers homemade organic bread and free-range eggs delivered to your tent – as well as breakfast if you want it. There's also an outside shower.

↑ Little Oxen Craig, a small detour if you want to collect all the high points on this clustered peak. (Spaceways)

GETTING INTO A HAMMOCK SAFELY

Don't be tempted to lie down straightaway. Instead sit as you would in a chair in the middle of your hammock and find your balance. Then swing your legs up and your body round into a lying position in one motion – voilà – you should still be in your hammock! Remember practice makes perfect.

WALK THIS WAY

❶ From the Forestry Commission car park at Back o' Bennachie (tinyurl.com/backobennachie), take the Mither Tap Quarry Trail (brown waymarkers) to climb steadily south through the woodland to a track where you turn right then immediately left to effectively continue going straight. Ignore the next turning, and carry on uphill. ❷ As you leave the trees the track enters heather-clad moorland. Rather than detour on to Little Oxen Craig, carry on and veer right at the fork to directly ascend to the summit of Oxen Craig (529m). This is the highest in Bennachie's small collection of hills above the treeline. ❸ To the east lies the neighbouring hill of Mither Tap with farmland stretching to the North Sea beyond. To the west, heather moors lead to Hermit Seat. When you've taken it all in, providing you don't want to tick off any more hillocks (see *Make it bigger*), simply retrace your steps to the start.

FOR ADRENALINE LOVERS

Though there's nothing directly on the mountain, just a 35km/22-mile drive south is the adrenaline-pumping Deeside Activity Park, where you can try your hand at quad biking, 4x4 driving and even learn how to manoeuvre a digger (!) on the site's own small hills (deesideactivitypark.com).

FOR HUNGRY HIKERS

In the nearby village of Oyne, try Lil C's BBQ (lilcbarbq.co.uk; Wed–Sun), which serves American diner-style food – think salty butter, sweetcorn, sugar-rubbed meats and wood smoke. If you're especially hungry there's even the Big Mouth challenge where if you can eat a set host of BBQ goodies and a milkshake you get the lot free of charge... and make the wall of shame. For pre-walk supplies try one of the several supermarkets in Inverurie, 11.2km (7 miles) southeast along the A96.

OTHER PRACTICALITIES

There are no buses to the start of this walk. From Aberdeen, you are best taking a train or bus (numbers 10, 41 or 416) to the village of Insch, 5km (3 miles) away. There are public toilets in Back o' Bennachie car park.

Look for common lizards basking in sheltered spots on the moorland. (James Lowen) ↑

60 BHRAGGIE RIGHTS

CONTEMPLATE SOCIAL INJUSTICE AS YOU HIKE UP A SUTHERLAND SUMMIT FEATURING A CONTROVERSIAL STATUE

WHERE	Ben Bhraggie, Highlands
STATS	↔ 7km (4¼ miles) ↕ 397m ↗ 397m ↻ 3½ hours
START/FINISH	Parking on Fountain Street, Golspie, at NH832999 (and also at train station)
TERRAIN	Forest paths and grassy tracks
MAPS	OS Explorer (1:25,000) 441; OS Landranger (1:50,000) 21, 17

I always think it's best to end with a bit of controversy, and nothing splits people's opinion quite like the statue that sits at the top of the small peak of Ben Bhraggie. This Sutherland summit dominates the skyline above the seaside town of Golspie, offering an array of footpaths and mountain-bike trails amid its high moorland and heath-clad slopes. Embellishing its humplike crest is a statue 30m (100ft) tall. Hewn from stone from the northeast side of this very hill, the memorial figure is that of George Leveson-Gower. This notorious local duke evicted his tenants to make way for much more profitable sheep farming during the notorious Highland Clearances which, here, took place during the early 19th century. After his death in 1833, subscriptions came in from across the UK to pay for this statue to be erected in Leveson-Gower's 'honour'.

Often called 'The Mannie' (colloquial work for 'the boy'), the memorial is a constant point of contention among villagers who cannot forget the trouble the laird caused to those who were forcibly evicted from

↑ Courting controversy – the disputed statue sits on Ben Bhraggie. (Ian Rowlinson)

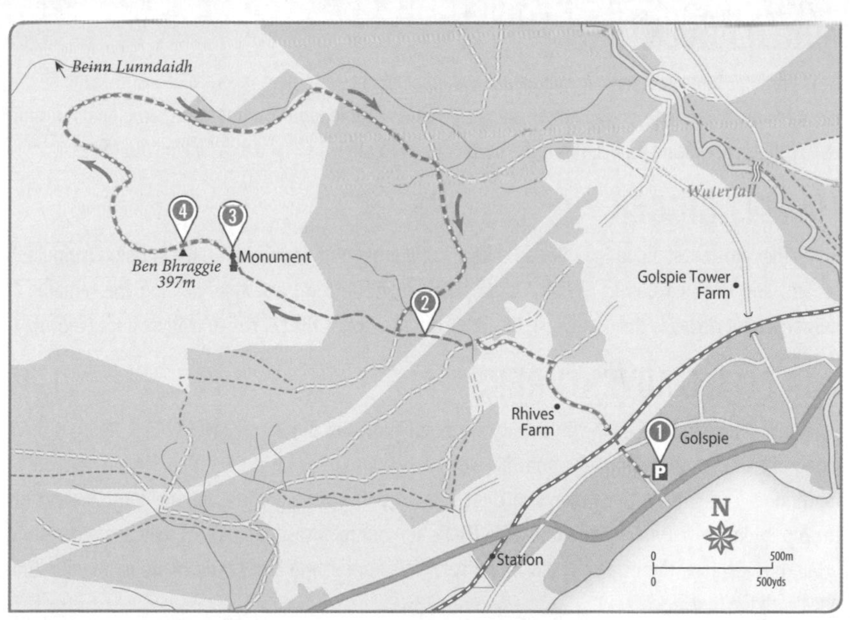
Beinn Lunndaidh
Waterfall
Monument
Ben Bhraggie
397m
Golspie Tower
Farm
Rhives
Farm
Golspie
Station
N
0
500m
0
500yds

his land. Local ire has resulted in several incidences of vandalism – both graffiti and attempts to topple the statue. However, despite campaigns to call for the permanent removal of the memorial, none has yet proved successful. Indeed, it's a war that seems to rage even longer than the actual clearances themselves.

All this is worth mulling over as you ascend the summit of Ben Bhraggie (397m). Should Gower's effigy be 'cleared' as retribution for the ousted or left as a memento to human cruelty, enabling future generations to vent their frustration at what remains of this man's reputation?

WALK THIS WAY

❶ From the car park on Fountain Road, walk northwest up Fountain Road and under the railway. Just before Rhives Farm, you'll see a car park on your right: ignore this and continue to the farm itself then take the path that forks right after passing it. ❷ Shortly after you pass a water tank, you'll come to a gate. Go through it and continue straight up the obvious forest track ignoring any of the arrowed turn-offs (intended for mountain bikers). You'll come to a path that veers off to the right that is signposted for Ben Bhraggie. Continue up through the woodland, under the power lines and across two forestry roads, all the time heading for The Mannie. You'll reach a wooden shelter with a bench inside it (a good place to take five and to look over the coastline which becomes visible as the trees relent). Continue along the path, still ignoring any turn-offs and soon the controversial statue will come into focus. ❸ Take a minute to look at the statue – whatever state it's currently in – and to contemplate its significance,

ADDED ADVENTURE

Go in winter: a blanket of snow makes an already great ascent even more spectacular – and as the height is not too overwhelming, you could consider attempting your inaugural winter wild camp on its summit too. With its east-facing aspect, this is the perfect place to catch a frosty dawn looking out to sea.

MAKE IT BIGGER

Go further northwest along the ridge to collect a few other pint-sized peaks. Take in Beinn Lunndaidh (446m) and Cnoc na Gamha (371m), then swing round into a horseshoe, passing the remains of numerous hut circles to the northwest, by adding on Aberscross Hill (277m) and Silver Rock (265m).

FOR LITTLE ADVENTURERS

Take them on a stroll to see the impressive waterfall known as Big Burn (NC837013). You get there along one of the delightful paths from Big Burn car park marked on the OS map. Here a network of footbridges criss-crosses the water as it cleaves its way down the gorge. Continue south afterwards to stop in on the fairytale-esque Dunrobin Castle (dunrobincastle.co.uk). As well as gardens and grounds to explore, there's a daily falconry display in summer: you could even photograph your little ones with the birds.

then continue up the track to take the summit of Ben Bhraggie. 4 From here the views of the Sutherland coast are stupendous and you'll find yourself questioning if the statue of this particular man truly deserves such a mighty panorama. To return, rather than simply returning the way you came, enjoy the variety, and no less hardship, of a longer route back. Continue inland following the track roughly north for yet more views. It then loops back east to start descending the slopes. Keep heading downhill, through a forested area until, at the far end of a clearing, you come to a major crossroads. Veer right here to head back to the area near the pylons (stage 2), then simply retrace your steps to the start.

FOR CAMPERS

The nearest one that takes tents is the beachside Dornoch Caravan & Camping (dornochcaravans.co.uk; from £11pn), 17km (11 miles) to the south.

FOR ADRENALINE LOVERS

Take your mountain bike. Some of the trails on which you will be walking are shared with bikers anyway so why not bring yours and have a pedal along 18km (11 miles) of forested tracks that lace the woodland below the summit. Known as the Highland Wildcat Trails (highlandwildcat.com), routes are graded by difficulty and which include the longest single-track descent in the UK (approximately 7km/4¼ miles).

FOR HUNGRY HIKERS

For coffee and breakfast check out Coffee Bothy on Fountain Road, Golspie (01408 633022). For a sit-down meal and drink head to Golspie Inn (golspieinn.co.uk), which has been in business since shortly before Leverson-Gower's clearances. Supplies can be bought from the Co-op in town.

OTHER PRACTICALITIES

Trains run from Inverness to Golspie station. There are toilets on Main Street in Golspie.

Entering the trees that cover the lower flanks of Ben Bhraggie. (David Simmonds) ↑

HILLWALKERS' GLOSSARY

ALTITUDE: the height of a hill or mountain as measured from sea level. This differs from total ascent – which is the elevational difference between the start of the walk and the **summit** of the hill.

BRIDLEWAY: **footpaths** that are also open for use by non-motorised traffic, ie: horseriders and bicycles.

CAIRN: a stack of stones that denotes a mountain **summit** or **spot height**. Also occasionally used, in a series, to mark the way to a summit.

CLAG: thick mist that tends to descend and linger around mountain **summits** and high moorland.

COIRE: a Scottish Gaelic term that describes a scooped-out hollow on a **plateau** or **ridge**; found in glaciated mountain ranges.

COL: (Scottish Gaelic: *bealach*; Welsh: *bwlch*) the lowest point of land between two **peaks**, forming a **ridge** or **pass**. Also known as a 'saddle'.

CONTOUR: the lines on a map that join parts of hills or landscapes that fall at an equal height, collectively showing their shape and steepness.

CORNICE: a windblown bank of snow overhanging the top of steep slopes and/or gullies. If walked upon or if thawing, the snow will break off. This makes it a danger to walkers, especially as it can crumble many metres away from the edge.

CRAG: steep, rocky and rough side of a mountain or hill.

ESCARPMENT: a steep, often cliff-like slope forming the edge of high land.

FLANK: the slopes of a hill or mountain.

FOOTPATH: a track solely for pedestrian use.

GLEN: a Gaelic term for valley.

GRID REFERENCE: a two-letter and (typically) six-figure reference that pinpoints a location on an Ordnance Survey (OS) map. The letters relate to 100km squares which cover the whole of Britain. On OS 1:25,000 Explorer maps and OS 1:50,000 Landranger maps each square represents 1km and can, for example, be divided into tenths (horizontally and vertically) so that you can work out the six-figure reference. The Easting (horizontal) number comes first, followed by the Northing (vertical).

GULLY: a crack or depression that runs up the side of a hill or mountain. Commonly used by climbers in winter as they tend to fill with snow and ice. Poses a high risk of avalanches.

MUNRO: a hill named on a list by Sir Hugh Munro in 1891, denoting a Scottish mountain over 3,000ft (914m) high. Munroists/Munro-baggers aim to climb them all. When successful, they are said to be a 'compleater' (sic).

PASS: a lower point between mountains or hills that connects two valleys.

PEAK: the highest and, usually, pointed top of a hill or mountain.

PERMISSIVE PATH: not a **right of way** but a **footpath** open for walkers by special arrangement with the landowner (who can remove the right to walk at any time).

PLATEAU: a flat-topped area of land raised above its surrounds.

RIDGE: a crest of land – usually quite narrow (though can be broad) that forms between two mountain or hill faces.

RIGHT OF WAY: a path that, legally, is supposed to be maintained and open at all times for use by walkers unless closed temporarily during exceptional circumstances, eg: for livestock control during outbreaks of foot-and-mouth disease.

SCREE: small, loose, stone shards that lie on the side of a mountain (usually a result of rock fall following weathering or erosion).

SCRAMBLE: a rocky walk where you will need to use your hands as well as feet. There are different grades of scramble – namely 1, 2, and 3. Grade 1 requires no technical training or equipment; Grades 2 and 3 normally require rope, climbing equipment and helmets. See www.bmc.co.uk for useful scrambling guides and on how to move from walking to this, the 'grey area' between walking and climbing.

SPOT HEIGHT: usually a point of some significance on a sprawling **ridge** or **plateau** (sometimes a **summit**), marked on a map by a figure indicating its height in metres. On the ground, it is often marked by a **cairn** or similar.

STILE: a wooden structure designed to help walkers cross hedges and fences without opening a gate. Sometimes features an adaption to allow dogs through.

SUMMIT: the highest point of any hill, mountain or land feature.

TRIG POINT: pillars and posts, usually on **summits** (though not always), used by the Ordnance Survey to triangulate, measure and map.

Small successes: nothing rivals that sense of achievement on reaching a summit. (Neil S Price) ↑

USEFUL WEBSITES

FOR PUBLIC TRANSPORT

traveline.info: national website for bus and train information. There are regional hubs for the following regions in England: northwest (traveline-northwest.co.uk); northeast (travelinenortheast.info); East Anglia (travelineeastanglia.org.uk); East Midlands (travelineeastmidlands.co.uk); West Midlands (travelinemidlands.co.uk); southeast (travelinesoutheast.org.uk); and southwest (travelinesw.com).

travelinescotland.com: Scotland-specific service providing bus and train information

traveline.cymru: same for Wales

rome2rio.com: how to get from a-to-b by various means of public transport

nationalrail.co.uk: train times, routes and tickets

seat61.com: train guru with lots of tips on cheap train travel and routes

sleeper.scot: Caledonian Sleeper train service from London, Crewe and Preston to various points in Scotland

FOR CAMPING

campingandcaravanningclub.co.uk: official friendly club website

ukcampsite.co.uk: for reviews and details of many campsites (including small ones) around Britain

nationaltrust.org.uk/camping: National Trust campsites and camping barns around England and Wales

PROVIDERS OF AUTHOR-RECOMMENDED COURSES IN HILL SKILLS

glenmorelodge.org.uk: Glenmore Lodge, Aviemore, Cairngorms

pyb.co.uk: Plas y Brenin Mountain Centre, Capel Curig, Snowdonia

expeditionguide.com: excellent courses and one-to-one tuition by Mountaineering Instructor Rob Johnson

climbmts.co.uk: Scottish mountain courses and guiding by Stuart Johnston Mountaineering

MAPS

ordnancesurvey.co.uk: best maps in the business for hillwalking

TOILET FINDER

greatbritishpublictoiletmap.rca.ac.uk: a vital resource to help find the nearest place to spend a penny

toiletfinder.org: an additional resource if the above does not yield results

PROTECT
LIGHTWEIGHT INSULATING JACKET
CompressLite II Jacket, RRP £65

CRAGHOPPERS

LIBERATE
STADSAAL CAVES
#MYCRAGHOPPERS

INDEX

Featured hill walks are highlighted in **bold**.

INDEX OF ADVERTISERS

First edition published September 2017
Bradt Travel Guides Ltd
IDC House, The Vale, Chalfont St Peter, Bucks SL9 9RZ, England
www.bradtguides.com
Print edition published in the USA by The Globe Pequot Press Inc,
PO Box 480, Guilford, Connecticut 06437-0480

Project Manager: Anna Moores
Book design: Pepi Bluck, Perfect Picture

ISBN: 978 1 78477 066 2 (print)
e-ISBN: 978 1 78477 514 8 (e-pub)
e-ISBN: 978 1 78477 415 8 (mobi)

British Library Cataloguing in Publication Data
A catalogue record for this book is available from the British Library

Photographs

All photographs © individual photographers credited beside images and also those from picture libraries/tourist boards, credited as follows: Alamy (A); Dreamstime.com (D); North York Moors National Park Authority (NYMNPA); Shutterstock.com (S).

Front cover **Top image**: Mam Tor (MCB Photography/Getty Images); **Bottom image**: Walking through Snowdonia National Park, near Betws-y-Coed (John Warburton-Lee/AWL Images/Getty Images)
Back cover On the flanks of Yr Arddu, Snowdonia, Cnicht in the distance (Neil S Price)
Title page Gazing out over Loch Katrine from Ben A'an, the Trossachs, Scotland (Neil S Price)

Maps David McCutcheon FBCart.S & Daniella Levin

Typeset by Pepi Bluck
Production managed by Jellyfish Print Solutions; printed in Turkey
Digital conversion by www.dataworks.co.in